IMAGES OF
ORGANIZATION
THE EXECUTIVE EDITION

Other books by Gareth Morgan

Imaginization: New Mindsets for Seeing, Organizing, and Managing

Creative Organization Theory

Riding the Waves of Change

Beyond Method: Strategies for Social Research

Organizational Symbolism (with L. Pondy, P. Frost, and T. Dandridge)

Sociological Paradigms and Organizational Analysis (with G. Burrell)

GARETH MORGAN

IMAGES OF ORGANIZATION

THE EXECUTIVE EDITION

 Berrett-Koehler Publishers, Inc.
San Francisco

 **SAGE Publications**
International Educational and Professional Publisher
Thousand Oaks   London   New Delhi

The hardcover and paperback of *Images of Organization*, Second Edition, was published by Sage Publications in 1997. The Executive Edition is co-published by Berrett-Koehler Publishers, Inc., and Sage Publications, Inc.

Berrett-Koehler Publishers, Inc.
235 Montgomery Street, Suite 650
San Francisco, California 94104-2916
Tel: (415) 288-0260, Fax: (415) 362-2512
www.bkconnection.com

Sage Publications, Inc.
2455 Teller Road
Thousand Oaks, California 91320
Tel: (805) 499-0721, Fax: (805) 499-0871
www.sagepub.com

Ordering information

Quantity sales. Special discounts are available on quantity purchases by corporations, associations, and others. For details, contact the "Special Sales Department" at the Berrett-Koehler or Sage Publications address above.

Individual sales. Images of Organization is available through most bookstores. It can also be ordered directly from Berrett-Koehler: Tel: (800) 929-2929; Fax: (802) 864-7626; www.bkconnection.com, or from Sage Publications, Inc., at the address above.

Orders for college textbook/course adoption use. Please contact Sage Publications, Inc., at the address above.

Orders by U.S. trade bookstores and wholesalers. Please contact Ingram Publisher Services, Tel: (800) 509-4887; Fax: (800) 838-1149; E-mail: customer.service@ingrampublisherservices.com; or visit www.ingrampublisherservices.com/Ordering for details about electronic ordering.

Berrett-Koehler and the BK logo are registered trademarks of Berrett-Koehler Publishers, Inc.

Library of Congress Cataloging-in-Publication Data

Morgan, Gareth, 1943–

     Images of organization: the international bestseller that revolutionized how we see organizations—newly abridged for today's manager / Gareth Morgan. — Executive ed.

     p. cm.

     Includes bibliographical references and index.

     ISBN 978-1-57675-038-4 (Berrett-Koehler; trade; alk. paper)

     ISBN 978-0-7619-1752-6 (Sage; academic; alk. paper)

     1. Organization. 2. Organizational behavior. 3. Management. I. Title.

     HD31.M628   1998

     658.4—dc21   98-10390

12 11   15 14 13 12

Developmental editing: Andrea Markowitz; Copyediting and proofreading: PeopleSpeak; Interior design and production: Joel Friedlander, Marin Bookworks; Indexing: Directions Unlimited; Cover design: Richard Adelson.

*In memory of my parents
Idris and Rachel Morgan*

Contents

List of Exhibits

Preface to the
Executive Edition

SEVERAL YEARS AGO COMMUNICATIONS THEORIST MARSHALL MCLUHAN REVOLUTIONIZED INSIGHTS ABOUT THE NATURE OF MEDIA through his famous dictum, "the medium is the message." While we tend to focus on the *content* of what is being communicated in the world around us, it is the medium itself that has the most impact on our lives. We read books. We listen to the radio. We watch television. We surf electronic webs. We are fascinated by what we see, hear, and learn. But we are oblivious to the way we are being shaped by the very nature of what we are doing as readers, listeners, watchers, or surfers.

Images of Organization–The Executive Edition brings a similar message to management. Leaders and managers tend to be preoccupied with the content of organizational activity, allowing the latest theory, technique, or preoccupation to dominate attention. But in doing so, they miss the powerful impact of the fundamental process that is framing their attention in the first place.

Images of Organization shows that the medium of organization and management is metaphor. Management theory and practice is shaped by a metaphorical process that influences virtually everything we do. In appreciating this, managers can begin to approach their craft at a new level and in a new way.

Metaphor, to use a metaphor, acts as the genetic code of management, producing all the detailed theories and ideas shaping management practice, exactly like genetic codes in the natural world shape the unfolding of nature. As the geneticists have shown, when we understand and master the code, the overwhelming diversity of nature is put in a completely new perspective.

So, too, in management. When managers appreciate the significance of metaphor in shaping their practice, they can master the fundamental code of organization and management instead of being at the mercy of detail. This is the fundamental message of *Images of Organization* and why the book deserves your attention. In "mastering the code," you'll discover key competencies that are vital for success in a turbulent world.

—Gareth Morgan
Toronto, Ontario
April 1998

Acknowledgments

IN PRODUCING THIS EXECUTIVE EDITION of *Images of Organization*, I am grateful for the excellent advice and guidance provided by Steven Piersanti at Berrett-Koehler and Sara Miller-McCune of Sage Publications and for the wonderful work of Andrea Markowitz, who has acted as the main editor. I am grateful for the way she has abridged the original work with care and sensitivity and for her enthusiasm and skill in guiding me to the parts of the manuscript needing fresh attention. She has proved an indispensable partner throughout.

My thanks also go to many other people over many years. Friends, colleagues, and students at Lancaster, Penn State, and York Universities, together with participants at executive and research workshops throughout Europe and North America, have contributed to many of the insights developed in this book. I am especially grateful to Asaf Zohar at York University for his valued contributions and to Dean Deszö Horvath at York's Schulich School of Business for his long-standing support. The Social Sciences and Humanities Research Council of Canada played an important role in launching my early research on the role of metaphor in the study of organization and have been helpful in supporting doctoral students working on the theory and practice of self-organization.

Rhea Copeland provided outstanding secretarial support, helping me produce the original manuscript, and as always, my friends at Berrett-Koehler and Sage Publications have made numerous contributions to the evolution of its final form.

My family provides an indispensable foundation for all that I do. Karen, Evan, and Heather have played a crucial role in helping me find the creative space needed to develop and work on my ideas. They provide a loving atmosphere full of positive energy and fun for which I am truly grateful.

To all, my sincere thanks.

I An Overview

On the nature of metaphor and its role in
understanding organization and management

1 The Promise of *Images of Organization*

ORGANIZATIONS ARE MANY THINGS AT ONCE!

They are complex and multifaceted.

They are paradoxical.

That's why the challenges facing managers and practitioners are often so difficult.

While managing and organizing are challenging in the best of times, the difficulties are compounding in today's environment of rapid change. If you want to be the type of leader or professional who helps your organization adapt to the multiple demands of an increasingly turbulent world, you need to become aware of the images and assumptions that are shaping your current thinking and develop the capacity to use new ones. You need to develop competencies that allow you to see, understand, and shape situations in new ways.

That is the focus of *Images of Organization.*

It is *not* a "quick fix" book.

It is *not* a book that offers a simple recipe for tackling organizational problems.

Rather, it is something that I hope you will find far more valuable: a *resource* that will help you challenge and transform your thinking about organization and management—a resource that you will want to visit time and again.

At first sight, *Images* may seem to be a very complex book because it embraces so many different management perspectives.

But the basic thesis underlying the book is a very simple one: that *all* organization and management theory and practice is based on images, or

3

metaphors, that lead us to understand situations in powerful yet *partial* ways. When we realize this, we learn to recognize that our favored ways of managing and organizing often lead us to miss out on other ways of managing and organizing. In addition, we recognize that since every metaphor has limitations as well as strengths, we must always be aware of the inherent blind spots that inevitably undermine our effectiveness.

To achieve greater effectiveness, managers must become skilled in identifying and using different approaches to organization and management. In *Images* terminology, they must become skilled at "reading" organizations from different perspectives and at developing action strategies that are consistent with the insights they glean. Some perspectives and insights may complement others. Some may contradict. When we master the art of working with these parallels and contradictions, we increase our peripheral ✳ vision, creating the flexibility needed to identify difficult organizational issues and to respond with appropriate strategies for change.

Managers who are skilled in the art of reading organizational life have a capacity to remain open and flexible, suspending immediate judgments whenever possible until a more comprehensive view of the situation emerges. They are aware that new insights often arise as they approach situations from new angles and that a wide and varied reading can create a wide and varied range of possibilities for action.

This is the new competency that *Images* promises. If you cannot wait to see this process in action, I encourage you to go directly to chapter 10, "Reading and Shaping Organizational Life." If you can wait, I invite you to explore first the power of metaphor and then the insights of eight metaphors that will help to change the way you think about organization.

THE POWER OF METAPHOR
IN ORGANIZATION AND MANAGEMENT

WHAT IS METAPHOR AND WHAT DOES IT DO?

Before we explore the many contributions of metaphor to organization and management, it would be helpful to explain "What is *metaphor*?"

Metaphor is a comparative figure of speech often used to add a creative flourish to the way we talk, such as when we say that "life is a game" or that "the world is a stage." But the nature and effect of metaphor is much more complex, much more fundamental. *It is a primal force through which humans create meaning by using one element of experience to understand another.* Think about how flat and static our communication would be if we could describe something only as itself: for example, "The world is a world."

Metaphor gives us the opportunity to stretch our thinking and deepen our understanding, thereby allowing us to see things in new ways and to act in new ways.

Applied in this manner, metaphor becomes a tool—indeed, I would say the primary tool—for creating an understanding about what we now recognize as organization and management. I don't know whether you have ever thought about this, but the concept of organization is itself a metaphor. It is based on an image taken from the ancient Greek word for a tool or instrument. Similarly, the concept of management is based on an old image of horsemanship and the challenge of putting a horse through its paces.

Metaphor exerts a formative influence on language, on science, on how we think, how we see, and how we express ourselves on a day-to-day basis, asserting that A is (or is like) B.

For example, when we say the man is a lion, we use the image of a lion to draw attention to the lionlike aspects of the man. The metaphor frames our understanding of the man in a distinctive yet partial way—partial, because metaphor always produces a *one-sided insight*. In highlighting certain interpretations, it forces others into a background role. So in drawing attention to the lionlike bravery, strength, or ferocity of the man, the metaphor glosses over the fact that the same person has other features that were eliminated from view.

Metaphor always creates *distortions*, too (exhibit 1.1). Metaphor uses evocative images to create what may be described as constructive falsehoods, which, if taken literally or to an extreme, become absurd:

- The man is a lion.
- He is brave, strong, and ferocious.
- But he is not covered in fur and does not have four legs, sharp teeth, and a tail!

When we approach metaphor in this way, we see that our simple premise that all management theory is metaphor has far-reaching consequences. We have to accept that any theory or perspective that we bring to the study of organization and management, while capable of creating valuable insights, is also incomplete, biased, and potentially misleading.

Consider the popular idea that the organization is a machine. The metaphor may create valuable insights about how an organization is structured to achieve predetermined results. But the metaphor is *incomplete:* it ignores the human aspects. The metaphor is *biased:* it elevates the importance of the rational and structural dimensions. The metaphor is

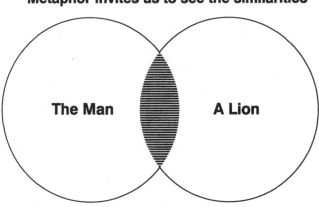

Metaphor invites us to see the similarities

The Man | A Lion

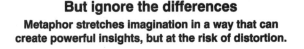

But ignore the differences
Metaphor stretches imagination in a way that can create powerful insights, but at the risk of distortion.

Exhibit 1.1. The nature of metaphor

misleading: the organization is not a machine and can never really be designed, structured, and controlled as a set of inanimate parts.

Metaphor is inherently paradoxical, as the way of seeing created through a metaphor becomes a way of not seeing.

Yet when we recognize this, we mobilize the true power of metaphor and its role in management. We quickly appreciate that no single theory will ever give us a perfect or all-purpose point of view. We realize that the challenge is to become skilled in the art of using metaphor—to find fresh ways of seeing, understanding, and shaping the situations that we want to organize and manage.

USING METAPHORS TO CREATE NEW WAYS OF SEEING AND SHAPING ORGANIZATIONAL LIFE

Using multiple metaphors to understand organization and management gives us a capacity to tap different dimensions of a situation, showing how different qualities of organization can co-exist, supporting, reinforcing, or contradicting one another:

- **In approaching the same situation in different ways, metaphors extend insight and suggest actions that may not have been possible before.**

For example, an understanding of the holographic nature of the brain, or of the "DNA" encoded in corporate culture, can help an enterprise break free of traditional structures and controls. An understanding of the uncon-scious psychic traps that are holding an organization in an undesirable "attractor pattern" can provide the all-important breakthrough for generat-ing new opportunities around organizational learning.

- **The insights generated by different metaphors are not just theoretical. They are incredibly practical.**

    For example, as we gain comfort in using the implications of differ-ent metaphors, we quickly learn that the insights of one metaphor can often help us overcome the limitations of another. This, in turn, encourages us to recognize and, indeed, search for the limitations of existing insights so that we can use them as springboards for new insight.

- **Metaphors lead to new metaphors, creating a mosaic of competing and complementary insights.**

    This is one of the most powerful qualities of the approach. When you recognize that your theories and insights are metaphorical, you also recog-nize your limitations and find ways of going beyond them. This results in a style of thinking that is always open and evolving and extremely well suited for dealing with the complexity of organizational life.

Using the complementarity inherent in different views

There are a lot of differences in the points of view that we will explore in this book. Different chapters pull us in very different directions, creating a great range of insights. Chapter by chapter, we will see how mechanistic imagery encourages us to structure and rationalize everything we do; organic imagery encourages a focus on adaptation and the satisfaction of needs; images of the brain focus on issues of organizational learning; the psychic prison metaphor points to ways out of conscious and unconscious traps; theories of autopoiesis encourage us to challenge and rethink our identities; images of mutual causality encourage us to transform problem-atic loops.

    But there is enormous complementarity as well. The insights of dif-ferent metaphors often support and reinforce each other. We will soon see how the challenge of creating organic organizations that can keep up with environmental change is assisted by an understanding of how we can use principles of holographic organization to enhance flexibility, or how corporate culture can help to create integration in the absence of formal structures and written rules.

Using the complexity and diversity of different views

We will also see how the insights of different metaphors can contribute to a rich understanding of the ways in which different features of organization are intertwined, suggesting multiple methods of tackling the issues at hand. For example, one simple aspect of organizational structure may embrace many dimensions. It may represent: an attempt to "mechanize" a particular set of activities; a particular manager's defense against anxiety; a key aspect of corporate culture; a mode of "single-loop learning"; a crucial part of a department's power base; or an anachronism that prevents the organization from dealing with the demands of the wider environment. *All these features can have a simultaneous presence.*

Using multiple images to capture these dimensions of organization may seem to complicate the nature of organizational reality to a terrible degree. But this *is* the reality with which managers have to deal. Continuing the above example, the aspect of organizational structure that seems such a hopeless and obvious anachronism may be the symbol and "carrier" of important elements of culture or corporate politics, or it may be playing a vital psychological role in how managers are coping with the uncertainties of the time. As such, its removal will generate all kinds of cultural, political, and psychological consequences.

It is vital that managers understand that any situation can have multiple interpretations. Otherwise they will find themselves falling into the unanticipated problems that have plagued so many corporate change programs seeking to restructure, reinvent, reengineer, or reform organizational life.

This view of organizational reality, of course, is completely consistent with what natural scientists have demonstrated in relation to the physical and biological worlds. These, too, possess paradoxical qualities. Consider the famous experiments on the nature of light. When scientists study light as a wave, it reveals itself as a wave. When it is studied as a particle, it reveals itself as a particle. Both wave-like and particlelike tendencies co-exist. The metaphor that the scientist uses to study these latent tendencies *shapes* what he or she sees.

The same is true of organizations.

Think "structure" and you'll see structure. Think "culture" and you'll see all kinds of cultural dimensions. Think "politics" and you'll find politics. Think in terms of system patterns and loops and you'll find a whole range of them.

This is the manager's dilemma: we tend to find and realize what we are looking for. This does *not* mean that there is no real basis to what we find. Rather, it is just that reality has a tendency to reveal itself in accordance with the perspectives through which it is approached. As Albert Einstein once noted, it is the theory through which we observe a situation that decides what we can observe.

Some theories and perspectives may prove weak or irrelevant, having little evocative or substantial power: scientists have generated powerful insights by studying light as a wave or a particle, but not as a grapefruit! In a similar way, managers face the challenge of finding or creating powerful metaphors that can help them understand and shape their organizations. The metaphors offered in this book provide examples but by no means exhaust the possibilities.

Living with the paradox of metaphor

Taken to an extreme, metaphors' insights encounter severe limitations. Any given metaphor can be incredibly persuasive, but it can also be blinding and block our ability to gain an overall view.

In terms of organization, we can be persuaded by the idea that management must engineer, reengineer, and operate an efficient organizational machine, only to find our designs undermined by a changing environment or by the human beings who ultimately have to bring the machine to life. Or, in becoming converts to the idea of developing "learning organizations" that can evolve in a brainlike way, we can easily overlook the political realities that block effective learning. Or, as enthused organizational politicians or social critics, we can find that while we are preoccupied with our political maneuvering or debates, key transformations in the external environment are "calling the tune."

Limited insight is inherent in the nature of metaphor and the theories and ideas it generates. It helps to explain the swings in management from fad to fad and why the latest theory is *always* in the process of giving way to another. Management theories tend to sell the positive insights of a metaphor while ignoring the limitations and distortions that it creates. IMPORTANT These insights attract. That's why they develop a following and become the trend of the day. But when managers get down to the business of applying the insights in practice, reality presents itself as being much more complicated. Most management theories are developed in a way that inevitably creates disillusionment and disappointment. They usually have an element of "truth," but it is a truth that, in effect, denies the complexity of the realities to which the theories are to be applied.

So the main invitation and challenge of this book is to recognize and cope with the idea that all theories of organization and management are based on implicit metaphors that persuade us to see, understand, and act on situations in partial ways:

- While metaphors create insight, they also distort.
- While they have strengths, they also have limitations.
- In creating ways of seeing and acting, metaphors tend to create ways of *not* seeing and acting.

Another challenge of this book is to learn to embrace multiple and diverse perspectives because there can be no single theory or metaphor that gives an all-purpose point of view, and there can be no one "correct theory" for structuring everything we do.

THE METAPHORS IN THIS BOOK

To illustrate the principles in action, chapters 2 through 9 explore the implications of different metaphors for thinking about the nature of organization. Some of the metaphors tap familiar ways of thinking; others develop insights and perspectives that will be rather new. Collectively, they demonstrate how we can use metaphor to generate a range of complementary and competing insights and learn to build on the strengths of different points of view.

Chapter 2 examines the image of organizations as machines and illustrates how the mechanistic style of thought underpins the development of bureaucratic organization. When managers think of organizations as machines, they tend to manage and design them as machines made up of interlocking parts that each play a clearly defined role in the functioning of the whole. At times, this can prove highly effective; at others, it can have many unfortunate results. One of the most basic problems of modern management is that the mechanical way of thinking is so ingrained in our everyday conceptions of organization that it is often very difficult to organize in any other way. In demonstrating our dependency upon mechanical thinking, the chapter helps us become more open to other ways of thinking.

Chapter 3 examines the idea that organizations are like organisms. This popular metaphor focuses attention on understanding and managing organizational needs and environmental relations. We come to see different types of organization as belonging to different species, of which the bureaucratic type is just one. We see that different species are suited to different environments. We are encouraged to understand how organizations are born, grow, develop, decline, and die and how they can adapt to changing circumstances. We are also encouraged to consider relations between species and the evolutionary patterns found in the broader ecology. As in the case of the mechanical metaphor, this kind of imagery leads us to see and understand organizations from a unique perspective that has already contributed a great deal to the theory of modern management.

In chapter 4 we pursue the implications of viewing organizations as brains. What if we attempt to design them as brains? The metaphor draws attention to the importance of information processing, learning, and intelligence and provides a frame of reference for understanding and assessing modern organizations in these terms. It also provides a set of principles for creating learning organizations.

Chapter 5 explores the idea that organizations are cultures. This focus gives us yet another way of managing and designing organizations: by recognizing the values, ideas, beliefs, norms, rituals, and other patterns of shared meaning that guide organizational life.

In chapter 6 we use a political metaphor to focus on the different sets of interests, conflicts, and power plays that shape organizational activities. The chapter explores organizations as systems of government and the detailed factors shaping the politics of organizational life.

In chapter 7 the focus shifts to a more abstract metaphor: the idea that organizations are psychic prisons where people become trapped by their conscious and unconscious thoughts, ideas, and beliefs. Could it be that our favored modes of organizing manifest an unconscious preoccupation with control? A form of repressed sexuality? A fear of death? The image of a psychic prison invites us to examine organizational life to see if, and in what ways, we have become trapped by cognitive processes of our own creation. It offers many important insights about the psychodynamic aspects of organization and favored styles of management.

Chapter 8 invites us to understand organization as flux and transformation by focusing on four "logics of change" that shape social life. One emphasizes how organizations are self-producing systems that create themselves in their own image. The second draws on insights from the study of chaos and complexity, viewing organizational life through images of competing attractor patterns. The third views organization as the product of circular flows of positive and negative feedback. The fourth explores how the features of modern organization are the product of a dialectical logic whereby every phenomenon generates its opposite. The insights help us to understand and manage organizational change and to appreciate some of the forces shaping the nature of organization at a societal level.

Chapter 9 explores the idea that organizations are instruments of domination. Here the focus is on the potentially exploitative aspects of corporate life. The chapter shows how organizations often use their employees, their host communities, and the world economy to achieve their own ends. An extension of the political metaphor examined in chapter 6, chapter 9 helps us understand aspects of modern organization that have radicalized labor-management relations and the negative impacts of global corporations. This metaphor is particularly useful for understanding organizations from the perspective of exploited groups and for understanding how actions that are rational from one viewpoint can prove exploitative from another.

Chapter 10 brings all the ideas together by presenting a practical case study that illustrates how we can use the metaphors presented in this book as practical frameworks for "reading and shaping" organizations. It shows how we can harness the power of metaphors to deepen our understanding of situations and create new, more effective ways of managing and organizing.

Chapter 11, "Using Metaphor to Manage in a Turbulent World," summarizes and synthesizes the major theses of *Images* and their implications for managers and practitioners seeking to negotiate the paradoxical and turbulent world in which we now find ourselves.

The book as a whole stands as a treatise on metaphorical thinking that contributes to both the theory and the practice of management. The metaphors discussed have been selected to illustrate a broad range of ideas and perspectives. But they by no means exhaust the possibilities. As you read, you may find yourself disagreeing with the importance of the metaphors that have been chosen and wish to add ones of your own. You are likely to be attracted to certain metaphors and be impatient with others. Or you may find competing metaphors equally compelling or attractive. That is the way it should be, for the aim is to open dialogue and extend horizons rather than to achieve closure around an all-embracing perspective.

In this respect, *Images of Organization* is very different from most management books. It has a clear point of view: that metaphor is central to the way we read, understand, and shape organizational life. But at no point will you find that view being brought down to advocacy of a single perspective. There are no right or wrong theories in management in an absolute sense, for every theory illuminates and hides.

See this book as a series of steps on a journey. Enjoy what you experience along the way as each chapter takes you inside a range of ideas that are crucial for understanding, managing, and designing organizations in a changing world. But be forewarned: it is not a quick read. And it is not a quick fix. It requires your attention and, above all, your openness and reflection.

I believe that the results will be worth the effort because the journey has the potential to revolutionize the way you think about organization and management.

Let this book challenge your thinking. Use it to gain new perspective on the issues you face. Use it to develop a key competency required by all managers in today's world.

Some Images of Organization

The following chapters demonstrate how metaphor can be used to develop theories of organization and management. Some focus on metaphors that have already been well explored. Others open newer territory. Collectively, they show how we can use metaphor to generate a range of complementary and competing insights about the nature of organizations and how they can be designed and managed.

2 Mechanization Takes Command: Organizations As Machines

WHEN WE THINK OF ORGANIZATIONS AS MACHINES we begin to see them as rational enterprises designed and structured to achieve predetermined ends.

- The organizational machine is given goals and objectives.
- It is designed as a rational structure of jobs and activities.
- Its blueprint becomes an organizational chart.
- People are hired to operate the machine and everyone is expected to behave in a predetermined way.

This is the theory that has driven much of organization and management since the industrial revolution. It has brought enormous benefits, increasing capacities for production a thousandfold. But its weaknesses have also been exposed as human beings have rebelled against being "mechanized," creating rigidities that prevent organizations from adapting and flowing with change.

Many of us are trapped by patterns of mechanistic thinking. By becoming aware of how this occurs, we can learn to tap its strengths while unleashing our ability to organize in new ways.

THE CHINESE SAGE CHUANG-TZU, who lived in the fourth century B.C., relates the following story:

> As Tzu-gung was traveling through the regions north of river Han, he saw an old man working in his vegetable garden. He had dug an irrigation ditch. The man would descend into the well, fetch up a vessel of water in his arms, and pour it out into the ditch. While his efforts were tremendous, the results appeared to be very meager.
>
> Tzu-gung said, "There is a way whereby you can irrigate a hundred ditches in one day, and whereby you can do much with little effort. Would you not like to hear of it?" Then the gardener stood up, looked at him, and said, "And what would that be?"
>
> Tzu-gung replied, "You take a wooden lever, weighted at the back and light in front. In this way you can bring up water so quickly that it just gushes out. This is called a draw-well."
>
> Then anger rose up in the old man's face, and he said, "I have heard my teacher say that whoever uses machines does all his work like a machine. He who does his work like a machine grows a heart like a machine, and he who carries the heart of a machine in his breast loses his simplicity. He who has lost his simplicity becomes unsure in the strivings of his soul.
>
> "Uncertainty in the strivings of the soul is something which does not agree with honest sense. It is not that I do not know of such things; I am ashamed to use them."

If the old man were to visit the modern world, he would no doubt be very dismayed. Machines now influence virtually every aspect of our existence. They have increased our productive abilities a thousandfold, but they have also done much more, shaping almost every aspect of our lives. The debate initiated by Tzu-gung and the old man continues. In the view of many, mechanization has brought mainly gain, raising mankind from competitors with nature to virtual masters of nature. For others, the old man's vision of human alienation recurs in various forms, as they contemplate the high price of mechanical progress in terms of the transition from craft to factory production, the exchange of rural community for urban sprawl, the general degradation of the environment, and the assault of rationalism upon the human spirit.

Regardless of the stand one takes, the wisdom of the old man's vision regarding the pervasive influence of machines remains beyond dispute. The use of machines has radically transformed the nature of productive activity and has left its mark on the imagination, thoughts, and feelings of humans throughout the ages. Scientists have produced mechanistic interpretations of the natural world, and philosophers and psychologists have articulated mechanistic theories of human mind and behavior. Increasingly, we have learned to use the machine as a metaphor for ourselves and our society and to mold our world in accordance with mechanical principles. *machine as metaphor*

This is nowhere more evident than in the modern organization.

Consider the mechanical precision with which many of our institutions are expected to operate. Organizational life is often routinized with the precision demanded of clockwork. People are frequently expected to arrive at work at a given time, perform a predetermined set of activities, rest at appointed hours, and then resume their tasks until work is over. In many organizations, one shift of workers replaces another in methodical fashion so that work can continue uninterrupted twenty-four hours a day every day of the year. Often, the work is very mechanical and repetitive. Anyone who has observed work in the mass-production factory or in any of the large "office factories" processing paper forms such as insurance claims, tax returns, or bank checks will have noticed the machinelike way in which such organizations operate. They are designed like machines, and their employees are in essence expected to behave as if they were parts of machines.

Fast-food restaurants and service organizations of many kinds operate in accordance with similar principles, with every action predetermined in a minute way, even in areas where personal interactions with others are concerned. Employees are frequently trained to interact with customers according to a detailed code of instructions and are monitored in their performance. Even the most casual smile, greeting, comment, or suggestion by a sales assistant is often programmed by company policy and rehearsed to produce authentic results. The management observation checklist used by a famous fast-food restaurant to monitor employee performance (exhibit 2.1) indicates the degree to which a simple task like serving a customer can be mechanized, observed, and evaluated in a mechanical way.

MACHINES, MECHANICAL THINKING, AND THE RISE OF BUREAUCRATIC ORGANIZATION

Organizations that are designed and operated as if they were machines are usually called bureaucracies. Yet most organizations are bureaucratized in some degree, for the mechanistic mode of thought has shaped our most basic conceptions of what organization is all about. When we talk about organization, we usually have in mind a state of orderly relations between clearly defined parts that have some determinate order. Although the image may not be explicit, we are talking about a set of mechanical relations. We talk about organizations as if they were machines, and as a consequence we

most org's are bureaucratized

Greeting the customer	Yes	No
1. There is a smile.		
2. It is a sincere greeting.		
3. There is eye contact.		
Other:		
Taking the order	Yes	No
1. The counter person is thoroughly familiar with the menu ticket (no hunting for items).		
2. The customer has to give the order only once.		
3. Small orders (four items or less) are memorized rather than written down.		
4. There is suggestive selling.		
Other:		
Assembling the order	Yes	No
1. The order is assembled in the proper sequence.		
2. Grill slips are handed in first.		
3. Drinks are poured in the proper sequence.		
4. Proper amount of ice.		
5. Cups slanted and finger used to activate.		
6. Drinks are filled to the proper level.		
7. Drinks are capped.		
8. Clean cups.		
9. Holding times are observed on coffee.		
10. Cups are filled to the proper level on coffee.		
Other:		
Presenting the order	Yes	No
1. It is properly packaged.		
2. The bag is double folded.		
3. Plastic trays are used if eating inside.		
4. A tray liner is used.		
5. The food is handled in a proper manner.		
Other:		
Asking for and receiving payment	Yes	No
1. The amount of the order is stated clearly and loud enough to hear.		
2. The denomination received is clearly stated.		
3. The change is counted out loud.		
4. Change is counted efficiently.		
5. Large bills are laid on the till until the change is given.		
Other:		
Thanking the customer and asking for repeat business	Yes	No
1. There is always a thank-you.		
2. The thank-you is sincere.		
3. There is eye contact.		
4. Return business was asked for.		
Other:		

Exhibit 2.1. A management observation checklist used to evaluate the performance of counter staff in a fast-food restaurant

tend to expect them to operate as machines: in a routinized, efficient, reliable, and predictable way.

When goals are fixed, environments are stable, and the workforce eager and compliant, a mechanical mode of organization can provide the basis for effective operation. But in other organizational contexts it can have many unfortunate consequences. So it is important to understand how and when we are engaging in mechanistic thinking, and how so many popular theories and taken-for-granted ideas about organization support this thinking. One of the major challenges facing many modern organizations is to replace mechanistic thinking with fresh ideas and approaches such as those discussed in subsequent chapters.

THE ORIGINS OF MECHANISTIC ORGANIZATION
Tools and instruments

Organizations are rarely established as ends in themselves. They are instruments created to achieve other ends. The word "organization" derives from the Greek *organon*, meaning a tool or instrument. No wonder ideas about tasks, goals, aims, and objectives have become such fundamental organizational concepts, for tools and instruments are mechanical devices invented and developed to aid in performing some kind of goal-oriented activity.

The instrumental nature of organizing is evident in the practices of the earliest formal organizations of which we know, such as those that built the great pyramids, empires, churches, and armies. However, it is with the invention and proliferation of machines that concepts of organization really became mechanized. The use of machines, especially in industry, required that organizations be adapted to the needs of machines.

Machines and the industrial revolution

If we examine the changes in organization accompanying the industrial revolution, we find an increasing trend toward the bureaucratization and routinization of life generally. Many self-employed family groups and skilled artisans gave up the autonomy of working in their homes and workshops to work on relatively unskilled jobs in factory settings. At the same time, factory owners and their engineers realized that the efficient operation of their new machines ultimately required major changes in the design and control of work. Division of labor at work became intensified and increasingly specialized as manufacturers sought to increase efficiency by reducing the discretion of workers in favor of control by their machines and their supervisors. New procedures and techniques were also introduced to discipline workers to accept the new and rigorous routine of factory production.

The military and human automation

Much about mechanistic organization was learned from the military, which since at least the time of Frederick the Great of Prussia had emerged as a prototype of mechanistic organization. Frederick, who ruled from 1740 to 1786, was fascinated by the workings of automated toys such as mechanical men, and in his quest to shape the army into a reliable and efficient instrument, he introduced many reforms that actually served to reduce his soldiers to automatons. Among these reforms were

- the introduction of ranks and uniforms,
- the extension and standardization of regulations,
- increased specialization of tasks,
- the use of standardized equipment,
- the creation of a command language, and
- systematic training that involved army drills.

Frederick's aim was to shape the army into an efficient mechanism operating through means of standardized parts by using

- *training procedures*—allowing the parts of the army to be forged from almost any raw material for easy replacement,
- *fear*—teaching the men to fear their officers more than the enemy to ensure the military machine would operate on command,
- *a distinction between advisory and command functions*—to free specialist advisers (staff) from the line of command so they could plan activities that would ensure the best use of the military machine, and
- *decentralization*—to allow greater autonomy of parts in different combat situations.

Many of Frederick's ideas and practices had great relevance for solving problems created by the development of factory systems of production, and were adopted in a piecemeal fashion throughout the nineteenth century as entrepreneurs struggled to find organizational forms suited to machine technology. The new technology was accompanied and reinforced by mechanization of human thought and action. Organizations that used machines became more and more like machines. Frederick the Great's vision of a "mechanized" army gradually became a reality in both factory and office settings.

THE ORIGINS OF CLASSICAL MANAGEMENT THEORY AND SCIENTIFIC MANAGEMENT

During the nineteenth century, a number of attempts were made to codify and promote the ideas that could lead to the efficient organization and management of work. However, it was not until the early twentieth century that these ideas and developments were synthesized in a comprehensive theory of organization and management.

Weber's bureaucracy

One of the first organizational theorists to observe the parallels between the mechanization of industry and bureaucratic forms of organization was Max Weber. He noted that the bureaucratic form routinizes the process of administration exactly as the machine routinizes production. In his work we find the first comprehensive definition of bureaucracy as a form of organization that emphasizes

- precision,
  - speed,
    - clarity,
      - regularity,
        - reliability, and
          - efficiency

achieved through the creation of

- a fixed division of tasks,
  - hierarchical supervision, and
    - detailed rules and regulations.

As a sociologist, Weber was interested in the social consequences of the proliferation of bureaucracy and, like the old man in Chuang-tzu's story, was concerned about the effect it would have on the human side of society. He saw that the bureaucratic approach had the potential to routinize and mechanize almost every aspect of human life, eroding the human spirit and capacity for spontaneous action. He also recognized that it could have grave political consequences in undermining the potential for more democratic forms of organization.

Two other major contributions to mechanistic theory were made by a group of management theorists and practitioners who set the basis for what is now known as "classical management theory" and "scientific management." In contrast with Weber, they were firm advocates of bureaucratization and devoted their energies to identifying detailed principles and methods through which this kind of organization could be achieved.

Whereas the classical management theorists focused on the design of the total organization, the scientific managers focused on the design and management of individual jobs. It is through the ideas of these theorists that so many mechanistic principles of organization have become entrenched in our everyday thinking. It is worth examining their work in some detail.

Classical management and mechanistic principles of organization

Typical of the classical theorists were Henri Fayol, F. W. Mooney, and Col. Lyndall Urwick. They were all interested in problems of practical management and sought to codify their experience of successful organization for others to follow. The basic thrust of their thinking is captured in the idea that management is a process of

- planning,
  - organization,
    - command,
      - coordination, and
        - control.

Collectively, they set the basis for many modern management techniques, such as management by objectives (MBO); planning, programming, budgeting systems (PPBS); and other methods stressing rational planning and control. Each theorist codified his insights, drawing on a combination of military and engineering principles, which we are quite familiar with today:

- unity of command (one manager per employee),
- lines of authority (the "scalar chain"),
- a limited span of control in terms of the ratio of workers reporting to one manager,
- a distinction between staff and line workers,
- encouraging initiative,
- the division of labor into specialized jobs,
- authority to be responsible for one's own work,
- centralized overall authority,
- employee discipline and obedience to management,
- subordination of individual interests to the interest of the organization,
- equity in treatment and remuneration,
- esprit de corps, and
- stability in the tenure of personnel.

If we implement these principles, we arrive at the kind of organization represented in the familiar organization chart—a pattern of precisely defined jobs organized in a hierarchical manner through precisely defined lines of command or communication. We see that the classical theorists were in effect designing the organization exactly as if they were designing a machine.

ORGANIZATION BECOMES A FORM OF ENGINEERING

When an engineer designs a machine, the task is to define a network of interdependent parts arranged in a specific sequence and anchored by precisely defined points of resistance or rigidity.

The classical theorists were attempting to achieve a similar design in their approach to organization:

- *They conceived organizations as a network of parts.* The focus is on functions and functional departments such as production, marketing, finance, personnel, and research and development, which are further specified as networks of precisely defined jobs. Job responsibilities interlock so that they complement each other as perfectly as possible and are linked together through the scalar chain of command expressed in the classical dictum "one man, one boss."

- *They designed the organizational structure to operate as precisely as possible* through patterns of authority, for example, in terms of job responsibilities and the right to give orders and exact obedience. Patterns of authority serve as points of resistance and coordinate activities by restricting activity in certain directions while encouraging it in others. By giving detailed attention to patterns of authority and to the general process of direction, discipline, and subordination of individual to general interest, the classical theorists sought to ensure that when commands were issued from the top of the organization they would travel throughout the organization in a precisely determined way to create a precisely determined effect.

Creating limited flexibility through decentralization

Classical management principles are basic to both centralized bureaucracy and the modified form found in the divisionalized and matrix forms of organization, where various units are allowed to operate in a semiautonomous manner under general rather than detailed supervision and control. Just as the military decentralized authority to cope with difficult combat situations, the classical management theorists recognized the necessity of reconciling the contrary requirements of centralization and decentralization to preserve an appropriate flexibility in different parts of large organizations.

Meeting goals through systems of top-down control

The ability to decentralize has been greatly advanced during the course of the twentieth century through the development of management techniques like MBO and PPBS and the design of sophisticated management information systems (MIS), which are often used to establish the kinds of top-down control advocated by the classical theorists. Forms of MBO are often used to impose a mechanistic system of goals and objectives on an organization. These are then used to control the direction in which managers and employees can take the organization—for example, through the development of performance targets consistent with these goals and various budgetary systems. Computerized information systems now allow performance to be subjected to almost complete surveillance and control. Despite an appearance of originality, they often reinforce the ideas of the classical management theorists, because they encourage people to fit into predetermined structures rather than exercise their initiative.

The whole thrust of classical management theory and its modern application is to suggest that organizations can or should be rational systems that operate in as efficient a manner as possible. While many will endorse this as an ideal, it is easier said than done because we are dealing with people, not inanimate cogs and wheels.

Dehumanizing workers to meet organizational objectives

The classical theorists gave relatively little attention to the human aspects of organization. Although they frequently recognized the need for leadership, initiative, benevolence, equity, esprit de corps, and a balance or harmony between the human and technical aspects, their main orientation was to make humans fit the requirements of mechanical organization. Organization was a technical problem!

For their neglect of the human side of organizing, classical theorists have been much criticized. Yet modern managers and management consultants often continue to introduce the mechanistic bias into their way of thinking.

The most recent example is found in the "reengineering movement" that swept across North America and much of Europe in the 1990s. Recognizing that the bureaucratic form of organization with its emphasis on rigid departmentalization had outlived its usefulness, the reengineering movement urged a new mechanistic design, building around key business processes instead of bureaucratic functions. As in the old classical theory, the basic assumption is that if you get the engineering right the human factor will fall into place. Needless to say, this is not always the case. As a result, the reengineering movement has encountered exactly the same problems and failures experienced by older-style classical management principles: the human factor often subverts the reengineering process, leading to massive failure rates.

"SCIENTIFIC MANAGEMENT": PERFECTING TECHNICAL DESIGN

The classical theorists elaborated upon many of the basic principles of Frederick the Great's approach to military organization. But it was another great Frederick of organization theory, Frederick Taylor, who developed them to a logical extreme.

Increasing efficiency by breaking work into its smallest parts

Taylor was an American engineer whose "principles of scientific management" provided the cornerstone for work design throughout the first half of the twentieth century, and they have prevailed in one form or another right up to the present day. His message was the following:

1. *Shift all responsibility for the organization of work from the worker to the manager.* Managers should do all the thinking relating to the planning and design of work, leaving the workers with the task of implementation.

2. *Use scientific methods* to determine the most efficient way of doing work. Design the worker's task accordingly, specifying the *precise* way in which the work is to be done.

3. *Select* the best person to perform the job thus designed.

4. *Train* the worker to do the work efficiently.

5. *Monitor* worker performance to ensure that appropriate work procedures are followed and that appropriate results are achieved.

Taylor also advocated the use of time-and-motion study as a means of analyzing and standardizing work activities. His scientific approach called for detailed observation and measurement of work to find the optimum mode of performance. Under Taylor's system even menial tasks such as pig-iron handling and earth shoveling became the subjects of science.

Prominent models of his approach to scientific management are found in numerous manufacturing firms, retail organizations, and offices.

Scientific management in fast food, assembly lines, and office work

Consider the fast-food chains serving hamburgers, pizzas, and other highly standardized products. Work is often organized in the minutest detail on the basis of designs that analyze the total process of production, find the most efficient procedures, and then allocate these as specialized duties to people trained to perform them in a very precise way. All the *thinking* is done by the managers and designers, leaving all the *doing* to the employees. The management observation checklist presented in exhibit 2.1 provides the perfect illustration of Taylor's approach to management, showing how a simple job such as taking and serving a customer's order can be split into many separate elements that can each be observed and evaluated.

Taylor's approach to work design is also found in traditional forms of assembly-line manufacturing and in production processes that are tightly controlled and monitored by computer technology. Here Taylor's ideas are built into the technology itself, making the workers servants or adjuncts to machines that are in complete control of the organization and pace of work.

Taylor's principles also had a major influence on the organization of office work through projects that broke integrated tasks into specialized components that could then be allocated to different employees. For example, in mechanized systems for processing insurance claim forms, one employee would often be responsible for checking a claim against a policy, another would initiate an evaluation process, another would conduct the evaluation, yet another would evaluate the evaluation, and so on. Systematically applied, Taylor's five principles led to the development of office factories where people performed fragmented and highly specialized duties in accordance with an elaborate system of work design and performance evaluation.

The effect of Taylor's scientific management on the workplace has been enormous, increasing productivity manyfold while accelerating the replacement of skilled craftspeople by unskilled workers. But the increases in productivity have often been achieved at great human cost, reducing many workers to automatons, just as the army reforms of Frederick the Great did to his soldiers over 150 years earlier.

Scientific management and dehumanization

The scientific management trend is so pervasive that it is now often described as one of "McDonaldization." This term captures how the organizational principles underlying the design of the McDonald's chain of fast-food restaurants, with its emphasis on efficiency, quantification, predictability, control, and deskilled jobs (often described as "McJobs"), is providing an icon for organization throughout society.

The human problems resulting from Tayloristic methods of organization have been glaringly obvious ever since they were first introduced:

- For most people, assembly-line work is simply boring or alienating. Job cycles are often very short, with workers sometimes being asked to complete work involving seven or eight separate operations every forty or fifty seconds, seven or eight hours a day, fifty weeks a year.

- When Henry Ford established his first assembly line to produce the Model T, employee turnover rose to approximately 380 percent per annum. Only by doubling wages to his famous "$5 a day" was he able to stabilize the work situation and persuade workers to accept the new technology.

- When General Motors (GM) decided to tighten up on efficiency in its Lordstown plant in the late 1960s, at the height of its commitment to this technology, the speed of the assembly line was raised to increase output from 60 to 100 cars per hour. At this new pace some workers had only thirty-six seconds to perform at least eight different operations, such as walking, lifting, handling, raising a carpet, bending to fasten bolts, fastening them by air gun, replacing the carpet, and putting a sticker on the hood.

- The principle of separating the planning and design of work from its execution is often seen as the most pernicious and far-reaching element of Taylor's approach to management, for it effectively "splits" the worker, advocating the separation of hand and brain. As Taylor was fond of telling his workers, "You are not supposed to think. There are other people paid for thinking around here."   — ov "headcount"

- Men and women were no more than "hands" or "manpower": the energy or force required to propel the organizational machine. The jobs they were required to perform were simplified to the ultimate degree so that workers would be cheap, easy to train, easy to supervise, and easy to replace.

Just as the system of mass production required that products be assembled from interchangeable parts, Taylor's system rationalized the workplace so that it could be "manned" by interchangeable workers.

The universal appeal of scientific management

Over the years, Taylor's approach to management has been extended and refined in many ways, most notably through the development of franchising systems that are faced with the challenge of offering consistent products and services through decentralized operations and through the science of ergonomics, which studies the use of energy in the workplace.

Interestingly, Taylor's principles have crossed many ideological barriers, being extensively used in the former USSR and Eastern Europe as well as in capitalist countries. This fact signifies that Taylorism is as much a tool for securing general control over the workplace as it is a means of generating profit. Although noncapitalist countries and institutions are rarely averse to profitable use of productive resources, one of the great attractions of Taylorism rests in the power it confers on those in control.

Although Taylor is often seen as the villain who created scientific management, it is important to realize that he was really part of a much broader social trend involving the mechanization of life generally. The principles underlying Taylorism are now found on the football field and athletics track, in the gymnasium, and in the way we rationalize and routinize our personal lives. Taylorism was typically imposed on the workforce. But many of us impose forms of Taylorism on ourselves as we train and develop specialized capacities for thought and action and shape our bodies to conform with preconceived ideals. Under the influence of the same kind of mechanism that has helped make Taylorism so powerful, we often think about and treat ourselves as if we were machines.

The really distinctive feature of Taylorism is not the fact that Taylor tried to mechanize the organization of people and work, but the *degree* to which he was able to do this. Taylor's workers were expected to be as reliable, predictable, and efficient as the robots that are now replacing them. History may well judge that Taylor came before his time. His principles of scientific management make superb sense for organizing production when robots rather than human beings are the main productive force, and then organizations can truly become machines.

The ultimate goal: Finding the one best way to organize

"Set goals and objectives and go for them."

"Organize rationally, efficiently, and clearly."

"Specify every detail so that all involved will be sure of the jobs that they have to perform."

"Plan, organize, and control, control, control."

These and other similar ideas are often ingrained in our way of thinking about organization and in the way we evaluate organizational practice. For many people, it is almost second nature to organize by setting up a structure of clearly defined activities linked by clear lines of communication, coordination, and control:

- When managers design organizations they frequently design a formal structure of jobs into which people can then be "fitted."

- When a vacancy arises in an organization, managers frequently talk about having "a slot" to fill.

- Much of our training and education is often geared to making us "fit in" and feel comfortable in our appointed place so that organization can proceed in a rational and efficient way.

Classical management theory and scientific management were each pioneered and sold to managers as the one best way to organize. The early theorists believed that they had discovered *the* principles of organization, which, if followed, would more or less solve managerial problems forever. Now, we only have to look at the contemporary organizational scene to find that they were completely wrong on this score. Indeed, we find that their management principles often lie at the basis of many modern organizational problems.

STRENGTHS AND LIMITATIONS OF THE MACHINE METAPHOR

As we noted in chapter 1, metaphors only create partial ways of seeing, for in encouraging us to see and understand the world from one perspective they discourage us from seeing it from others. This is exactly what has happened in the course of developing mechanistic approaches to organization.

In understanding organization as a rational, technical process, mechanical imagery tends to underplay the human aspects of organization and to overlook the fact that the tasks facing organizations are often much more complex, uncertain, and difficult than those that can be performed by most machines.

The strengths and limitations of the machine as a metaphor for organization are reflected in the strengths and limitations of mechanistic organization in practice.

STRENGTHS

■ Mechanistic approaches to organization work well under conditions when machines work well.

- when there is a straightforward task to perform,
- when the environment is stable and predictable enough to ensure the products produced will be appropriate,
- when one wishes to produce exactly the same product time and again,
- when precision and efficiency are at a premium, and
- when the human "machine" parts are required to be compliant and behave as they have been designed to do.

Some organizations have had spectacular success using the mechanistic model because these conditions are all fulfilled. McDonald's and many firms in the fast-food industry provide the best examples.

McDonald's built a solid reputation for excellent performance in the fast-food industry by mechanizing the organization of all its franchise outlets all over the world so that each can produce a uniform product. It serves a carefully targeted mass market in a perfectly regular and consistent way. The firm is exemplary in its adoption of Tayloristic principles and recruits a nonunionized labor force, often made up of high school and college students and part-time workers, who can be molded to fit the organization as designed. And the "machine" works perfectly most of the time. Of course, the company also has a dynamic and innovative character, but this is for the most part confined to its central staff who do the thinking (i.e., the policy development and design work) for the corporation as a whole.

Many franchising systems have used the same Tayloristic approach with great effect, centralizing the design and development of products or services and decentralizing implementation in a highly controlled way. The use of scientific methods to determine the work to be performed, manuals that set standards and codify performance in minute detail, well-developed recruitment and training plans, and comprehensive systems of job analysis often provide the recipe for success, provided that the service or product is amenable to definition and control in this way.

Surgical wards, aircraft maintenance departments, finance offices, courier firms, and other organizations where precision, safety, and clear accountability are at a premium are also often able to implement mechanistic approaches successfully in some, if not all, aspects of their operations.

LIMITATIONS

■ **Mechanistic approaches create organizational forms that have difficulty in adapting to change.**

Like machines, mechanistic organizations are designed to achieve predetermined goals. They are *not* designed for innovation.

■ **Mechanistic approaches can result in mindless and unquestioning bureaucracy.**

The flexibility and creative action that are so important in changing circumstances are often blocked by the barriers inherent in mechanistic divisions between different hierarchical levels, functions, and roles. As a result

- problems can be ignored because there are no ready-made responses;

- communications can be ineffective because standardized procedures and channels of communication are often unable to deal with new circumstances;

- paralysis and inaction can lead to backlogs of work;
- senior managers can become remote because they have no *direct* contact with front-line issues;
- high degrees of specialization can create myopic views because there is no overall grasp of the situation facing the enterprise as a whole; and
- mechanistic definitions of job responsibilities can encourage many organizational members to adopt mindless, unquestioning attitudes, such as "It's not my job to worry about that," "That's his responsibility, not mine," or "I'm here to do what I'm told."

Although all these problems are often seen as being caused by poor execution or by the attitudes that employees "bring to work," they are actually inherent in the mechanistic approach. This is due to the irony that defining work responsibilities in a clear-cut manner has the advantage of letting all organization members know what is expected of them. But it also lets them know what is *not* expected of them. Initiative is discouraged because people are expected to obey orders and keep their place, not question what they are doing.

As we enter the twenty-first century, we find bureaucracies and other modes of mechanistic organization coming under increasing attack because of all these dysfunctional consequences. The total quality movement and emphasis on flexible, team-based organization that came into prominence in the 1980s and 1990s are examples of the response to these problems and the need to find new, nonmechanical ways of organizing. From a historical perspective, the mechanistic approach to organization belongs to the mechanical age. Now that we are entering an age with a completely new technological base drawing on microelectronics, new organizational principles are likely to become increasingly important.

The images of organization considered in the following chapters give a glimpse of what may be both possible and appropriate for managing in these new times.

[handwritten annotation] WHAT MAY BE POSSIBLE MOVING FORWARD →

3

Nature Intervenes: Organizations As Organisms

THE IMAGE OF AN ORGANISM SEEKING TO ADAPT AND SURVIVE IN A CHANGING ENVIRONMENT offers a powerful perspective for managers who want to help their organizations flow with change.

- The metaphor helps us to understand organizations as clusters of interconnected human, business, and technical needs.

- It encourages us to learn about the art of corporate survival.

- It urges us to develop vibrant organic systems that remain open to new challenges.

The metaphor offers powerful ways of thinking about strategy and organizational design, showing that the mechanical perspective, so popular in management, is just one of many approaches. It encourages us to see how whole populations of organizations may rise and fall along with the transformation of the niches and resource flows on which they depend, and to understand that, as in nature, the evolution of the corporate world reflects a "survival of the fitting," not just the survival of the fittest.

The metaphor suggests that different environments favor different species of organizations based on different methods of organizing and that congruence with the environment is the key to success.

LET'S THINK ABOUT ORGANIZATIONS AS IF THEY WERE ORGANISMS.
We find ourselves thinking about them as living systems, existing in a wider environment on which they depend for the satisfaction of various needs. And as we look around the organizational world, we begin to see that it is possible to identify different species of organization in different kinds of environments. Just as we find polar bears in arctic regions, camels in deserts, and alligators in swamps, we notice that certain species of organization are better "adapted" to specific environmental conditions than others. We find that bureaucratic organizations tend to work most effectively in environments that are stable or protected in some way and that very different species are found in more competitive and turbulent regions, such as the environments of high-tech firms in the aerospace and microelectronics industries.

In this simple line of inquiry we find many of the key ideas in organization theory throughout the second half of the twentieth century. The problems of mechanistic organization resulted in shifting attention away from mechanical science and toward biology as a source of ideas for thinking about organization. In the process, organization theory has become a kind of biology in which the distinctions and relations among *molecules, cells, complex organisms, species,* and *ecology* are paralleled in those between *individuals, groups, organizations, populations (species) of organizations,* and their *social ecology.* This has generated many new ideas for understanding how organizations function and the factors that influence their well-being.

In this chapter, we will explore how the organismic metaphor has helped organization theorists identify and study different organizational needs, and focus on the following:

- organizations as "open systems,"
- the process of adapting organizations to environments,
- organizational life cycles,
- factors influencing organizational health and development,
- different species of organization, and
- the relations between species and their ecology.

Collectively, these ideas have had an enormous impact on the way we now think about organization. Under the influence of the machine metaphor, organization theory was locked into a form of engineering preoccupied with relations between goals, structures, and efficiency. The idea that organizations are more like organisms guided our attention toward the more general issues of survival, organization-environment relations, and organizational effectiveness. Goals, structures, and efficiency now become subsidiary to problems of survival and other more biological concerns.

DISCOVERING ORGANIZATIONAL NEEDS

Organization theory began its excursion into biology by developing the idea that employees are people with complex needs that must be satisfied if they are to lead full and healthy lives and to perform effectively in the workplace. In retrospect, this seems an obvious fact of life. We all know that employees work best when motivated by the tasks they have to perform and that the process of motivation hinges on allowing people to achieve rewards that satisfy their personal needs. However, in the nineteenth and early twentieth centuries for many people work was a basic necessity, and those who designed and managed early organizations treated it as such.

[handwritten margin note: work was seen as a basic necessity]

As we saw in the previous chapter, the design of organizations was viewed as a *technical* problem, and the task of encouraging people to comply with the requirements of the organizational machine was reduced to a problem of "paying the right rate for the job." Although esprit de corps was viewed as a valuable aid, management was viewed primarily as a process of controlling and directing employees in their work.

IDENTIFYING SOCIAL AND PSYCHOLOGICAL NEEDS

Much of organization theory since the late 1920s has focused on the limitations of the machine perspective. We can start the story with the Hawthorne studies, conducted in the 1920s and 1930s under the leadership of Elton Mayo. At the outset, the studies were primarily concerned with investigating the relation between conditions of work and the incidence of fatigue and boredom among employees. As the research progressed, it left this narrow perspective to focus on many other aspects of the work situation, including the attitudes and preoccupations of employees, and factors in the social environment outside work.

The studies are now famous for identifying the importance of social needs in the workplace and the fact that work groups can satisfy these needs by restricting output and engaging in other unplanned activities. In identifying that an "informal organization" based on friendship groups and unplanned interactions can exist alongside the formal organization documented in the "blueprints" designed by management, the studies showed that work activities are influenced as much by the nature of human beings as by formal design, and that we must pay close attention to this human side of organization.

[handwritten margin note: WE MUST PAY ATTENTION]

The question of work motivation became a burning issue, as did the relations between individuals and groups. A new theory of organization began to emerge, built on the idea that individuals and groups, like biological organisms, operate most effectively only when their needs are satisfied.

For example, Abraham Maslow's theory of motivation (exhibit 3.1) presented the human being as a kind of psychological organism struggling to satisfy its needs in a quest for full growth and development. This theory, which suggested that humans are motivated by a hierarchy of needs progressing through the physiological, the social, and the psychological, had very powerful implications, for it suggested that bureaucratic organizations that sought to motivate employees through money or by merely providing a secure job confined human development to the lower levels of the need hierarchy. Many management theorists were quick to see that jobs and interpersonal relations could be redesigned to create conditions for personal growth that would simultaneously help organizations achieve their aims and objectives.

[handwritten margin note: IMPORTANT MASLOW IMPACT]

INTEGRATING THE NEEDS OF INDIVIDUALS AND ORGANIZATIONS

The idea of integrating the needs of individuals and organizations became a powerful force. Alternatives to bureaucratic organization began to emerge as research showed how bureaucratic structures, leadership styles, and work organization generally could be modified to create "enriched," motivating jobs that would encourage people to exercise their capacities for self-control and creativity.

Particular attention was focused on the idea of making employees feel more useful and important by giving them meaningful jobs and by giving as much autonomy, responsibility, and recognition as possible as a means of getting them involved in their work. Job enrichment, combined with a more participative, democratic, and employee-centered style of leadership, arose as an alternative to the excessively narrow, authoritarian, and dehumanizing work orientation generated by scientific management and classical management theory.

Since the 1960s, management and organizational researchers have given much attention to shaping the design of work to increase productivity and job satisfaction while improving work quality and reducing employee absenteeism and turnover. Human resource management has become a major focus of attention, and the need to integrate the human and technical aspects of work an important principle.

TYPE OF NEED

Self-actualizing

- Encouragement of complete employee commitment
- Job a major expressive dimension of employee's life

Ego

- Creation of jobs with scope for achievement, autonomy, responsibility, and personal control
- Work enhancing personal identity
- Feedback and recognition for good performance (e.g., promotions, "employee of the month" awards)

Social

- Work organization that permits interaction with colleagues
- Social and sports facilities
- Office and factory parties and outings

Security

- Pension and health care plans
- Job tenure
- Emphasis on career paths within the organization

Physiological

- Salaries and wages
- Safe and pleasant working conditions

Exhibit 3.1. Examples of how organizations can satisfy needs at different levels of Maslow's hierarchy

Sociotechnical systems

This dual focus on people and technology is now captured in the view that organizations are best understood as "sociotechnical systems"—one element in this configuration *always* has important consequences for the other. When we choose a technical system (whether in the form of an organizational structure, job design, or particular technology), it always has human consequences, and vice versa. This was clearly illustrated in Eric Trist and Ken Bamforth's study on technological change in coal mining in England in the late 1940s.

The attempt to mechanize coal mining through the introduction of the "long-wall method" in effect brought assembly-line coal cutting to the coal face and created severe problems by destroying the informal fabric of social relations present in the mine. The new technology promised increases in efficiency yet brought all the social problems now associated with the modern factory. It isolated the miners, broke group cohesion and support, and prevented individuals from exercising control over their work. The resolution of the problems rested in finding a means of reconciling human needs and technical efficiency.

Work in most parts of the world has shown that in designing or managing any kind of social system, whether it be a small group, an organization, or a society, the interdependence of technical and human needs must be kept firmly in mind.

The sociotechnical principle now seems very obvious and is clearly recognized in most popular theories of organization, leadership, and group functioning. But there is still a tendency in management to fall back into a strictly technical view of organization. As noted in the machine chapter, this has been the primary problem facing the reengineering movement. By placing primary emphasis on the design of technical "business systems" as the key to change, the majority of reengineering programs mobilized all kinds of social, cultural, and political resistance that undermined their effectiveness.

RECOGNIZING THE IMPORTANCE OF ENVIRONMENT: ORGANIZATIONS AS OPEN SYSTEMS

When we recognize that individuals, groups, and organizations have needs that must be satisfied, attention is invariably drawn to the fact that they depend on a wider environment for various kinds of sustenance. It is this kind of thinking that now underpins the "open systems approach" to organization, which builds on the principle that organizations, like organisms, are "open" to their environment and must achieve an appropriate relation with that environment if they are to survive.

The open systems approach has generated many new concepts for thinking about social systems and organizations, which are often presented as general principles for thinking about *all* kinds of systems.

- *An open system* is one in which there is a continuous exchange with the environment. Cycles of input, internal transformation, through-put, output, and feedback exchange are crucial for sustaining the life and form of the system. The open nature of biological and social systems contrasts with the "closed" nature of many physical and mechanical systems, although the degree of openness can vary. Towers, bridges, and clockwork toys with predetermined motions are closed systems. A machine that is able to regulate its internal operation in accordance with variations in the environment may be considered a partially open system. A living organism, organization, or social group is a fully open system.

- *Homeostasis* refers to self-regulation and the ability to maintain a steady state. Biological organisms seek a regularity of form and distinctness from the environment while maintaining a continuous exchange with that environment through "negative feedback," where deviations from standards or norms initiate actions to correct the deviation. When body temperature rises above normal limits, certain bodily functions try to counteract the rise (e.g., we begin to perspire and breathe heavily). Likewise, social systems require homeostatic control processes to maintain their social structure.

- *Entropy* refers to the tendency of closed systems to deteriorate and run down.

- *Negative entropy* refers to open systems' attempts to sustain themselves by importing energy to offset entropic tendencies.

- *Requisite variety* refers to the internal complexity of a system. The law of requisite variety states that the internal regulatory mechanisms of a system must be as diverse as its environment in order to deal with the variety and challenge posed by the environment. Any system that insulates itself from diversity in the environment tends to atrophy and lose its complexity and distinctive nature.

- *Equifinality* refers to the fact that in an open system there may be many different ways of arriving at the same end. Living systems have flexible patterns of organization that allow the achievement of specific results from different starting points with different resources in different ways. The structure of the system at a given time does not determine the process but rather is a manifestation of the process. In contrast, closed systems relations are fixed to produce specific patterns of cause and effect.

- *System evolution* refers to a cyclical process of variation, selection, and retention of selected system characteristics that allow the system to move to more complex forms of differentiation and integration in order to allow the system to deal with challenges and opportunities posed by the environment.

PRACTICAL IMPLICATIONS OF OPEN SYSTEMS

Open systems principles have been extremely influential and have refocused understanding of organization in several ways.

1. *Open systems theory emphasizes the importance of the environment in which organizations exist.* The classical management theorists devoted relatively little attention to the environment. They treated the organization as a closed mechanical system and became preoccupied with principles of internal design. The open systems view suggests that we should always organize with the environment in mind. It devotes much attention to understanding the immediate task or business environment, defined by the organization's direct interactions with customers, competitors, suppliers, labor unions, and government agencies, as well as the broader contextual or general environment.

   All this has important implications for organizational practice, stressing the importance of being able to

   • scan and sense changes in task and contextual environments,

   • bridge and manage critical boundaries and areas of interdependence, and

   • develop appropriate operational and strategic responses.

   Much of the widespread interest in corporate strategy is a product of this realization that organizations must be sensitive to what is occurring in the world beyond.

2. *Organizations are seen as sets of interrelated subsystems.* Systems are like Chinese boxes in that they always contain wholes within wholes. Likewise, organizations contain individuals (who are systems on their own account) who belong to groups or departments that belong to larger organizational divisions. And so on.

If we define the whole organization as a system, then the other levels can be understood as subsystems, just as molecules, cells, and organs can be seen as subsystems of a living organism, even though they are complex open systems on their own account.

The sociotechnical view of organization is often expanded to take account of relations between technical, social, managerial, strategic, and environmental requirements (exhibit 3.2). This way of thinking has helped us to recognize how everything depends on everything else

---

Organizations, like organisms, can be conceived of as sets of interacting subsystems. These subsystems can be defined in many ways. Here is one example stressing relations between the different variables that influence the functioning of an organization, thereby providing a useful diagnostic tool.

Organizational Subsystems

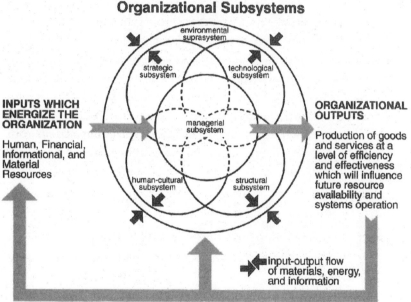

Exhibit 3.2. How an organization can be seen as a set of subsystems, adapted from F. E. Kast and J. E. Rosenzweig, *Contingency Views of Organization and Management*, p 36. © 1973, Science Research Associates, Inc.

---

and to find ways of managing the relations between critical subsystems and the environment.

3. *The open systems approach encourages us to establish congruencies or "alignments" between different systems and to identify and eliminate*

potential dysfunctions. Just as a sociotechnical approach to work design emphasizes the importance of matching human and technical requirements, open systems theory more generally encourages a matching of the kind of subsystems illustrated in exhibit 3.2. The principle of requisite variety is particularly important in designing control systems or for the management of internal and external boundaries—for these must embrace the complexity of the phenomena being controlled or managed to be effective.

Collectively, these three ideas have helped organization and management theory to break free of bureaucratic thinking to organize in a way that meets the requirements of the environment. They are now usually marshaled under the perspective known as "contingency theory" and in the practice of organizational development.

CONTINGENCY THEORY: ADAPTING ORGANIZATION TO ENVIRONMENT

- Organizations are open systems that need careful management to satisfy and balance internal needs and to adapt to environmental circumstances.

- There is no one best way of organizing. The appropriate form depends on the kind of task or environment with which one is dealing.

- Management must be concerned, above all else, with achieving alignments and "good fits."

- Different approaches to management may be necessary to perform different tasks within the same organization.

- Different types or "species" of organizations are needed in different types of environments.

In a nutshell, these are the main ideas underlying the contingency approach to organization, which has established itself as a dominant perspective in modern organizational analysis.

MECHANISTIC VERSUS ORGANIC ORGANIZATIONS

One of the most influential studies establishing the credentials of this approach was conducted in the 1950s by Tom Burns and G. M. Stalker. Their work is famous for establishing the distinction between "mechanistic" and "organic" approaches to organization and management.

Focusing on firms in a variety of industries (e.g., man-made fibers, engineering, and electronics), Burns and Stalker illustrated that when change in the environment becomes the order of the day, as when changing technological and market conditions pose new problems and challenges, open and flexible styles of organization and management are required. Exhibit 3.3 captures salient aspects of their study, illustrating patterns of organization and management in four successful firms experiencing different rates of environmental change.

The rayon mill: A mechanistic approach

The rayon mill faced a relatively stable environment, employed a technology that was routine and well understood, and was organized in a highly mechanistic way. The firm had a "factory bible," which was held by every head of a department and defined required action in almost every situation. People in the organization knew precisely what was expected of them and attended to their job responsibilities in a narrow yet efficient way to create a competitively priced product. The firm was relatively successful in meeting the demands placed upon it, treating problematic situations as temporary deviations from the norm and doing whatever it could to stabilize its operating environment. For example, the sales office was sometimes asked to restrain sales in the interest of sustaining an even and trouble-free production schedule.

The switch-gear firm: Modifications to embrace change

In other successful organizations facing more uncertain and turbulent environmental conditions, the mechanistic approach to organization tended to be abandoned; more flexible approaches to organization were required for successful operation. In a switch-gear firm operating in an area of the engineering industry, where product developments hinged on improvements in design and cutting costs and where products were frequently made to customer specifications, systems of authority, communication, and work organization were geared to the contingencies of changing situations. Great use was made of meetings as a means of exchanging information and identifying problems, particularly those relating to the coordination of work, so that an alternative system of organization existed alongside the formal hierarchy defining relationships between specialist tasks.

The radio and television manufacturing firm: A more organic approach

In successful firms in the electronics industry, the departure from the mechanistic mode was even more pronounced. For example, in a firm involved in radio and television manufacture, at the more stable end of the electronics spectrum, the need to keep abreast of market and technological change through frequent product modification and the need to link developments in research and production called for free and open collaboration

	Rayon Mill	Switch-Gear Firm	Radio and Television Firm	Electronics Firm
Nature of environment	Relatively stable: technological and market conditions well understood	Moderate rate of change: expanding market coupled with opportunities for improved products	High degree of change: dynamic technological and market conditions with predictable rate of novelty	Highly unpredictable: rapid technological advance and boundless market opportunities
Nature of task facing the firm	Efficient production of standard product	Efficient production and sale of basic product, subject to modification according to customer requirements	Efficient design, production, and marketing of new products highly competitive in environment	Exploitation of rapid technical change through innovation and exploration of new market situations
Organization of work	Clearly defined jobs arranged in hierarchical pattern	Rough division of job responsibilities according to functional and hierarchical pattern, modified to meet contingencies; no stable division of functions.	Consistent blurring of organizational positions; every section of management concerned with the focal task of competitive selling.	Deliberate attempt to avoid specifying individual tasks; jobs defined by the individuals as concerned through interaction with others
Nature of authority	Clearly defined and vested in formal position in hierarchy; seniority important	Not clearly defined but following the hierarchy except in specially convened committees and meetings	Limits of authority and responsibility not defined; authority vested in people with ability to solve problems at hand	Pattern of authority informal and constantly changing as roles become redefined with changing circumstances; vested in individuals with appropriate skills and abilities

	Mechanistic			Organic
Communications system	According to pattern specified in various rules and regulations; mainly vertical	According to rules and conventions but supplemented by regular system of committees and meetings; junior staff free to consult with top management group	Frequent meetings in a context of constant consultation across all levels and parts of the firm	Completely free and informal; the process of communication was unending and central to the concept of organization
Nature of employee commitment	Commitment to responsibilities associated with their own particular jobs; loyalty and obedience important	Commitment to own job but recognizing the need for flexibility in dealing with contingencies arising from the total situation	Commitment to demands of own functional positions reconciled with wider demands for cooperation and flexible interpretation of function	Full commitment to the central tasks facing the concern as a whole and an ability to deal with considerable stress and uncertainty

Mechanistic ⟷ Organic

Exhibit 3.3. Patterns of organization and management in four successful organizations facing different rates of environmental change, based on T. Burns and G. M. Stalker, *The Management of Innovation*. © 1961, Tavistock.

and communication across departments and levels of seniority. Meetings were again a central feature, driving and dominating day-to-day work activities. This approach to organization has grown in prominence since the publication of Burns and Stalker's work. It is most evident in the "project" or "matrix" form of organization, which makes use of project teams to deal with the continuous flow of problems and projects associated with changes in corporate policy and the external environment.

The electronics firm: Fully organic

In successful organizations in even more unpredictable areas of the electronics field, where the need to innovate was an essential condition for survival, the mode of organization was even more open. Here, jobs were allowed to shape themselves, because people were appointed to the organization for their general ability and expertise and were allowed and encouraged to find their own place and define the contributions that they could make.

This style of open, organic management is consistent with the way the electronics industry has evolved. When the first commercial electronics firms began operating at the end of World War II, there was no commercial market for electronics products to speak of, for peacetime applications of this newly emerging technology had yet to be found. The electronics industry literally had to invent both products and markets and at the same time cope with the rapid technological change that has converted computers from room-sized giants into devices that fit our pockets. Countless new applications have been found for the basic technology.

From the start, firms in this industry operated in an organic and flexible manner, creating or searching for opportunities in the environment and adapting themselves to take advantage of these opportunities. In the firms observed by Burns and Stalker, the process of finding out what one should be doing proved unending, defining a mode of organization linking inquiry and action, and the process has continued. Successful electronics firms avoided organizational hierarchies and avoided narrow departmentalization, with individuals and groups defining and redefining roles in a collaborative manner in connection with the tasks facing the organization as a whole. They created innovative, team-based organizations having more in common with an amoeba than a machine.

Burns and Stalker's ideas, that it is possible to identify various organizational forms ranging from mechanistic to organic, and that more flexible forms are required to deal with changing environments, quickly received support from other studies. These studies demonstrated that in the process of organizing, a lot of choices have to be made, and that effective organization depends on achieving a balance or compatibility between strategy, structure, technology, the commitments and needs of people, and the external environment. We find here the essence of modern contingency theory. But it took an important study, led by Paul Lawrence and Jay Lorsch, to hammer the point home.

AWARENESS OF THE NEED FOR INTERNAL DIFFERENTIATION AND INTEGRATION

Lawrence and Lorsch's research was built around two principal ideas:

1. that different kinds of organizations are needed to deal with different market and technological conditions, and

2. that organizations operating in uncertain and turbulent environments need to achieve a higher degree of internal differentiation (e.g., between departments) than those in environments that are less complex and more stable.

They studied high- and low-performance organizations in three industries experiencing high, moderate, and low rates of growth and technological and market change:

- The *plastics industry* was selected as an example of a turbulent environment.

- The *standardized container industry* was selected as an example of a stable environment.

- The *food industry* served as an example that falls between a stable and a turbulent environment.

Lawrence and Lorsch's results supported their hypotheses, showing that successful firms in each environment achieved an appropriate degree of differentiation and integration and that the degree of differentiation between departments tended to be greater in the plastics industry than in the food industry, which was in turn greater than that in the standardized container industry.

The Lawrence and Lorsch study thus refined the contingency approach by showing that styles of organization may need to vary between organizational subunits because of the detailed characteristics of their subenvironments. At the time of their study, production departments typically faced task environments characterized by more clear-cut goals and shorter time horizons. They adopted more formal or bureaucratic modes of interaction. Research and development departments, especially those engaged in fundamental as opposed to applied research, faced even more ambiguous goals, had longer time horizons, and usually adopted even more informal modes of interaction. The study showed that the degree of required differentiation in managerial and organization styles between departments varied according to the nature of the industry and its environment and that an appropriate degree of integration was also needed to tie the differentiated parts together again.

The study also yielded important insights on modes of integration: In relatively stable environments, conventional bureaucratic modes of integration such as hierarchy and rules appeared to work quite well. But in more turbulent environments, they needed to be replaced by other modes, such as the use of multidisciplinary project teams and the appointment of personnel skilled in the art of coordination and conflict resolution. The successful use of these integrative devices was also shown to be dependent on achieving an intermediate stance between the units being coordinated; on the power, status, and competence of those involved; and on the presence of a structure of rewards favoring integration.

Lawrence and Lorsch gave precision and refinement to the general idea that certain organizations need to be more organic than others, suggesting that the degree of organicism required varies from one organizational subunit to another. Even in the dynamic context of an electronics firm, where the dominant ethic may be to remain open, flexible, and innovative, certain aspects of production or financial administration may require clearer definition and control than work in other areas.

THE VARIETY OF THE SPECIES

Since the 1960s, hundreds of research studies have further addressed the job of specifying organizational characteristics and their success in dealing with different tasks and environmental conditions, adding rich insight to the mechanistic-organic continuum developed by Burns and Stalker. The idea has developed that different "species" of organization are needed to cope with the demands of different environments.

For example, Henry Mintzberg has identified five types of organization:

- the *machine bureaucracy,*
- the *divisionalized form,*
- the *professional bureaucracy,*
- the *simple structure,* and
- the species that we refer to as the *adhocracy.*

Within each species, effective organization depends on developing a cohesive set of relations between structural design; the age, size, and technology of the firm; and the conditions of the industry in which it is operating.

The machine bureaucracy and the divisionalized form (as seen in the machine chapter) tend to be ineffective except under conditions where tasks and environment are simple and stable. Their highly centralized systems of control tend to make them slow and ineffective in dealing with changing circumstances. While appropriate for firms that are production driven or efficiency driven, they are often inappropriate for firms that are market or environment driven.

The professional bureaucracy modifies the principles of centralized control to allow greater autonomy to staff and is appropriate for dealing with relatively stable conditions where tasks are relatively complicated. This has proved an appropriate structure for universities, hospitals, and other professional organizations where people with key skills and abilities need a large measure of autonomy and discretion to be effective in their work. But since the 1980s, the profesional bureaucracy's effectiveness has been severely challenged by the changing environments with which these kinds of organizations have had to deal. The structure of the professional bureaucracy tends to be fairly flat with tall hierarchies being replaced by a decentralized system of authority. Standardization and integration are achieved through professional training and the acceptance of key operating norms rather than through more direct forms of control.

The simple structure and adhocracy tend to work best in unstable environmental conditions.

The simple structure usually comprises a chief executive, often the founder or an entrepreneur, who may have a group of support staff along with a group of operators who do the basic work. Organization is very informal and flexible and, although run in a highly centralized way by the chief executive, is ideal for achieving quick changes and maneuvers. This form of organization works very well in entrepreneurial organizations where speedy decision making is at a premium, provided that tasks are not too complex. It is typical of successful young and innovative companies.

The adhocracy characterizes organizations that are temporary by design, approximating Burns and Stalker's organic form of organization. It is a form highly suited for the performance of complex and uncertain tasks in turbulent environments. It usually involves project teams that come together to perform a task and disappear when the task is over, with members regrouping in other teams devoted to other projects. Sometimes, this kind of enterprise is called a "virtual" or "network" organization, especially when teams and team members are spread geographically, using electronic technology and occasional face-to-face meetings to integrate their activities.

Adhocracies, "virtual teams," and "virtual organizations" now abound in innovative firms in the electronic and other high-tech and rapidly changing industries. They are the norm in all kinds of project-oriented companies, such as consulting firms and advertising agencies, and in the movie industry. This form of organization also sometimes emerges as a differentiated unit of a larger organization: for example, an ad hoc task group or project team performing a limited assignment or contributing to the strategic planning and development of the organization as a whole. It is also frequently used in research and development (R&D).

Each species of organization seems to have distinct characteristics and distinctive niches in which it excels. Like organizations in the natural world, it seems that successful organizations evolve appropriate structures and processes for dealing with the challenges of their external environment, and the proliferation of species equipped to deal with high degrees of change seems to be a major trend. As technological and market changes challenge traditional niches, many old-style bureaucracies are becoming extinct and being replaced by more nimble competitors.

Despite a high degree of consensus about the nature of this basic trend, organization and management researchers are deeply split in terms of their explanations of *how* organizations can strike an appropriate relationship with the environment:

- One school of thought argues that managers can use the insights of contingency theory to develop a "good fit" between organization and environment.

- The other argues that, although short-term innovation and adjustments are always possible, the forces of natural selection and the environment are ultimately in control.

These contrasting views are explored in the following sections of this chapter.

CONTINGENCY THEORY: PROMOTING ORGANIZATIONAL HEALTH AND DEVELOPMENT

DIAGNOSING ORGANIZATION–ENVIRONMENT COMPATIBILITY

- How can an organization systematically achieve a good fit with its environment?

- How can it adapt to changing environmental circumstances?

- How can it ensure that internal relations are balanced and appropriate?
- What does this mean in operational terms?

These and related questions have become the focus of attention for numerous consultancy-oriented researchers working in the field of organizational development. They have helped bring the insights generated by the contingency theorists and by the systems approach down to earth by developing diagnostic and prescriptive models to identify organizational ailments and to prescribe some kind of cure. To diagnose and prescribe, they usually pose a series of questions about the existing internal organizational relations and between the organization and environment, for example:

1. *What is the nature of the organization's environment?*

    Is it simple and stable or complex and turbulent? Is it easy to see interconnections between various elements of the environment?

    What changes are occurring in the economic, technological, market, labor relations, and sociopolitical dimensions?

    What is the chance of some development transforming the whole environment—some development that will create a new opportunity or challenge the viability of existing operations?

2. *What kind of strategy is being employed?*

    Is the organization adopting a nonstrategy, simply reacting to whatever change comes along?

    Is the organization attempting to defend a particular niche that it has created in the environment?

    Is the organization systematically analyzing the environment to identify new threats and opportunities?

    Is the organization adopting an innovative, proactive stance, constantly searching for new opportunities and evaluating existing activities?

    Is the stance toward the environment competitive or collaborative?

3. *What kind of technology (mechanical and nonmechanical) is being used?*

    Are the processes used to transform inputs into outputs standardized and routinized?

    Does the technology create jobs with high or low scope for responsibility and autonomy?

Does the technology rigidify operations, or is it flexible and open-ended?

What technological choices face the organization?

Can it replace rigid systems with more flexible forms?

4. *What kinds of people are employed, and what is the dominant "culture" or ethos within the organization?*

What orientations do people bring to their work? Is a narrow "I'm here for the money" commitment the norm, or are people searching for challenge and involvement?

What are the core values and beliefs shaping patterns of corporate culture and subculture?

5. *How is the organization structured, and what are the dominant managerial philosophies?*

Is the organization bureaucratic, or are matrix/organic forms of organization the norm?

Profile of Organizational Characteristics

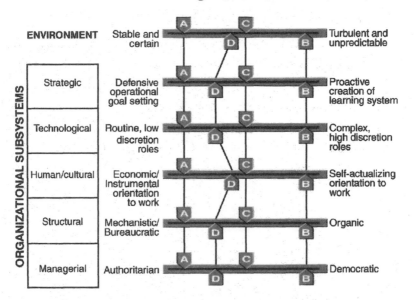

Lines A, B, and C illustrate congruent, and line D illustrates incongruent, relations between systems.

Exhibit 3.4. Congruence and incongruence between organizational subsystems, adapted from G. Burrell and G. Morgan, *Sociological Paradigms and Organizational Analysis*, p. 177. © 1979, Heinemann Educational Books.

Is the dominant managerial philosophy authoritarian, stressing accountability and close control?

Or is it more democratic, encouraging initiative and enterprise throughout the organization?

Does the philosophy stress safe but sure approaches, or is it innovative and risk taking?

[handwritten margin note: WHAT WAS MY OWN MANAGERIAL PHILOSOPHY?]

This scheme of questioning builds on the idea that the organization consists of interrelated subsystems of a strategic, human, technological, structural, and managerial nature (see exhibit 3.2). From a contingency standpoint, these subsystems need to be both internally consistent and adapted to environmental conditions. Exhibit 3.4 shows how we can plot our answers to create a practical tool that reveals congruencies and incongruencies between organization and environment.

Three examples of congruent relations between organizational and environmental characteristics are represented by the positions A, B, and C in exhibit 3.4. In accordance with the conclusions of contingency theory, each is likely to be highly effective.

Position A represents an organization in a stable environment adopting a defensive strategy to protect its niche. Perhaps it is an organization commanding a secure market on the basis of a good quality product produced in a cost-efficient way. The organization employs a mass-production technology and is structured and managed mechanistically. The people employed are content with their narrowly defined roles, and the organization operates in an efficient and trouble-free manner.

Position C represents an organization encountering a moderate degree of change in its environment. Technological developments are occurring at a regular pace, and markets are in a constant state of transition. The organization has to keep abreast of these developments, analyzing emergent trends, updating production methods, and creating a flow of product modifications rather like the radio and television firm in Burns and Stalker's study. It is not on the cutting edge of innovation. Its competitive advantage rests in being able to produce a better product in a cost-effective way. The organization adopts an effective project-driven matrix organization and commands the required flexibility and commitment from its staff.

Position B represents the case of a firm in a highly turbulent environment where products and technologies are constantly changing and often have a very short life span. This means that the firm has to search for new ideas and opportunities on a continuous basis. The firm is a kind of "prospector," always looking for new places where it can strike gold. It relies on getting there first, recognizing that type C organizations will soon move in with a competitive product. Innovation is the lifeblood of this organization. It employs people who are prepared to make massive commitments to their work and who are motivated and managed in an organic way. Again, this organization is balanced internally and in relation to its environment.

Position D, on the other hand, presents an example of a set of organization-environment relations where the strategic stance, technology, and approach to organization and management are incongruent with the nature of the environment and the general orientations of the people within the organization. The conclusions of contingency theory suggest this would be ineffective. The situation is characteristic of an organization that is over-bureaucratized, being more inclined to defend the position it has achieved than to search out new opportunities. It is a frustrating place in which to work because the employees are looking for more open and demanding jobs than the strategy, technology, organization, and managerial style allow. Contingency theorists suggest that the organization should be designed and managed like organization C. If a way could be found to allow the people who are highly involved with the organization to initiate changes in the required direction, the organization could achieve a much more effective configuration of relations. At present, the incongruencies get in the way of effective operations, and the organization is likely to find difficulty in sustaining its position within the industry.

Organizational development practitioners confronted with the situation in organization D would attempt to improve the alignment of relations by persuading management to move closer to a C configuration. This organizational change strategy could involve action on a number of fronts—in relation to strategy, technology, organization structure, and management style. It would also involve an attempt to change the culture of the organization, namely, the systems of belief and practice that hold the organization in its ineffective configuration.

Balancing relations at the subunit level

The analytical diagnosis presented above can be conducted at the level of a total organization or major division, but it will also need to be conducted at the level of subunits within the organization to take account of Lawrence and Lorsch's point about the need for appropriate differentiation and integration.

Analysis at the subunit level identifies the pattern of relations necessary for dealing with various subenvironments and shows the required differentiation and integration. However, contingency theory suggests that care must be taken to ensure that the requirements of the parts do not take priority over those of the whole and that critical competencies are kept firmly in mind. For example, in organizations where frontline innovation is the basis of survival, the design and management of subunits must accommodate the primary task of innovation rather than the reverse.

The task of successful organizational change and development usually hinges on bringing variables into closer alignment so that an organization can meet the challenges and opportunities posed by its environment. In nature we find that organisms are endowed with a harmonious pattern of internal and external relations as a result of evolution. In organizations, however, the degree of internal harmony and fit with the environment is a product of human decision, action, and inaction so that incongruence and conflict are often the rule. As a result, there are usually many problems to keep managers and organizational consultants favoring a contingency approach very busy.

NATURAL SELECTION: THE POPULATION ECOLOGY VIEW OF ORGANIZATIONS

Up to now our use of the organismic metaphor has focused on organizations as the key units of analysis. We have discussed how organizations and their members can be seen as having different sets of needs and examined how organizations can develop patterns of relations that allow them to adapt to their environment. Survival has been presented as a problem of adaptation, with contingency theory offered as a means of identifying patterns of good fit and showing how these can be achieved.

Popular as this approach has been, in recent years it has attracted growing criticism from theorists and researchers subscribing to a "natural selection" view of organizations. In their opinion, the idea that organizations can adapt to their environment attributes too much flexibility and power to the organization and too little to the environment as a force in organizational survival. They advocate that we must counteract this imbalance by focusing on the way environments "select" organizations and that this can best be done by analysis at the level of *populations* of organizations and their wider ecology.

The "population ecology" view of organization brings Darwin's theory of evolution right into the center of organizational analysis. In essence, the argument is as follows: Organizations, like organisms in nature, depend for survival on their ability to acquire an adequate supply of the resources necessary to sustain existence. They have to face competition from other organizations, and since there is usually a resource scarcity, only the fittest survive. The nature, numbers, and distribution of organizations at any given time are dependent on resource availability and on competition within and between different species of organizations, making the environment the critical factor in determining which organizations succeed and which fail, by "selecting" the most robust competitors through elimination of the weaker ones.

Although selection may be the mechanism through which evolution occurs, it depends on there being variation in individual characteristics. Without variation there is nothing to select. So most applications of Darwin's theory build on a cyclical model that allows for the *variation, selection, retention*, and *modification* of species characteristics. Variations in a species typically arise as a result of cross-reproduction and random variation of characteristics. Some of these variations may confer a competitive advantage on the survival process, leading to a better chance of selection or of evolving along with changes in the environment. Because the surviving members of a species, or emerging new species, provide a foundation for the next stage of reproduction, there is a strong chance that the new characteristics will be retained. In turn, these characteristics will be subject to random modification, creating the variety that allows the process to continue. In this way, new species and ecological patterns evolve from variations in the old.

Although evolution occurs through modification of individual members of a species, the population ecologists argue that it is more important to understand evolutionary dynamics at the level of the population. When the environment changes or when a new species makes an inroad on the resource niche traditionally held by another, ultimately the change is reflected in population structure. Because members of a species tend to share similar strengths and weaknesses, it is the whole species that tends to survive or fail. Although some individual members may be fitter than others, they are often not as fit as the incoming species and tend to share the fate of their population in the long run.

This population perspective encourages us to understand the dynamics influencing whole populations of organizations. It suggests that organizational analysis should shift from explaining how individual organizations adapt to their environments to understanding how different species rise and decline in importance.

- Why are there so many different kinds of organizations?
- What factors influence their numbers and distribution?
- What factors influence a population's ability to acquire or retain a resource niche?

Under the influence of these and related questions, the population ecologists have begun to develop a form of organizational demography. Numerous research studies are attempting to identify species or populations (typically defined as sets of organizations sharing certain characteristics or a common fate with regard to environmental circumstances) and the birth rates, death rates, and general factors influencing organizational life cycles, growth, and decline. Considerable attention has also been devoted to understanding organizations and their environments in terms of "resource dependencies" and the patterning and availability of resource niches.

INSIGHTS CREATED BY THE POPULATION PERSPECTIVE

1. *Inertial pressures may prevent organizations from changing in response to their environment.* These inertial pressures include specialization of production plants and personnel; established ideas and "mindsets" of top managers; inadequate information; the difficulty of restructuring technology and personnel in unionized plants; the force of tradition; barriers to entry created by legal, fiscal, and other circumstances; and many other factors that make it impossible for organizations to engage in timely and efficient changes.

2. *Faced with new kinds of competition or environmental circumstances, whole industries or types of organization may come and go.* Large traditional steel mills may give way to small, technologically advanced competitors; department stores may give way to specialty stores in shopping malls or to "factory outlets"; coal mines and oil companies may give way to entrepreneurial solar energy firms; bureaucracies may give way to more flexible project-oriented firms, or market driven competitors; firms offering traditional products and services throughout the economy may find themselves eliminated by information technology companies serving customers in a completely different way; and public sector organizations in government, education, or health care may find once secure niches completely eroded by more nimble service-oriented firms in the private sector.

3. *The ability to obtain a resource niche and outperform one's competitors is all-important, and in the long run, relative superiority in being able to command resources applies to whole populations of organizations.* Perhaps one particularly skillful or efficient steel mill or department store may be able to hold off new forms of competition a little longer than other members of its species, but in the long run it too may become extinct, as a result of environmental changes that favor species of better fit.

4. *An awareness of the changing structure of critical resource niches and patterns of resource dependencies can make important contributions to our understanding of the success and power of different organizations.* The way that new populations of organizations can emerge through the dissemination of innovations or new practices, as has happened in the computer and electronics sector, does much to explain the changing structure of industry.

CRITICISMS OF POPULATION ECOLOGY THEORY

This kind of thinking has proved persuasive in many management circles, drawing attention to how organizations can be buffeted by broad environmental forces over which they have little control. However, there are counterviews. In particular

1. *The theory is seen as too deterministic.* If we accept at face value the theory that environments select organizations for survival, then in the long run it really doesn't matter what managers and decision makers do. Even efficient and successful firms that adapt to their environment are liable to fail as the result of environmental changes that influence the structure of their resource niche.

    The population ecology view has been much criticized for downplaying the importance of the choice of strategic direction for an organization. Despite inertial pressures, an organization may be able to transform itself from one kind of organization into another or shift from a declining niche to a more profitable one. For example, companies like General Electric have shifted out of their core business, in this case the electrical business, to become diversified conglomerates spanning many different sectors.

2. *The theory is seen as placing too much emphasis on resource scarcity and competition.* The emphasis on resource scarcity and competition, which lie at the basis of selection, underplays the fact that resources can be abundant and self-renewing and that organisms can collaborate as well as compete. Organizations that focus on creating value for existing new customers may be able to generate resource niches that never existed before. Many aspects of development in the information technology industry, bioengineering, and the electronic media business are fueled by this kind of process. Social and economic resources, especially in a knowledge economy, are inherently self-generating. When these neglected aspects of population ecology are brought into consideration, a more optimistic view of the ecology of organizations begins to emerge. It is to this that we now turn.

ORGANIZATIONAL ECOLOGY:
THE CREATION OF SHARED FUTURES

The population ecology and contingency views of organization both view organizations as existing in a state of tension or struggle with their environments. Both presume that organizations and environments are separate phenomena. Under the influence of developments in modern systems theory, however, this kind of assumption has attracted increasing criticism. Organizations, like organisms, are not really discrete entities, even though it may be convenient to think of them as such. They do not live in isolation and are not self-sufficient. Rather, they exist as elements in a complex ecosystem.

SURVIVAL = "SURVIVAL OF THE FITTING"

Many biologists now believe that it is the whole ecosystem that evolves and that the process of evolution can really be understood only at the level of the total ecology. This has important implications because it suggests that organisms do not evolve by adapting to environmental changes or as a result of these changes selecting the organisms that are to survive. Rather, it suggests that evolution is always evolution of a pattern of relations embracing organisms *and* their environments. It is the *pattern,* not just the separate units comprising this pattern, that evolves. Or as Kenneth Boulding has put it, evolution involves the "survival of the fitting," not just the survival of the fittest.

Organizations and their environments are engaged in a pattern of cocreation, where each produces the other. Just as in nature, where the environment of an organism is composed of other organisms, organizational environments are in large measure composed of other organizations. Once we recognize this, it becomes clear that organizations are, in principle, able to influence the nature of their environment. They can play an active role in shaping their future, especially when acting in concert with other organizations. Environments then become in some measure negotiated environments rather than independent external forces.

COLLABORATION, COMPETITION AND THE EVOLUTIONARY PROCESS

In the organizational world we find that, as in nature, collaboration is often as common as competition. Organizations in the same industry frequently get together under the umbrella of trade and professional associations to collaborate in relation to shared interests. Formal and informal cartels for price fixing, agreements regarding areas of competition and market sharing, and the joint sponsorship of lobbies designed to influence government legislation are obvious examples.

Examples of day-to-day collaborative relations between organizations in different industries or in different parts of the same industry are also very common. Firms often cultivate interlocking directorships to create a measure of shared decision making and control, engage in joint ventures to pool expertise or share risk in research and development, strike agreements with suppliers or manufacturers to achieve a measure of "vertical integration" of production, and engage in numerous kinds of informal networking. They sometimes establish informal joint organizations to link firms that have an interest in special problems or lines of development. For example, in the financial services industry it is not uncommon for banks, trust companies, insurance firms, and other interested agencies to offer joint services, in effect creating a new form of organization at the level of the industry. And in the high technology sector it is now quite common to find clusters of organizations collaborating and competing in a way that enhances the fitness of the whole niche.

An ecological perspective that emphasizes the importance of collaboration as well as competition can make an important contribution to how we understand and manage the world of organizations. Under the influence of interpretations of evolution that emphasize the survival of the fittest, competition is often encouraged as the basic rule of organizational life. Under the influence of more ecological interpretations stressing the survival of the fitting, the ethic of collaboration receives much more attention.

Inspired by this idea, social scientists have begun to investigate the possibility of developing new patterns of interorganizational relations that can help shape the future in a proactive way. Building on the observation that these relations emerge as a natural response to complexity and turbulence in the environment, it is argued that these relations should be encouraged to help make the turbulence more manageable. For example, the late Eric Trist came up with the idea of developing domain-based organizations that can embrace the organization-environment relations of a whole set of constituent organizations so that what were once external relations—for example, between competing or interdependent firms or between labor and management—now in some measure become internal relations that are open to collaborative action. The approach has been applied in a wide variety of settings to tackle problems of environmental pollution and regional and community economic development, as well as in the development of industrial associations.

Trist and his colleagues also encourage the development of informal learning networks that can generate domain-based exchange and discussion, promote shared appreciations of concerns and problems, facilitate the emergence of common values and norms, and find new solutions to shared problems.

The concern is to allow the ecology of organizational relations to evolve and survive. Just as natural ecologists are concerned about the disastrous effects of industrial pollution on the natural world, Trist and his successors believe that our organizational ecology is menaced by highly individualistic lines of action that threaten to make the social world completely unmanageable. The concept of organizational ecology marshals a new and creative way of thinking and acting in relation to these problems.

STRENGTHS AND LIMITATIONS OF THE ORGANISMIC METAPHOR

We began this chapter with the invitation to view organizations as organisms and have ended up with a review of some of the central ideas of modern organization theory. This is because most modern organization theorists have looked to nature to understand organizations and organizational life. The ideas identified provide an excellent illustration of how a metaphor can open our minds to a systematic and novel way of thinking. By exploring the parallels between organisms and organizations in terms of organic functioning, relations with the environment, relations between species, and the wider ecology, it has been possible to produce different theories and explanations that have very practical implications for organization and management.

Given the rich and varied insights, it is difficult to identify strengths and limitations that apply equally to all variations of the metaphor. However, there are a number of important commonalities.

STRENGTHS

■ The metaphor suggests that organizations must always pay close attention to their external environments.

Earlier mechanical theories (explored in the machine chapter) more or less ignored the role of the environment, treating organizations as relatively closed systems that could be designed as clearly defined structures of parts. In contrast, the ideas considered in this chapter stress that organizations must take close account of their environments to stand any chance of surviving. They must look externally, not just at issues of internal design.

■ Survival and evolution become central concerns.

The organismic metaphor emphasizes survival as the key aim facing any organization. This contrasts with the classical focus on the achievement of specific operational goals. Survival is a process. Goals and targets are often endpoints. This reorientation adds flexibility and warns of the dangers of goals becoming ends in themselves, a common fate in many organizations. The focus on the use and acquisition of resources and the satisfaction of different "needs" also encourages a broader and more flexible approach.

- **Achieving congruence with the environment becomes a key managerial task.**

In identifying different "species" of organization, we are alerted to the fact that in organizing we always have a range of options. It would be an exaggeration to suggest that mechanistic organizations do not innovate, but the point contains an important kernel of truth. The ideas explored in this chapter are at one in suggesting that if innovation is a priority, then flexible, dynamic, project-oriented matrix or organic forms of organization will be superior to the mechanistic-bureaucratic form.

- **The perspective contributes to the theory and practice of organization development.**

By focusing on key organizational subsystems and "needs," the organismic metaphor offers a methodology for transforming organizations to achieve effective relations with the environment. As shown, it has provided a powerful base for much management and consulting practice.

- **We acquire a new understanding of organization ecology.**

Whether we listen to "population ecologists" or advocates of collective evolution, the message of the organismic metaphor is the same. Organizations cannot survive as independent entities. Their future is bound with that of the wider context to which they belong. Here again, the metaphor invites us to broaden insight well beyond the boundaries of classical management theory.

LIMITATIONS

A way of seeing is a way of not seeing. Now that the organismic image of organization has established its powerful credentials, it is difficult to see how the classical theorists could have given so little attention to the influence of the environment. It is also difficult to see how they could have believed that there are uniform principles of management worthy of universal application. But we have to remember that the organizational world was much simpler then. The rise in importance of the organismic metaphor is in many respects a product of changing times that have undermined the efficiency of bureaucratic organizations. Organization theorists did not simply discover the organismic metaphor; they needed it to keep abreast of developments, and as we have seen, they have exploited its insights in many different ways.

Interestingly, most of the organismic metaphor's limitations are associated with the basic way of seeing that the metaphor encourages. Specifically

- **Organizations are *not* organisms, and their environments are far less concrete than the metaphor presumes.**

We know that organisms live in a natural world with material properties that determine the life and welfare of its inhabitants. We can see this world. We can touch and feel it. Nature presents itself as being objective and real in every aspect. However, this image breaks down when applied to society and organization because organizations and their environments can, at least to some extent, be understood as socially constructed phenomena. As we will discuss in the culture chapter, organizations are very much products of visions, ideas, norms, and beliefs, so their shape and structure is much more fragile and tentative than the material structure of an organism. True, there are many material aspects of organization, such as the land, buildings, machines, and money, but organizations fundamentally depend for life—in the form of ongoing organizational activity—upon the creative actions of human beings. Organizational environments can also be seen as being products of human creativity because they are made through the actions of the individuals, groups, and organizations who populate them.

It is thus misleading to suggest that organizations need to "adapt" to their environment, as do the contingency theorists, or that environments "select" the organizations that are to survive, as do the population ecologists. Both views tend to make organizations and their members dependent upon forces operating in an external world rather than recognizing that they are active agents operating with others in the construction of that world. The natural selection view of organizational evolution in particular gives the individual organization little influence in the struggle for survival. This view undermines the power of organizations and their members to help make their own futures. Organizations, unlike organisms, have a choice as to whether they are to compete or to collaborate. We may agree that an organization acting in isolation can have little impact on the environment, and hence that the environment presents itself as external and real in its effects, but it is quite a different matter when we consider the possibility of organizations collaborating in pursuit of plural interests to shape the environment they desire.

- **The metaphor overstates the degree of "functional unity" and internal cohesion found in most organizations.**

If we look at organisms in the natural world, we find them characterized by a functional interdependence where every element of the system, under normal circumstances, works for all the other elements. In the human body the blood, heart, lungs, arms, and legs normally work together to preserve the homeostatic functioning of the whole. The system is unified and shares a common life and a common future. Circumstances in which one element works in a way that sabotages the whole, as when appendicitis or a heart attack threatens one's life, are exceptional and potentially pathological.

If we look at most organizations, however, we find that the times at which their different elements operate with the degree of harmony discussed above are often more exceptional than normal. Most organizations are not as functionally unified as organisms. The different elements of an organization are usually capable of living separate lives and often do so. Although organizations *may* at times be highly unified, with people in different departments working in a selfless way for the organization as a whole, they may at other times be characterized by schism and major conflict.

The organismic metaphor has had a subtle yet important impact on our general thinking by encouraging us to believe that the unity and harmony characteristic of organisms can be achieved in organizational life. We often tend to equate organizational well-being with a state of unity where everyone is "pulling together." This style of thought usually leads us to see "political" and other self-interested activity as abnormal or dysfunctional features that should be absent in the healthy organization. As we will see in the politics chapter, the emphasis upon unity rather than conflict as the normal state of organization may be an inherent weakness of the organismic metaphor. In recent years, those favoring the metaphor have begun to recognize this weakness by giving more attention to the role of power in organizations, but they rarely have gone so far as to abandon the ideal of functional unity. There are good reasons for this. The idea that organizations can work in a functionally unified way is popular, particularly among managers charged with the task of holding organizations together.

- **The metaphor can easily become ideology.**

The danger of metaphor becoming an ideology is always a problem in applied social science where images or theories come to serve as normative guidelines for shaping practice. We have already seen the impact of the machine metaphor on classical management theory: the idea that the organization is a machine sets the basis for the idea that it ought to be run like a machine.

With the organismic metaphor, this "ought" takes a number of forms. The fact that organisms are functionally integrated can easily set the basis for the idea that organizations *should* be the same way. Much of organizational development attempts to achieve this ideal by finding ways of integrating individual and organization—for example, by designing work that allows people to satisfy their personal needs *through* the organization. Whereas Frederick Taylor's scientific management provided an ideology based on the idea that "efficiency and productivity are in the interests of all," ideologies associated with organizational development tend to emphasize that we can live full and satisfying lives if we fulfill our personal needs through our organizations.

Many argue that this style of thinking runs the danger of producing an organizational society populated by the "organization man" and the "organization woman." People become resources to be developed rather than human beings who are valued in themselves and who are encouraged to choose and shape their own future. This issue directs attention to the values that underlie much organizational development and, by implication, to the values associated with the use of the organismic metaphor as a basis for theorizing.

Another important ideological dimension of some of the theories discussed in this chapter is found in their links with the social philosophy of the nineteenth century. The population ecology view of organizations revives the ideology of social Darwinism, which stressed that social life is based on the laws of nature and that only the fittest will survive. Social Darwinism arose as an ideology supporting the early development of capitalism in which small firms competed for survival on a free and open basis. The population ecology view of organization in effect develops an equivalent ideology for modern times, holding up a mirror to the organizational world and suggesting that the view we see reflects a law of nature. In effect, natural law is invoked to legitimize the organization of society. Obviously, there are real dangers in doing this because when we take the parallels between nature and society too seriously, we fail to see that human beings, in principle, have a large measure of influence and choice over what their world can be. This is a theme that will receive a lot of attention in future chapters.

4 Learning and Self-Organization: Organizations As Brains

WHAT IF WE THINK ABOUT ORGANIZATIONS AS BRAINS?

- We focus on their learning abilities and the processes that can either stunt or enhance organizational intelligence.
- We discover how the findings of modern brain research can be translated into design principles for creating learning organizations.
- We learn how intelligence can be distributed throughout an enterprise.
- We see how the power of information technology can be used to develop decentralized modes of organization that are simultaneously global and local.

As we move into a knowledge-based economy where information, knowledge, and learning are key resources, the inspiration of a living, learning brain provides a powerful image for creating organizations ideally suited to the requirements of a digital age.

IN HIS BOOK *The Natural History of the Mind,* science writer G. R. Taylor offers the following observations on some of the differences between brains and machines:

> In a famous experiment, the American psychologist Karl Lashley removed increasing quantities of the brains of rats which had been taught to run in a maze. He found that, provided he did not remove the visual cortex and thus blind them, he could remove up to ninety percent of their cortex without significant deterioration in their power to thread their way through the maze. There is no man-made machine of which this is true. Try removing nine-tenths of your radio and see if it still brings in a signal! It would seem that each specific memory is distributed in some way over the brain as a whole.
>
> Similarly, you can remove considerable amounts of the motor cortex without paralyzing any one group of muscles. All that happens is a general deterioration of motor performance. The evolutionary advantages of such an arrangement are manifest: when pursued, it is better to run clumsily than not at all. But how this remarkable distribution of function is achieved we do not really understand. We see, at all events, that the brain relies on patterns of increasing refinement and not (as man-made machines do) on chains of cause and effect.

Taylor's comments raise intriguing questions.

- Is it possible to design "learning organizations" that have the capacity to be as flexible, resilient, and inventive as the functioning of the brain?
- Is it possible to distribute capacities for intelligence and control *throughout* an enterprise so that the system as a whole can self-organize and evolve along with emerging challenges?

These issues are the focus of this chapter, which pursues the basic question, *"What if we think about organizations as living brains?"*

IMAGES OF THE BRAIN

In the twenty-four hundred years since Hippocrates located the seat of intellect in the skull, scientists and philosophers of all kinds have been fascinated by the mysteries of the brain. As might be expected, numerous metaphors have been summoned to shape understanding. Many of these images focus on the idea that the brain is an information-processing system similar to a complex computer, telephone switchboard, or memory bank. More recently, the brain has been compared with a holographic system, one of the marvels of laser science.

THE BRAIN AS A HOLOGRAPHIC SYSTEM

Holography uses lensless cameras to record information in a way that stores the whole in all the parts. One of the interesting features is that, if the holographic plate recording the information is broken, any single piece can be used to reconstruct the entire image. Everything is enfolded in everything else, just as if we were able to throw a pebble into a pond and see the whole pond and all the waves, ripples, and drops of water generated by the splash *in each and every one of the drops of water.*

Holography demonstrates that it is possible to create processes where the whole can be encoded in all of the parts, so that each and every part represents the whole. Neuroscientist Karl Pribram has suggested that the brain functions in accordance with holographic principles: that memory is distributed throughout the brain and therefore can be reconstituted from any of the parts. If he is correct, this may explain why the rats in Karl Lashley's experiments were able to function reasonably well even when major portions of their brains had been removed.

Debate about the true nature and functioning of the brain continues at an intense level, and the evidence remains inconclusive. Each metaphor used to shape understanding seems to catch key insights but falls short on other accounts. For example, the information-processing images capture how the human brain manages to process billions of bits of data every second, transforming them into patterns and routines that help us deal with the world around us. But the explanations tend to overcentralize the process.

The holographic evidence favors a more decentralized, distributed form of intelligence. When it comes to brain functioning, it appears that there is no center or point of control. The brain seems to store and process data in many parts simultaneously. Pattern and order *emerge from the process*—it is not imposed.

The paradox of being holographic and specialized

Holographic explanations stress the "all over the place" character of brain functioning. Different elements are involved in systems of "parallel processing," generating signals, impulses, and tendencies that make contributions to the functioning and character of the whole. But the holographic explanation can go too far in that it underplays the fact that despite this distributed character there is also a strong measure of system specialization. The brain, it seems, is *both* holographic *and* specialized!

This paradox is clearly illustrated in the results of "split brain" research, which shows how the brain's right hemisphere plays a dominant role in creative, intuitive, emotional, acoustic, and pattern recognition functions and controls the left side of the body. The left hemisphere is more involved with rational, analytic, reductive, linguistic, visual, and verbal functions while controlling the right side of the body. There is undoubtedly a high degree of specialization on the part of each hemisphere, but both are always involved in any given activity. It is just that one hemisphere seems to be more active or dominant than the other as different functions are brought into play. The complementarity is also illustrated in the evidence that although different people may bring a right- or left-brain dominance to a specific task, both hemispheres are necessary for effective action or problem solving to occur.

To understand the brain we have to embrace several paradoxes and develop explanations that acknowledge

- how logical reduction and creative expansiveness may be elements of the same process,
- how high degrees of specialization and distributed function can coexist,
- how high degrees of randomness and variety can produce a coherent pattern,
- how enormous redundancy and overlap can provide the basis for efficient operation, and
- how the most highly coordinated and intelligent system of which we are aware has no predetermined or explicit design.

Interestingly, some of the most powerful insights on these issues are emerging from the field of artificial intelligence, where experiments in the construction of brainlike machines are actually showing how we can create the capacities that G. R. Taylor refers to in the quotation about experiments with rats' brains at the beginning of this chapter.

In the construction of mobile robots, called "mobots," ways are being found of reconciling principles of centralized and decentralized intelligence. Mobots with large centralized "brains" require so much supporting hardware that they get overwhelmed and immobilized by the high ratio of body to brain. And when the "body problem" is solved by putting "the brain" in a central but remote location, communication processes tend to get distorted by all kinds of random "noise" that create a constant tendency toward system failure. The most successful innovations seem to involve systems of distributed intelligence where integration and coherence are built from the "bottom up" in a way that allows "higher" or more evolved forms of intelligence to emerge.

Consider the mobot called "Genghis," created by Rodney Brooks at MIT, which is a kind of "mechanical cockroach" that has six legs but no brain. Each leg has its own microprocessor that can act as a sensing device that allows it to "think for itself" and determine its actions. When faced with a "local" situation it initiates a local response. Within the body of the machine other semi-independent "thinking" devices coordinate communications between the legs. The walking process emerges as a result of the piecemeal intelligence. The independence of the legs gives great flexibility and avoids the mammoth task of processing all the information that would be necessary to coordinate the operation of the six legs as an integrated process.

Genghis offers a metaphor for understanding how intelligent action can emerge from quasi-independent processes linked by a minimal set of key rules, making the whole system appear to have an integrated, purposeful, well-coordinated intelligence. By building around a pattern of simple if-then routines, the "cockroach" walks without knowing how it does so.

Now return to the brain. Could it be that sophisticated forms of intelligence emerge from the bottom up as the result of the integration of more modest capacities and intelligences? This, indeed, is close to the view offered by Daniel Dennett, who suggests that what we see and experience in the brain as a highly ordered stream of consciousness is really the result of a more chaotic process where multiple possibilities are generated as a result of activity distributed throughout the brain. There is no master, centralized intelligence! The brain as a system engages in an incredibly diverse set of parallel activities that make complementary and competing contributions to what eventually emerges as a coherent pattern.

So the question, "What if we view organizations as brains?" raises many interesting possibilities for organizations, which we will explore and develop by viewing organizations in three interconnected ways:

- as information processing brains,
- as complex learning systems, and
- as holographic systems combining centralized and decentralized characteristics.

ORGANIZATIONS AS INFORMATION PROCESSING BRAINS

Every aspect of organizational functioning depends on information processing of one form or another. Bureaucrats make decisions by processing information with reference to appropriate rules. Strategic managers make decisions by developing policies and plans that then provide a point of reference for the information processing and decision making of others. Computers automate complex information flows, and with the development of the Internet, corporate "intranets," and other webs of electronic communication, we are finding that organizations are becoming synonymous with the decisions, policies, and data flows that shape day-to-day practice.

Organizations are information systems. They are communication systems. And they are decision-making systems. So it is not a far stretch to think of them as information-processing brains!

Scientists working in the fields of operations research (OR), management decision systems (MDS), and management information systems (MIS) have been inspired by this idea to find ways of developing information-processing and decision-making tools that can lead to more rational decisions. This has resulted in complex theories and systems for data management in relation to logistics, production, distribution, finance, sales, marketing, and other areas of activity and to the creation of planning, design, and implementation teams and departments that can "think" for the rest of the organization and control overall activities. In effect, this development has given many complex organizations the equivalent of a centralized brain that regulates overall activity. Large, complex organizations that rely on vast amounts of data processing to manage their customers, production, or distribution activities would now find it impossible to function without this kind of support.

With new decentralizing capacities of information technology, the process is also reshaping organizational design.

ELECTRONICS AND NETWORKED INTELLIGENCE

Consider how computerized stock control and checkout facilities in supermarkets and other large retail stores have transformed the organizations using them. In applying a laser beam to precoded labels on the items being sold, the sales assistant records price and product and inputs data into various kinds of financial analyses, sales reports, inventory controls, reordering procedures, and numerous other automated information and decision-making activities.

The system of organization embedded in the design of such information systems replaces more traditional modes of human interaction, eliminating armies of clerks, stockroom attendants, and middle managers. It also links organizations that used to have distinct identities—manufacturers, suppliers, banking and finance companies—into an integrated information web.

MICROPROCESSING TECHNOLOGY AND VIRTUAL ORGANIZATIONS

Microprocessing technology has also created the possibility of organizing without having an organization in strictly physical terms.

For example, a manufacturing organization "based" in the outskirts of New York City may coordinate the assembly of parts delivered from several Asian manufacturing plants at a location in Taiwan. The resulting product will be delivered to retailers throughout Europe and North America by independent distributors. Customer inquiries or problems with the product may be routed via a "help line" to customer service representatives employed in Ireland, Denmark, or New Brunswick, Canada. The accounting to support such transactions is performed in the Far East, and "accounts receivable" is delegated to a firm in Atlanta. The company based in New York City has a small staff of central coordinators and provides a marketing and R&D function.

It is a "virtual organization." Information technology dissolves the constraints of space and time, linking knowledge workers and factory operators in remote locations across the globe into an integrated set of activities.

JUST-IN-TIME MANUFACTURING

We find the same pattern in "just-in-time" (JIT) systems of manufacturing, where the components to be used in producing a product are delivered by independent suppliers just minutes or hours before they are needed. This innovation has transformed the very concept of what it means to be "an organization."

Under older systems of production, where suppliers provided the parts or raw materials to be used in manufacturing a product such as an automobile, the automobile manufacturer (e.g., Ford, General Motors, or Volkswagen) was a clearly defined organization. It had a physical boundary and a distinct workforce. But with JIT such boundaries and patterns of membership dissolve. Suppliers may locate their production activities on the premises of Ford or GM to streamline the delivery process and make the just-in-time period shorter and more reliable.

To an outsider, it may be impossible to distinguish who is working for whom. The fundamental organization really rests in the complex information system that coordinates the activities of all the people and firms involved rather than in the discrete organizations contributing different elements to the process. JIT has transformed organizational relationships throughout the world, linking what used to be discrete organizations into integrated systems of intelligence and activity. We see the same process occurring in financial services and throughout the service sector.

THE INTERNET AND THE TRANSFORMATION OF COMMERCE

Consider how the Internet and other webs of electronic information exchange are transforming retailing and electronic commerce. Large computer software companies are collaborating with manufacturers, distributors, and credit card and finance companies to produce a pattern of direct interaction between customers and manufacturers. Besides eliminating intermediary firms, such as retailers, the development is enhancing possibilities for mass customization. For example, a person wishing to order a shirt or suit of clothes from a manufacturer can select the desired product from an electronic catalogue, submit height, weight, and other personal measurements for complete customization, pay electronically, and expect to receive delivery without further action.

We have here a system of organization. Or is it better described and understood as a system of intelligence? It reflects the shift that is occurring toward a fully fledged information economy. Organizations are rapidly evolving into global information systems that are becoming more and more like electronic brains. What once seemed to rest within the domain of science fiction—peopleless factories coordinated by peopleless offices, producing services on demand—is rapidly becoming reality.

All these developments break the old assumptions that the structure and capacities of our organizations are limited by constrained information processing, or what Nobel laureate Herbert Simon called the "bounded rationality" of human beings. While human intelligence is still the driving force, networked computing is able to realize organizational possibilities that, just a few decades ago, were no more than a dream.

In this world, where rapid change and transformation are becoming the norm, organizations face new challenges. In addition to planning and executing tasks in an efficient, rational way, they face the challenge of constant learning and, perhaps even more important, of learning to learn. It is to this aspect of the brain that we now turn.

CREATING LEARNING ORGANIZATIONS

How can one design complex systems that are capable of learning in a brainlike way? This question has been of special concern to a group of information theorists who have interested themselves in problems of artificial intelligence under the umbrella of what is now known as cybernetics.

CYBERNETICS, LEARNING, AND LEARNING TO LEARN

Cybernetics is an interdisciplinary science focusing on the study of information, communication, and control. The term was coined as a metaphorical application of the Greek *kubernetes,* meaning "steersman." The Greeks developed the concept of steersmanship, probably from their understanding of the processes involved in the control and navigation of watercraft, and extended its use to the process of government and statecraft. Today cybernetics characterizes processes of information exchange through which machines and organisms engage in self-regulating behaviors that maintain steady states.

The core insight emerging from early cybernetic theory was that the ability of a system to engage in self-regulating behavior depends on processes of information exchange involving *negative feedback*. This concept is central to the process of steersmanship. If we shift a boat off course by taking the rudder too far in one direction, we can get back on course again only by moving it in the opposite direction. Systems of negative feedback engage in this kind of error detection and correction automatically so that movements beyond specified limits in one direction initiate movements in the opposite direction to maintain a desired course of action.

The concept of negative feedback explains many kinds of routine behavior in a very unconventional way. For example, when we pick up an object from a table we typically assume that our hands, guided by our eyes, move directly toward the object. Cybernetics suggests not. This action occurs through a process of error elimination, whereby deviations between hand and object are *reduced at each and every stage of the process,* so that in the end no error remains. We pick up the object by avoiding not picking it up (exhibit 4.1).

These cybernetic principles are evident in many kinds of systems. In the "governor" that regulated the speed of the steam engine invented by James Watt, two steel balls were suspended from a central shaft attached to the engine. The shaft rotated with the speed of the engine, swinging the balls in an outward direction as speed increased, closing the throttle. The reverse actions occurred when speed was reduced. The machine acted as a form of communication system in which an increase in speed initiated actions leading to a decrease in speed and vice versa.

This is negative feedback: more leads to less, and less to more. So to self-regulate, learning systems must be able to

1. sense, monitor, and scan significant aspects of their environment,

2. relate this information to the operating norms that guide system behavior,

3. detect significant deviations from these norms, and

4. initiate corrective action when discrepancies are detected.

We pick up an object by avoiding not picking it up!

In a similar way, we manage to ride a bicycle by means of a system of information flows and regulatory actions that help us to avoid falling off.

Negative feedback eliminates error: it creates desired system states by avoiding noxiant states.

Exhibit 4.1. Negative feedback in practice

If these four conditions are satisfied, a continuous process of information exchange is created between a system and its environment, allowing the system to monitor changes and initiate appropriate responses. In this way, the system can operate in an intelligent, self-regulating manner.

However, these learning abilities are limited in that the system can maintain only the course of action determined by the operating norms or standards guiding it. This is fine so long as the action defined by those standards is appropriate for dealing with the changes encountered. But when this is not the case, the intelligence of the system breaks down, because the process of negative feedback ends up trying to maintain an inappropriate pattern of behavior.

This has led modern cyberneticians to draw a distinction between the process of learning and the process of *learning to learn*. Simple cybernetic systems, like house thermostats, are able to learn in the sense of being able to detect and correct deviations from predetermined norms, but they are unable to question the appropriateness of what they are doing.

A simple thermostat is unable to determine what level of temperature is appropriate to meet the preferences of the inhabitants of a room and to make adjustments to take account of this. More complex cybernetic systems, such as the human brain or advanced computers, have this capacity.

They are often able to detect and correct errors in operating norms, thereby influencing the standards that guide their detailed operations.

It is this self-questioning ability that underpins the activities of systems that are able to learn to learn and self-organize. The essential difference between these two types of learning is identified in terms of a distinction between "single-loop" and "double-loop" learning (exhibit 4.2).

CAN ORGANIZATIONS LEARN TO LEARN?

All the above ideas raise very important questions for modern organizations:

- Are they able to learn in an ongoing way?
- Is this learning single-loop or double-loop?
- What are the main barriers to learning?
- Are these barriers intrinsic to the nature of human organization?
- Can they be overcome?

As a result of the pioneering work conducted by Chris Argyris at Harvard University and by Donald Schön at MIT, these issues have now been brought to the forefront of management attention. Conceived as a challenge of creating "learning organizations," and popularized by the work of Peter Senge in the United States and independently through Reg Revans's concept of "action learning" in Europe, the idea of developing capacities for individual and organizational learning has established itself as a key priority in designing and managing organizations that can deal with the challenges of a turbulent world. The principles of modern cybernetics provide a framework for thinking about how this can be achieved. But first, organizations must be aware of ways in which they are unintentionally reinforcing single-loop learning.

Barriers to double-loop learning

Many organizations have become proficient at single-loop learning, developing an ability to scan the environment, set objectives, and monitor the general performance of the system in relation to these objectives. This basic skill is often institutionalized in the form of information systems designed to keep the organization "on course," such as in the following three systems:

1. *Budgets and other management controls* often maintain single-loop learning by monitoring expenditures, sales, profits, and other indications of performance to ensure that organizational activities remain within established limits. Advances in computing have done much to foster the use of this kind of single-loop control. Double-loop learning, however, requires institutionalizing systems that review and challenge basic paradigms and operating norms. Many organizations,

Single-loop learning rests in an ability to detect and correct error in relation to a given set of operating norms:

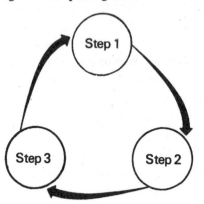

Double-loop learning depends on being able to take a "double look" at the situation by questioning the relevance of operating norms:

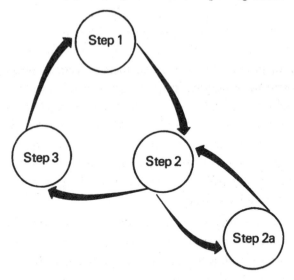

Step 1 = the process of sensing, scanning, and monitoring the environment.

Step 2 = the comparison of this information against operating norms.

Step 2a = the process of questioning whether operating norms are appropriate.

Step 3 = the process of initiating appropriate action.

Exhibit 4.2. Single- and double-loop learning

especially bureaucratized organizations, have fundamental organizing principles that actually *obstruct* the learning process.

2. *Bureaucratization* tends to create fragmented patterns of thought and action. Where hierarchical and horizontal divisions are particularly strong, information and knowledge rarely flow in a free manner. Different sectors of the organization often operate on the basis of different pictures of the total situation, pursuing subunit goals almost as ends in themselves. The existence of such hierarchical and horizontal divisions tends to emphasize the distinctions between different elements of the organization and fosters the development of political systems that place yet further barriers in the way of learning. Employees are usually encouraged and rewarded for occupying and keeping a predefined place within the whole. Situations in which policies and operating standards are challenged tend to be exceptional rather than the rule. Under these circumstances, single-loop learning systems are reinforced and may actually serve to keep an organization on the wrong course.

3. *Processes of bureaucratic accountability and other systems for rewarding or punishing employees* may threaten employees and activate defensive behaviors. To protect themselves and their colleagues, people find ways of obscuring or burying issues and problems that will put them in a bad light and of deflecting attention elsewhere. They become skilled in making situations for which they are responsible look better than they actually are. They often ignore or fail to report deep-seated problems and often hold back or dilute other bad news, giving senior managers rosy pictures of a situation or telling them what they think they would like to hear.

The sequence of events leading to the U.S. space shuttle *Challenger* disaster provides an excellent example of burying problems. The desire to launch on time overrode knowledge of serious problems with the O-ring seals that triggered the shuttle explosion.

Such problems can be systemic and universal. They are found in many different kinds of organizations and transcend cultural boundaries. In organizational contexts, formal structures, rules, job descriptions, and various conventions and beliefs offer themselves as convenient allies in the process of self-protection. Defensive behaviors can also become a central part of the culture of an organization, generating shared norms and patterns of conformity that prevent people from addressing key aspects of the reality with which they are dealing.

GUIDELINES FOR CREATING "LEARNING ORGANIZATIONS"

Given all these potential pathologies, it is not surprising that so many organizations find difficulty in learning and evolving in a fluid way. But the good news is that awareness of a problem is often the first important step toward a solution. We can take the insights about cybernetics and learning and begin to define the requirements of learning organizations in practice.

In a nutshell, cybernetics suggests that learning organizations must develop capacities that allow them to do the following:

- scan and anticipate change in the wider environment to detect significant variations,

- develop an ability to question, challenge, and change operating norms and assumptions, and

- allow an appropriate strategic direction and pattern of organization to emerge.

To achieve these aims they must evolve designs that allow them to become skilled in the art of double-loop learning.

The task of realizing these characteristics in practice is difficult and very much a "work in progress." Many organizations are struggling to find ways of breaking free of traditional modes of operation to enhance continuous learning. However, the above guidelines provide clear indications of the direction in which to move.

Scanning and anticipating environmental change

Learning organizations have to develop skills and mindsets that embrace environmental change as a norm. They have to be able to detect early warning signals that give clues to shifting trends and patterns. And they often have to invent completely new ways of seeing their industry and activities in order to envisage and create new possibilities.

Many of the most innovative companies worldwide possess an ability to envisage and create completely new industries or business niches. This allows them to invent and reinvent themselves and their relationships with competitors, customers, and the broader environment on a continuous basis. For example:

- Apple Computer's vision of a world where everyone has a PC helped reinvent the computer industry.

- CNN's vision of an international around-the-clock system of news reporting helped create a major transformation in broadcasting.

- Canon's vision of small user-friendly photocopiers using disposable parts created a major new niche in the maturing photocopier business.

- British Airways' drive to globalization initiated major transformations in the airline industry.

- The vision of a world where everyone will possess a personal mobile telephone number and where telecommunications and other media services will be completely user driven is setting a new stage for the development of media, computer, and other electronic services.

- The vision of electronic merchandising is changing the shape of retailing and creating personal relationships between mass, yet fully customized, manufacturers and the people who buy their products and services.

Intelligent learning systems use information about the present to ground their activities in a business reality. But they are also skilled in spotting the "fracture lines," signals, and trends that point to future possibilities. They are skilled at imagining and anticipating possible futures and acting in the present in ways that help make those futures reality. Often, the skill is not just cognitive but intuitive, emotional, and tactile as well.

It is impossible to truly know our customers, potential customers, or products and services at a distance. We have to join them, share their experiences, and understand products and services from their point of view. A learning organization has to become skilled in breaking the boundaries separating it from its environment to engage and experience the environment as fully as possible.

The view of learning involved here goes well beyond the passive information-processing characteristics of simple cybernetic machines. It embraces the kind of active intelligence characteristic of the human brain and its extension through the nervous system. And, like the products of the human brain, the actions of a learning organization actually change the environment in which it exists. We are a long way from the bounded rationality of a mechanistic organization monitoring its environment, shielding itself from uncertainty and seeking to maintain a stable internal system and a fixed niche. We are involved with a much more fluid sense of intelligence that uses, embraces, and at times creates uncertainty as a resource for new patterns of development.

QUESTIONING, CHALLENGING, AND CHANGING OPERATING NORMS

The kind of learning orientation described above must be rooted in key competencies within the organization. The principles of double-loop learning give clear guidance on what's needed. To learn and change, organizational members must be skilled in understanding the assumptions, frameworks, and norms guiding current activity and be able to challenge and change them when necessary. In this way the organization can adjust internal operations to meet changing strategic and environmental requirements and avoid being locked into the past.

Double-loop learning depends on what is sometimes described as the art of framing and reframing, which is crucial for the kind of self-reflective practice that underpins intelligent action. In concrete terms, it means that organizational members must be skilled in understanding the paradigms, metaphors, mindsets, or mental models that underpin how the organization operates. They must be able to develop new ones when appropriate. They need to ask the following questions:

- What business are we in, and is it the right business?
- Can we create fundamentally new products and services?
- Can we redefine the boundaries between different industries and services so that new niches emerge?
- Can we structure our organization around business processes that reflect a customer viewpoint rather than the influence of traditional departmental structures?
- Can we redesign business processes in a way that will increase the quality of production and reduce costs?
- Can we replace our organizational hierarchy with a network of self-managing teams?

All these questions contain a double-loop learning potential because they invite the questioner to examine the status quo and consider alternative modes of operation. They encourage us to understand key organizational attributes from the standpoint of a new frame of reference. This is what it takes to reinvent existing modes of operation. Many organizations get trapped by the status quo. They become myopic, accepting their current reality as *the* reality. To learn and change, they must be prepared to challenge and change the basic rules of the game at both strategic and operational levels.

The practice of double-loop learning has become well established at a strategic level. Most organizations have recognized the importance of challenging key business paradigms, using brainstorming sessions and other forms of creative thinking to create new directions. As a result of the pathbreaking work by W. Edwards Deming, Joseph Juran, and other leaders of the quality movement, the philosophy of promoting continuous improvement (the Japanese concept of *Kaizen*) and total quality management (TQM) has done much to institutionalize the practice of challenging taken-for-granted norms and practices at an operational level (exhibit 4.3).

The challenge is to ensure that the strategic and operational dimensions are in synchronization, and this is where problems often arise. Strategic development may run ahead of organizational reality because of the tendency for current operations to get caught in patterns of single-loop learning. Indeed, the TQM movement has suffered badly from this problem. Despite an outright commitment to constant improvement, many TQM programs have become caught in old bureaucratic patterns and cultural norms, leading to failure rates in the region of 70 percent. Such is the strength of pressures toward single-loop learning. When change threatens the status quo, defensive routines "kick in," diluting or diverting the attack on established practice.

The power of TQM, *Kaizen*, and other methods of generating continuous improvement rests in the fact that they foster double-loop learning. Employees are encouraged to

- dig beneath the surface of recurring problems and uncover the forces that are producing them,
- examine existing modes of practice and find better ones, and
- create "languages," mind-sets, and values that make learning and change a major priority.

In challenging operating norms and assumptions in this way, the approaches create information, insights, and capacities through which a system can evolve to new levels of development.

Exhibit 4.3. TQM and double-loop learning

For successful double-loop learning to occur, organizations must develop cultures that support change and risk taking; embrace the idea that in rapidly changing circumstances with high degrees of uncertainty, problems and errors are inevitable; promote an openness that encourages dialogue and the expression of conflicting points of view; recognize that legitimate error, which arises from the uncertainty and lack of control in a situation, can be used as a resource for new learning; recognize that since genuine learning is usually action based, organizations must find ways of helping to create experiments and probes so that they learn through doing in a productive way.

All this, of course, can raise high levels of anxiety in an organization. In particular, it is difficult for managers who want to be on top of the facts and in control to ride the kind of creative chaos on which innovation thrives. Yet this is precisely the competence that double-loop learning requires. Under its reign, managers and employees at all levels have to find ways of embracing uncertainty in a manner that allows new patterns of action to emerge.

Encouraging "emergent" organization

The intelligence of the human brain is not predetermined, predesigned, or preplanned. Indeed, it is not centrally driven in any way. It is a decentralized, *emergent* phenomenon. Intelligence *evolves*. This aspect of the brain metaphor has enormous implications because it counters the traditional view of management as requiring strong direction, leadership, and control that, in effect, imposes goals and objectives from "above" for execution "below."

But a top-down approach to management, especially one focusing on control through clearly defined targets, encourages single-loop learning and discourages the double-loop thinking that is so important for an organization to evolve.

This creates interesting paradoxes for management, for how can one manage in a coherent way without setting clear goals and objectives?

The answer derived from cybernetics is that the behavior of intelligent systems requires a sense of the vision, norms, values, limits, or "reference points" that are to guide behavior. Otherwise, complete randomness will prevail. *But* these reference points must be defined in a way that creates a space in which many possible actions and behaviors can emerge, *including those that can question the limits being imposed!*

Targets tend to create straitjackets. Cybernetic points of reference create space in which learning and innovation can occur.

The contrast between the top-down and cybernetic approaches is beautifully illustrated in a story told by management writer William Ouchi, in his book *Theory Z*. It describes how American and Japanese managers, working in the U.S. headquarters of a Japanese bank, view objectives:

> The basic mechanisms of management control in a Japanese company are so subtle, implicit, and internal that they often appear to an outsider not to exist. That conclusion is a mistake. The mechanisms are thorough, highly disciplined, and demanding, yet very flexible. Their essence could not be more different from methods of managerial control in Western organizations.
>
> In an interview with the American vice presidents, I asked how they felt about working for this Japanese bank. "They treat us well, let us in on the decision making and pay us well. We're satisfied." "You're very fortunate," I continued, "but tell me, if there were something that

you could change about this Japanese bank, what would it be?" The response was quick and clearly one that was very much on their minds: "These Japanese just don't understand objectives, and it drives us nuts!"

Next I interviewed the president of this bank, an expatriate Japanese who was on temporary assignment from Tokyo headquarters to run the United States operation, and asked about the two American vice presidents. "They're hard-working, loyal, and professional. We think they're terrific," came the reply. When asked if he would like to change them in any way, the president replied, "These Americans just don't seem to be able to understand objectives."

With each side accusing the other of an inability to understand objectives, there was a clear need for further interviewing and for clarification. A second round of interviews probed further into the issue. First, the American vice presidents: "We have all the necessary reports and numbers, but we can't get specific targets from him. He won't tell us how large a dollar increase in loan volume or what percent decrease in operating costs he expects us to achieve over the next month, quarter, or even year. How can we know whether we're performing well without specific targets to shoot for?" A point well taken, for every major American company and government bureau devotes a large fraction of its time to the setting of specific, measurable performance targets. Every American business school teaches its students to take global, fuzzy corporate goals and boil them down to measurable performance targets. Management by objective (MBO), program planning and evaluation, and cost-benefit analysis are among the basic tools of control in modern American management.

When I returned to reinterview the Japanese president, he explained, "If only I could get these Americans to understand our philosophy of banking. To understand what the business means to us— how we feel we should deal with customers and our employees. What our relationship should be to the local communities we serve. How we should deal with our competitors, and what our role should be in the world at large. If they could get that under their skin, then they could figure out for themselves what an appropriate objective would be for any situation, no matter how unusual or new, and I would never have to tell them, never have to give them a target."

In the American view, objectives should be hard and fast and clearly stated for all to see. In the Japanese view, objectives *emerge* from a more fundamental process of exploring and understanding the values through which a firm is or should be operating.

As the Japanese bank president in Ouchi's example suggests, if his managers could absorb the basic philosophy of the bank and how it wants its staff to deal with customers and competitors, appropriate objectives and behaviors in any situation would become very apparent. They wouldn't have to be set or be imposed by a third party.

The core values of the bank are cybernetic reference points that allow self-regulating behavior to occur. They create coherence. But they also give a lot of space. In any situation, a manager is free to choose whatever action or behavior seems appropriate to the situation at hand. This opens the way to sustained innovation at a local level. This, in turn, creates a potential for double-loop learning, as significant innovations can be used to modify operating norms.

Suppose that managers working within the framework of the bank's philosophy and values find means of meeting customer needs in a new way or of providing a new service. A system that is open to this kind of innovation from below can acknowledge, disseminate, and use the information and ideas in a way that actually influences the operating rules of the system, and the principles or values through which the bank seeks to serve its customers or deal with a competitor or potential competitor can evolve in a way that incorporates and builds on the successful innovation.

Fostering an ability to challenge norms

Many aspects of Japanese management have a cybernetic quality that promotes learning through innovation and the questioning of operating norms. It is no accident that the quality movement first took off in Japan. Quality circles, where people come together to share issues and problems and find ways of making improvements to the overall system in which they are working, offer a perfect illustration of double-loop learning in practice.

Cybernetic principles are also evident in the ritual of *ringi,* a collective decision-making process through which companies seek to test the robustness of policy initiatives and other developments. Under this process, a policy document is circulated among a group of managers or other personnel for approval. If a person disagrees with what is being proposed, he or she is free to amend the document, and it is circulated again. The process explores the values, premises, and details relating to a project from multiple points of view until an agreed-on position that satisfies all critical concerns and parameters emerges. It can be extremely time consuming. But when the decision is made, one can be fairly certain that key assumptions will have been challenged and that most errors will have been detected and corrected.

This is what double-loop learning is all about. The *ringi* serves the dual function of allowing people to challenge core operating principles and, in both the process and the outcome, to affirm and reaffirm the values that are to guide action. Paradoxically, it is a process that mobilizes disagreement to create consensus. It is also a process that allows innovation to be driven from all directions and for intelligence to evolve to higher and higher levels.

Cybernetic functioning based on double-loop learning can allow a system to get smarter and smarter. Interestingly, the process is completely paradoxical because learning has to be guided by key operating norms that, in turn, have to be constantly challenged.

Learning always seems to involve this kind of paradox because whenever we try to do something new, established modes of behavior are threatened.

When a corporation seeks to reinvent itself and create a new business orientation, it often encounters resistance from the old business. The fear is that everything will be lost in the transition. Or when a traditional bureaucracy tries to create "empowered teams," they are often undermined as the old hierarchy tries to retain control. The existing norms of a system rise up and in effect say "don't change."

To facilitate the double-loop process of learning to learn, people have to be skilled in managing paradox, a point to which we will return in the flux and transformation chapter. They have to be able to find ways of managing the tensions generated through the learning process in a way that allows new operating norms to emerge. Otherwise, the system will almost certainly remain trapped in the old pattern.

Cybernetics also shows us that in facilitating double-loop learning managers have to be aware of the importance of understanding the *limits* to be placed on action. Here again we find ourselves challenging central principles of Western management theory.

The importance of limits

Let's return to the issue of setting objectives and targets. When we try to achieve goals or targets as end states, for example, a cost reduction of 20 percent or sales growth of $200 million, the target can dominate attention and obliterate other key aspects of the overall situation. Attention and action tend to be oriented to a fixed point in the future and the environment tends to be manipulated in a way that will allow the organization to get there. In the process, all kinds of dysfunctions and unintended consequences arise:

- Managers may gain their 20 percent cut in costs but in the process do irreversible damage to the corporate culture as a result of employee layoffs.

■ The sales department may achieve its new target of $200 million but alienate a part of the company's future customer base because a substandard product has been shipped to get the sales on time.

Corporate life is full of these kinds of horror stories. In retrospect, they always seem blatantly stupid and short-sighted. More fundamentally, they are systemic. They are inevitable in any situation where people are encouraged to edit their understanding of reality to suit narrow purposes.

A cybernetic view of the problem shows us that while goals and targets often reflect noble *intentions*, the achievement of any goal must always be moderated by an understanding of the *limits* that need to be placed on behavior. Put more forcefully, successful system evolution has to be guided as much by the avoidance of noxiants as the pursuit of desired ends.

To illustrate, return to the operation of a simple cybernetic system. Look at how system behavior is guided by the *avoidance of undesirable system states*. A thermostat achieves its "goal" of a warm, comfortable room by ensuring that the room does *not* get too warm or too cold. The system avoids noxious outcomes.

We see the same cybernetic principle operating in more complex areas of social life. It is no coincidence, for example, that most of the great codes of behavior are framed in terms of "Thou shalt *not.*" Whether we examine the Ten Commandments or contemporary legal systems, we find that the principle of avoiding noxiants is defining a space of acceptable behavior within which individuals can act, innovate, or self-organize as they please.

Interestingly, the same process is evident in the evolution of the Internet, which offers a perfect example of the problems of design in complex, open-ended systems.

No one can say what form the Internet should take. No one knows its true potential or what its future should look like. It cannot be pre-designed in any authoritative way. Hence, the de facto design principle: give would-be users advice on what they should *not* do. For example, "Don't offend other users." "Don't overload them with information." "Don't send junk mail." "Don't reveal confidential information." "Never respond to provocation."

As a result, the Internet is evolving within the space defined by key parameters. Experience and practice test the limits giving rise to a redefinition of limits when appropriate. In this way, the Internet is self-organizing in a manner that is producing an emergent design. As in the developing intelligence of the brain, resonant innovations become embedded in the evolving "architecture." Inappropriate lines of development stall or die.

Western management, with its enormous emphasis on the achievement of predetermined goals, objectives, and operational targets, overasserts desired *intentions* and underplays the importance of recognizing the *limits* that need to guide behavior. Much of the turbulence of the modern environment is created as a by-product. Independent lines of action collide as organizations jostle to achieve their targets, with a solution *here* creating a problem elsewhere.

These are the messages of cybernetics:

- Learn from *ringi*.
- Be sure to surface the "do nots."
- Effective management depends as much on the selection of the limits that are to be placed on behavior as on the active pursuit of desired goals.

If management encourages an appropriate dialogue about the limits or constraints to be placed on action, they create a space in which desirable futures and appropriate strategies and modes of organization can develop. The system becomes "learning driven." Detailed goals become an emergent phenomenon. They look after themselves! These ideas challenge many established management assumptions.

Evolving designs for double-loop learning

This chapter has intentionally placed considerable emphasis on how the creation of double-loop learning and emergent forms of organization depend on an ability to transcend the constraints of the single-loop processes that tie an organization to the past. As we have seen, the challenge hinges on adopting an appropriate management philosophy that views and encourages the capacity of learning to learn as a key priority. It also rests in encouraging organizational principles and designs that can support this process.

This brings us to the topic of our next section: the holographic approach to organization. The ideas generated through this image provide many interesting and practical insights into the qualities that organizations must possess if they are to have the flexible self-organizing capacities of a brain.

ORGANIZATIONS AS HOLOGRAPHIC BRAINS: SELF-ORGANIZATION AND REGENERATION

The metaphor of a hologram invites us to think of systems where qualities of the whole are enfolded in all the parts so that the system has an ability to self-organize and regenerate itself on a continuous basis.

- Think of a broken holographic plate, where any part can be used to regenerate the information contained in the whole.

- Think of a holographic sculpture of a dancer in an art gallery. As you walk around the laser beam the dancer changes position as the information encoded in the beam is engaged in different ways.

- Or think of how the brain is able to reorganize itself when specific parts are injured or removed.

  - Rats are able to thread their way through a maze with up to 90 percent of the cortex missing.

  - Young children who lose a complete hemisphere of their brain are often able to recover lost functions as the remaining hemisphere takes over.

  - Adults experiencing severe brain injury involving amnesia sometimes develop completely new personalities as the brain self-organizes and relearns all the skills, emotions, and capacities needed to create a new life.

Now think of designing organizations that possess these abilities:

- They have wonderful memories that are organized and accessed in a highly decentralized way.

- They are capable of processing massive amounts of information and of shaping it for different purposes.

- They are comfortable with managing many different points of view.

- They have individuals, teams, and other units that are able to take on almost any challenge and find ways of organizing for the needs at hand.

- They are capable of functioning when major sections become obliterated or immobilized.

- Their capacities, intelligence, and control are distributed in a way that allows any single element to become a vital part of the whole.

- They are able to grow, develop, and change their personalities along with changing experiences.

They are, in short, intelligent, self-organizing brains that reflect all the qualities of what we have described as a "learning organization."

The holographic image seems to offer an almost impossible ideal. But if one examines existing organizational reality it is surprising to find that many of these qualities already exist. Every individual working in an organization has a wonderful brain. Even though it may not be used effectively, the potential is there. Decentralized local computer networks as well as the Internet, the World Wide Web, and other electronic databases extend and distribute memory and intelligence in a way that can be accessed at many points and in many forms. The potential for new forms of intelligence to emerge from this vast network of connections is enormous.

The regenerative capacities that allow an organization to form and reform itself to deal with destructive circumstances are also present. When organizations encounter disaster that immobilizes major functions, the healthy parts often rise to the new challenge:

- Government, health, telecommunications, transportation, and other service companies in San Francisco were able to reorganize in response to the great earthquake of 1989. Within hours or days, revised services were in operation. Staid organizations transformed themselves. Dynamic organizations became even more dynamic.

- When a small Norwegian shipping company lost half its employees, including many managers, as a result of a charter plane crash, the company was initially shocked and immobilized. But as Epsen Andersen, who reports the story, observes, it was soon able to function very much as before. The remaining staff shared much of the original intelligence of the company and by pooling their knowledge were able to reconstruct the functions performed by the people who perished.

Holographic aspects of organization are always asserting their presence. But in many situations they are suppressed or negated by conventional assumptions about organization design. So let's explore some ways that holographic qualities can be encouraged.

PROMOTING SELF-ORGANIZATION THROUGH PRINCIPLES OF HOLOGRAPHIC DESIGN

In certain respects it is a paradox to talk of "holographic design" because the holographic style of organization is very much a self-organizing, emergent phenomenon. However, there are several key principles that can help create contexts in which holographic self-organization can flourish. They are discussed here under the five headings summarized in exhibit 4.4.

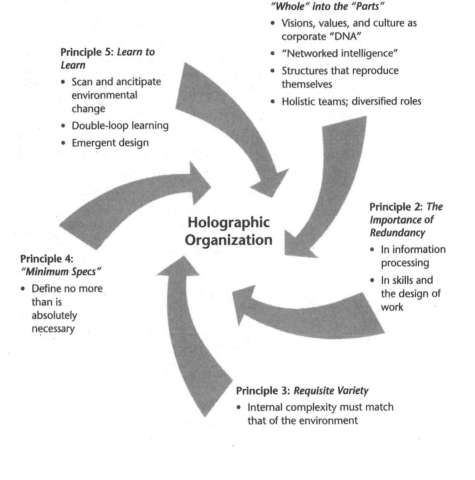

Exhibit 4.4. Principles of holographic design

Principle 1: Build the "whole" into all the "parts"

This principle seems to express an impossible ideal. But there are at least four ways in which the "whole in parts" philosophy can be realized in practice: by focusing on corporate culture, information systems, structure, and roles.

1. *Corporate DNA.* The visions, values, and sense of purpose that bind an organization together can be used as a way of helping every indi-

vidual understand and absorb the mission and challenge of the whole enterprise. Just as DNA in nature carries a holographic code that contains the information required to unfold the complete development of the human body, it is possible to encode key elements of a complete organization in the cultural and other codes that unite its members.

An appreciation of an organization's vision, aspirations, core values, operating norms, and other dimensions of corporate culture creates a capacity for each person to embody and act in a way that represents the whole. This is one of the reasons why companies like the Norwegian shipping firm discussed earlier, are able to re-create themselves in new situations. Culture has a holographic quality—a quality that is arguably its major source of power as a factor influencing effective management.

To create brainlike capacities for self-organization, however, it is vital that the cultural codes uniting an organization foster an open and evolving approach to the future. Cultures that embody closed visions and self-sealing values tend to die. In line with the principles of cybernetic learning discussed earlier, visions, values, and other dimensions of culture must create space in which productive innovation can occur. In this way, the culture that unites an organization can have an enduring yet changing form, as the visions, values, and operating codes get expressed in different ways at different times and evolve with changing circumstances.

2. *"Networked intelligence."* The second way of building the whole into the parts of an organization is through the design of appropriate information systems. Information systems that can be accessed from multiple points of view create a potential for individuals throughout an enterprise, even those in remote locations, to become full participants in an evolving system of organizational memory and intelligence. They can learn from and contribute to the organization's information base and the ideas expressed. Just as the Internet and the World Wide Web create an opportunity for the evolution of a kind of "global mind," organizational information systems create a capacity for the evolution of a shared "organizational mind."

Developments in information technology and associated global networks are creating quantum breakthroughs insofar as the holographic metaphor is concerned. They create a practical context in which information that used to be shaped, manipulated, and controlled through organizational hierarchies in an exclusive manner can become widely assembled and disseminated and used as a new source of intelligence and growth throughout an enterprise.

3. *Holographic structures that reproduce themselves.* A third way of building the whole into the parts rests in the design of organizational structures that can grow large while staying small.

   Consider Magna International, an auto parts manufacturer that has grown at a rapid rate from a single factory employing twenty people in the mid-1950s to a corporation with sales in excess of $4 billion in the mid-1990s. The Magna philosophy is encoded in a simple set of business principles and the rule that operating factories must remain on a small scale to avoid becoming impersonal. Once an enterprise reaches a size in the region of two hundred people, the only way it can grow is by spinning off another unit. In this way, Magna spawns clusters of organizations that, in turn, spawn further clusters (exhibit 4.5), creating a highly diversified enterprise where each part develops as an integrated whole. The process has a "fractal" quality in that the same basic pattern reproduces itself over and over again.

   As a second example, consider an information processing company that has achieved a spectacular rate of growth over the past ten years through a process of holographic reproduction.

   Within the context of a broadly defined vision of superior customer service, it has formulated the broad operational rule that growth can occur only through the development of new service units. When a unit reaches an optimal size, yet wishes to serve a larger customer base, three people from the unit, typically a manager and two service specialists, break away to launch a new enterprise. In this way the culture, character, and skill base of the whole organization are encoded into the new part. The part quickly becomes synonymous with the whole as new staff joining the unit absorb and "live" the qualities that lend the organization its distinctive character.

   Using information technology and a strong sense of values and corporate culture as unifying forces, it is able to operate in a completely decentralized fashion, adjusting to the special circumstances met in local environments. Yet it remains a tightly integrated enterprise.

4. *Holistic teams and diversified roles.* A fourth way of building the whole into the parts rests in how work tasks are designed. Under old mechanistic principles, work processes were usually fragmented into narrow and highly specialized jobs linked through some means of coor-

It is possible to grow large while staying small.

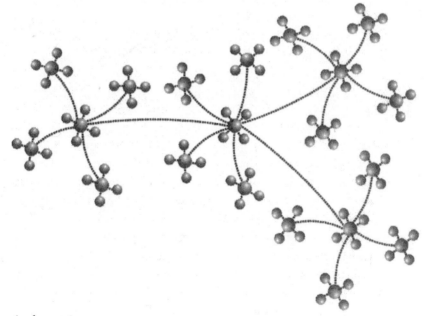

And so on!

Exhibit 4.5. Holographic reproduction

dination. The whole was the sum of the designed parts. Fragmentation ruled.

The holographic approach to job design moves in exactly the opposite direction by defining work holistically. The basic unit of design is a work team that is made responsible for a complete business process, such as assembling the seat of a car, meeting the needs of a group of customers, or steering the development of a new product from inspiration to prototype production. Within the team, roles or jobs are then broadly defined with individuals being trained in multiple skills so that they are interchangeable and can function in a flexible, organic way.

The prototype of this mode of operation is found in offices and factories built around self-managing work groups. Consider an electronics firm that assembles modular units for use in computers through the work of autonomous work teams. These operating teams have complete responsibility for production from the arrival of supplies in the plant to the shipment of finished products.

Every employee is multiskilled and able to perform the operating tasks needed to produce the whole product. The teams meet daily to make decisions about production, to divide work, and to attend to special issues such as improvements in work design, problems in supplies or shipping, or the hiring of new members. Members of the team are responsible for setting their own hours of work and production schedules and conducting their own quality control. They even administer skills-certification tests to their colleagues. Each operating team has a leader or manager who acts as a resource, coach, and facilitator and who has special concern for the team's identity.

In effect, the teams have absorbed many of the functions that, in a bureaucratic organization, would be performed by staff in many separate departments, such as planning, personnel, training, quality control, and engineering. This pattern is evident in autonomous work groups of all kinds. There seems to be a natural tendency to "embrace the whole," in the sense that teams that are responsible and rewarded for effective performance of a set of tasks soon realize that work becomes a lot easier and more effective if they are able to influence and shape the context and conditions influencing their performance.

So rather than just trying to achieve their production bonus through methods and guidelines suggested by production engineering staff, teams frequently develop innovations of their own. They see how a simplification of product design could lead to many production efficiencies. Rather than accept new team members chosen by the personnel department, they realize the benefits of handling the recruitment process themselves. Rather than relying on training programs mandated by the training department, they prefer to shape and select their own.

Although the teams may require professional support from outside their ranks from technical, administrative, and other specialist staff, especially in terms of ongoing development and integration with the wider enterprise, they approximate the whole organization just as each multiskilled team member embodies the vision, outlook, and skills of the whole team.

The four broad practices discussed above offer concrete strategies through which holographic organization can become a reality. Although at first sight, the notion of "building the whole into all the parts" seems a paradoxical and unattainable ideal, there are clear ways in which it can be made to happen.

There is, however, an important qualification that needs to be made with regard to the balance that often has to be struck between demands for specialization and demands for generalization. Recall the earlier discussion of the brain. The brain is both specialized and generalized. While memory and the capacity to perform different functions have a strong holographic quality, it is also possible to see strong specialist tendencies, for example, in the orientations of the left and right hemispheres, in how the cortex has distinct functional areas, in how the hypothalamus is concerned with survival activity, and so on.

A similar synthesis may be required in organizational contexts.

In a company like Magna International, the whole-in-parts philosophy does not lead to the development of identical units. There may be considerable differences between parts of the company specializing in the assembly of electrical components compared with those producing car seating modules. The company's central office will be different from the manufacturing cells.

Likewise, in the information-processing company discussed above, the process of holographic diffusion may produce a variety of "spin-off" units that are differentiated in terms of the relations struck with different clients. Different environmental niches may require that the company avoid producing clones and find ways of delivering core services in a manner that's tailored to meet specific needs. Different spin-offs may develop distinct competencies.

This "whole in parts" principle does not always result in "clones."

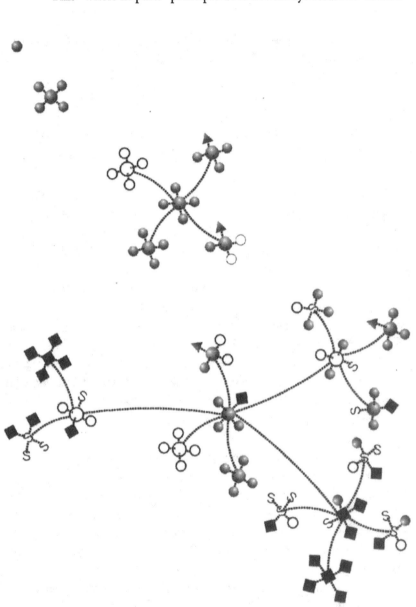

Exhibit 4.6. Holographic yet differentiated

Self-organizing work groups in office or factory settings are also likely to reflect similar variations as they develop their own modes of operation and distinctive character.

The pattern reflected in each of these examples is illustrated in exhibit 4.6. The point is that, in practice, the whole-in-parts principle does not always result in clones and has to be interpreted and implemented in a creative manner.

As another source of inspiration, recall our earlier discussion about mobots. They provide an excellent image for thinking about the whole/part problem.

Consider Genghis, the mechanical cockroach. It is a system composed of six "thinking legs" linked by a few simple rules that allow walking, as a kind of higher-order intelligence, to emerge. It operates through loosely coupled subsystems that are skilled in dealing with the challenges of their immediate environment. When bound together, Genghis becomes more than the sum of its parts.

There is an important lesson for organizational design: When organizational units are allowed to develop in a manner that enhances local intelligence, whether in the form of a self-organizing work group committed to continuous process and product innovation or a decentralized company with semiautonomous units each meeting the needs of different environmental niches, capacities for intelligent self-organization of the whole system are much enhanced.

The whole-in-parts principle is perhaps the key idea underlying holographic design. But it needs to be supported by an understanding of the four other principles illustrated in exhibit 4.4.

Principle 2: The importance of redundancy

Any system with an ability to self-organize must have a degree of "redundancy," a kind of excess capacity that can create room for innovation and development to occur. Without redundancy, systems are fixed and completely static.

In the human brain we find this redundancy in the vast networks of connectivity through which each neuron, or nerve cell, is connected with thousands upon thousands of others. This enormous capacity generates considerable evolutionary potential. It allows vast amounts of information processing from which thousands of potential patterns of development can emerge, contributing to the brain's constantly evolving structure, refinement, and intelligence.

A lot of the brain's activity seems to be completely random and characterized by a massive amount of distributed and parallel information processing. At any one time many parts of the brain may be involved with the same activity or information. This redundancy allows initiatives to be generated from many locations at once, reducing dependence on the activities of any single location. The process generates the multiple, competing "drafts" of intelligence from which an evolving pattern eventually emerges. The redundancy reflected in this system of parallel processing is vital in generating a range of potential outcomes, in coping with error, and in contributing to the brain's flexibility, creativity, and adaptiveness.

In an organizational context, redundancy can play a similar role. "Parallel processing" and sharing of information can be a source of creativity, shared understanding, trust, and commitment. We see this in the *ringi* process discussed earlier. This shared decision-making system contains massive redundancy. It is, however, very effective in exploring issues from multiple perspectives and in testing the robustness of emerging decisions and actions. The process offers a wonderful example of how intelligent action can emerge from multiple drafts.

We see the same process in the way Japanese and many Western companies approach problem solving or product innovation from multiple perspectives: by giving the same project to different teams who work independently and then come together to share progress, information, ideas, and insights. The process, like the *ringi*, creates an enormous degree of shared understanding of issues and problems. It broadens the range of investigation. It opens the process to random variation. It counteracts premature group conformity. It creates a fertile ground in which promising ideas or innovations can strike resonant chords of acceptance and appreciation.

Redundancy can also be built into the skills and mindsets within an organization. Fred Emery suggests that there are two methods for designing redundancy into a system:

1. *Redundancy of parts.* Each part is precisely designed to perform a specific function, special parts being added to the system for the purpose of control and to back up or replace operating parts whenever they fail. This is the old mechanistic design principle, creating a hierarchy of roles where managers and supervisors become responsible for the work of others. In effect, managers are "spare parts" that come into operation when things go wrong.

2. *Redundancy of functions.* Instead of spare parts being added to a system, extra functions are added to each of the operating parts so that each part is able to engage in a range of functions. This is the principle guiding self-organizing work groups. Members acquire multiple skills so that they are able to perform each other's jobs and substitute

as the need arises. And the team as a whole absorbs an increasing range of functions as it develops more effective ways of approaching its work. At any one time, each team member possesses skills that are redundant in the sense that they are not being used for the job at hand. However, this organizational design possesses great flexibility and creates a capacity for self-organization within each and every part of the system.

The two design principles show us different ways of creating flexibility. Holographic, self-organizing processes require a *redundancy of functions* approach. The shift to self-organizing work groups, the use of quality circles and TQM, and the flattening of organizational structures all reflect a major shift to this in practice. Holographic design encourages people to get involved in the challenges at hand, whatever they may be and wherever they come from, rather than focusing on narrow job descriptions and adopting the "that's not my responsibility" attitude typical of more mechanistic approaches to management.

From a mechanistic standpoint, redundancy seems unnecessary and inefficient. It is something that needs to be eliminated. That is why it is so important to understand its role in fostering self-organization and innovative practice. However, as discussed in relation to the whole-in-parts principle, another paradox arises: *How much redundancy should be built into a system?* This is where the principle of requisite variety comes into play.

Principle 3: Requisite variety

Clearly, it is impossible to give everybody all possible information about everything. It is impossible for people to become skilled in all possible tasks and activities. So where does one draw the line?

The cybernetic principle of "requisite variety" suggests that the internal diversity of any self-regulating system must match the variety and complexity of its environment if it is to deal with the challenges posed by that environment. Or, to put the matter slightly differently, any control system must be as varied and complex as the environment being controlled.

In the context of holographic design, this means that all elements of an organization should embody critical dimensions of the environment with which they have to deal so that they can self-organize to cope with the demands they are likely to face.

The principle of requisite variety gives clear guidelines as to how the ideas about getting the whole into the parts and redundant functions should be applied. It suggests that redundancy (variety) should always be built into a system where it is *directly* needed rather than at a distance. This means that close attention must be paid to the boundary relations between organizational units and their environments to ensure that requisite variety always falls within the unit in question.

To build redundancy into an organization we must consider the following:

- What is the nature of the environment being faced?
- Can all the skills for dealing with this environment be possessed by every individual?
  - If so, then build around multifunctioned people, as in the model of the self-organizing work groups discussed earlier.
  - If not, then build around multifunctioned teams that collectively possess the requisite skills and abilities and where each individual member is as generalized as possible, creating a pattern of overlapping skills and knowledge bases in the team overall.

Multifunctional teams offer a means of coping with the problem that everyone cannot be skilled in everything. Organization can be developed in a cellular manner around self-organizing, multidisciplined groups that have the requisite skills and abilities to deal with the environment in a holistic and integrated way.

Requisite variety has important implications for the design of almost every aspect of organization. Whether we are talking about the creation of a strategic business unit, a corporate planning group, a product development or research team, or a work group in a factory, requisite variety argues in favor of a proactive embracing of the environment in all its diversity.

Very often managers do the reverse, reducing variety to achieve greater internal consensus.

Corporate planning teams are often built around people who think along the same lines rather than around a diverse set of stakeholders who can actually represent the complexity of the problems with which the team ultimately has to deal. Or in launching a strategic business unit, corporate headquarters may be persuaded to retain vital functions for themselves so that they can continue to exert a measure of direction and control.

Requisite variety points to the fallacy of these practices. If a business unit or team is to be successful in dealing with the challenges of a complex task or of a difficult environment, it is vital that the unit be allowed to possess sufficient internal complexity. As indicated in our earlier discussion of the development of self-organizing work teams, teams absorb more and more functions—recruitment, training, quality control, process, and product design—so that they can become more effective in dealing with their environment.

The principle of requisite variety is not just an abstract concept. It is a vital management principle. If a team or unit is unable to recognize, absorb, and deal with the variations in its environment, it is unlikely to evolve and survive.

The principle suggests that when variety and redundancy are built at a local level—at the point of interaction with the environment rather than at several stages removed, as happens under hierarchical design—evolutionary capacities are enhanced. Individuals, teams, and other units are empowered to find innovations around local issues and problems that resonate with their needs. This also provides a resource for innovation within the broader organization, as the variety and innovation experienced is shared and used as a resource for further learning. The principle of requisite variety can play a vital role in developing evolutionary capacities throughout an enterprise.

Principle 4: Minimum specs

The first three principles of holographic design create a capacity to evolve. But systems also need the freedom to evolve. This is where the principle of minimum critical specification, or "minimum specs," comes into play.

The central idea here is that if a system is to have the freedom to self-organize, it must possess a certain degree of "space" or autonomy that allows appropriate innovation to occur. This seems to be stating the obvious. But the reality is that in many organizations the reverse occurs because management has a tendency to overdefine and overcontrol instead of just focusing on the critical variables that need to be specified, leaving others to find their own form.

For example, a senior manager responsible for a strategic business unit may fall under the influence of the old bureaucratic mindset, trying to define relations as clearly and as precisely as possible. Instead of focusing on critical elements, such as the vision or strategy that will guide the unit, expected resource flows, time lines, and anticipated results, and using these to create a broad structure of accountability, he or she ends up specifying detailed rules, protocol, and targets that in effect bind the organization into a specific mode of operation. The overcontrol negates any redundancy, variety, and innovative potential that the unit may possess because attention gets focused on the internal rules and controls instead of absorbing and dealing with the external challenges being faced.

The principle of minimum specs suggests that managers should define no more than is absolutely necessary to launch a particular initiative or activity on its way. They have to avoid the role of "grand designer" in favor of one that focuses on facilitation, orchestration, and boundary management, creating "enabling conditions" that allow a system to find its own form.

- One challenge is to help operating units, whether they be spin-off businesses, work teams, research groups, or individuals, find and operate within a sphere of "bounded" or "responsible autonomy."
- Another challenge is to avoid the anarchy and the completely free flow that arises when there are no parameters or guidelines, on the one hand, and overcentralization, on the other.

If a manager does a good job in creating a holographic sense of the vision that is to guide a subunit's operation, discussed earlier as a strategy for getting the whole into the parts, the additional specifications can often be quite minimal because an element of guidance is already built into the system. The experience and needs of the unit or work group concerned can then become the driving force in the emerging design. The manager plays an integrating role, with a focus on the issues linking the team to the wider organization.

The principle of minimum specs helps preserve the capacities for self-organization that bureaucratic principles and mindsets usually erode. It helps create a situation where systems can be self-designing as opposed to being "designed" in a traditional sense.

Principle 5: Learning to learn

As this chapter has emphasized, there is a strong tendency in most organizations to get trapped in single-loop systems that reinforce the status quo. Continuous self-organization requires a capacity for double-loop learning that allows the operating norms and rules of a system to change along with transformations in the wider environment.

The holographic design principles presented above create a potential for this to occur. But they must be supported by managerial philosophies that help to create a context that encourages the process of "learning to learn." All the ideas discussed in the section on creating learning organizations are critical to learning to learn.

As we see in the exhibit on principles of holographic design (4.4), our design principles have a circular quality. They are interconnected and blend with each other. Although presented as *design principles,* they don't offer a blueprint or recipe. Rather, they define a mindset and approach through which we can mobilize key insights about the holographic qualities of the brain in organizational contexts.

STRENGTHS AND LIMITATIONS OF THE BRAIN METAPHOR

Discussion in much of this chapter has looked to the future of organizational design. While our chapters on the machine and organismic metaphors were able to focus on how these metaphors have already been used to shape organization theory and practice, our discussion of the brain metaphor has had to chart newer ground and adopt a more normative and prescriptive tone.

STRENGTHS

■ **The metaphor gives clear guidelines for creating learning organizations.**

Leaders and managers in a variety of organizations are stressing the importance of creating organizations that are able to innovate and evolve to meet the challenges of changing environments. The ideas presented in this chapter offer concrete guidelines on how this can be achieved.

As we shift into what Peter Drucker has described as the new "knowledge economy," where human intelligence, creativity, and insight are the key resources, we can expect the ideas and principles involved in creating brainlike organizations to become more and more a reality. The potential is already there. Every person has a brain, and developments in electronic technology are demonstrating how we can mobilize intelligence on a broad front.

The brain metaphor identifies the requirements of learning organizations in a comprehensive way, and how different elements need to support each other.

■ **We learn how information technology can support intelligent evolution.**

Historically, there has been a tendency to use the new technology to reinforce bureaucratic principles and centralized modes of control. This misses the true potential of information technology, which rests in creating networks of interaction that can self-organize and be shaped and driven by the intelligence of everyone involved. The holographic design principles presented in this chapter show how this can be achieved.

■ **We gain a new theory of management based on principles of self-organization.**

Consider how an understanding of the functioning of the brain challenges traditional assumptions about the importance of strong central leadership and control, about the wisdom of setting clear goals and objectives, about the role of hierarchy, about the concept of organizational design, and about the wisdom of trying to develop and impose systems from the top down.

All these ideas are central to the managerial mindsets that have dominated the industrial age. But they are all open to major challenge as organizing principles for the new information age. The ideas explored in this chapter point to a completely new mode of leadership and management where the desire to stimulate learning and evolution are key priorities.

The message, in short, is that

- leadership needs to be diffused rather than centralized,
- even though goals, objectives, and targets may be helpful managerial tools, they must be used in a way that avoids the pathologies of single-loop learning,
- goal seeking must be accompanied by an awareness of the *limits* needed to avoid noxious outcomes, and
- hierarchy, design, and strategic development must be approached and understood as self-organizing, emergent phenomena.

The detailed principles of holographic self-organization show how this can be achieved.

■ **We recognize the importance of dealing with paradox.**

The brain is a paradoxical phenomenon, and the management principles it inspires are equally paradoxical. That is the main reason why the design principles offered here have been presented as aspirations rather than blueprints. Traditional management practice based on a mechanical frame of reference thrives on checklists and how-to manuals. The message of the brain is that we need to remain more open and trust that when key capacities and organizing principles are in place, intelligent forms of organization will usually result.

LIMITATIONS

The brain metaphor thus has many strengths insofar as the development of intelligent organization is concerned. But there are also several limitations.

■ **There may be conflict between the requirements of organizational learning and the realities of power and control.**

Any move away from hierarchically controlled structures toward more flexible, emergent patterns has major implications for the distribution of power and control within an organization, as the increase in autonomy granted to self-organizing units undermines the ability of those with ultimate power to keep a firm hand on day-to-day activities and developments.

Moreover, the process of learning requires a degree of openness and self-criticism that is foreign to traditional modes of management.

Both these factors tend to generate resistance from the status quo. Managers are often reluctant to trust self-organizing processes among their staff and truly let go. Many early experiments in self-organizing work designs encountered this problem, and they still do. There is such a strong belief that order means clear structure and hierarchical control that any alternative seems to be a jump in the direction of anarchy and chaos. Successful self-organizing systems always require a degree of hierarchical ordering. But this hierarchy must be allowed to emerge and change as different elements of the system take a lead in making their various contributions. In such systems, hierarchy and control have an emergent quality: they cannot be predesigned and imposed.

Application of ideas associated with the brain metaphor requires both a power shift and a mind shift. Few will probably quarrel with the ideal of creating learning organizations that are able to evolve and adapt along with the challenges they encounter. But when ideal comes to reality, many forces of resistance can be unleashed.

■ **Learning for the sake of learning can become just another ideology.**

Finally, we have to be aware of the strong normative bias of the brain metaphor. Few will quarrel with the aim of increased learning. But what are the purposes to be served? As we will see in the flux and transformation chapter, a future where organizations devote all their energies to outwitting other organizations is a recipe for enormous turbulence. Imagine the uncertainty and upheaval that this would create. Continuous learning may seem fine as an end in itself. But in practice it needs to be accompanied by an awareness of the cybernetic limits that will help make it a positive process from a societal perspective.

5 Creating Social Reality: Organizations As Cultures

WHEN WE VIEW ORGANIZATIONS AS CULTURES, we see them as minisocieties with their own distinctive values, rituals, ideologies, and beliefs.

- We see important cross-national variations in cultural style.
- We see that individual organizations may also have their own unique cultures.
- We learn that what unfolds in any organization is a reflection of what is in people's minds.
- We note that while some corporate cultures may be uniform and strong, others are often fragmented by the presence of subcultures.
- We realize that organization rests in the shared meanings that allow people to behave in organized ways.

The metaphor helps us to rethink almost every aspect of corporate functioning, including strategy, structure, design, and the nature of leadership and management. Once we understand culture's influence on workplace behaviors, we realize organizational change is cultural change and that all aspects of corporate transformation can be approached with this perspective in mind.

EVER SINCE THE RISE OF JAPAN as a leading industrial power, organization theorists and managers alike have become increasingly aware of the relationship between culture and management.

During the 1960s, the confidence and impact of American management and industry seemed supreme. Gradually, but with increasing force, throughout the 1970s the performance of Japanese automobile, electronics, and other manufacturing industries led Japan to take command of international markets, establishing a solid reputation for quality, reliability, value, and service. With virtually no natural resources, no energy, and over 110 million people crowded in four small mountainous islands, Japan succeeded in achieving the highest growth rate, the lowest level of unemployment, and, at least in some of the larger and more successful organizations, one of the best-paid and healthiest working populations in the world.

Although different theorists argued about the reasons for this transformation, most agreed that the culture and general way of life in Japan played a major role. Culture became a hot topic in management in the 1980s and early 1990s, prompting Western management theorists to take special interest in the culture and character of their *own* countries and the links with organizational life.

CULTURE AND ORGANIZATION

What is this phenomenon we call culture?

The word derives metaphorically from the idea of cultivation: the process of tilling and developing land. When we talk about culture we are usually referring to the pattern of development reflected in a society's system of knowledge, ideology, values, laws, and day-to-day ritual. The word is also frequently used to refer to the degree of refinement evident in such systems of belief and practice, as in the notion of "being cultured."

The concept of culture signifies that different groups of people have different ways of life. It is a metaphor that has considerable relevance for our understanding of organizations.

In our pursuit of understanding organizational culture, we will

- explore the idea that organization is itself a cultural phenomenon that varies according to a society's stage of development,

- focus on the idea that culture varies from one society to another and examine how this helps us understand cross-national variations in organizations,

- explore patterns of corporate culture and subculture between and within organizations, and

- take a detailed look at how patterns of culture are created and sustained and how organizations are socially constructed realities.

ORGANIZATION AS A CULTURAL PHENOMENON

Robert Presthus suggests that we now live in an "organizational society." Whether in Japan, Germany, Hong Kong, Great Britain, Russia, the United States, or Canada, large organizations are likely to influence most of our waking hours in a way that is completely alien to life in a remote tribe in the jungles of South America. This may seem to be stating the obvious, but many characteristics of culture rest in the obvious.

For example, why do so many people

- build their lives around distinct concepts of work and leisure,
- follow rigid routines five or six days a week,
- live in one place and work in another,
- wear uniforms,
- defer to authority,
- and spend so much time in a single spot performing a single set of activities?

To an outsider, daily life in an organizational society is full of peculiar beliefs, routines, and rituals that identify it as a distinctive cultural life when compared with that in more traditional societies. For example, in communities where households rather than formal organizations are the basic economic and productive units, work has a completely different meaning and often occupies far less of a person's time. The distinctions drawn between occupational activities and other aspects of social life tend to be far more blurred.

In a sense, we can say that people working in factories and offices in Detroit, Moscow, Liverpool, Paris, Tokyo, and Toronto all belong to the same "industrial culture." They are all members of organizational societies. Their work and life experience seem qualitatively different from those of individuals living in more traditional societies dominated by domestic systems of production. If nothing else, modern office and factory workers share basic expectations and skills that allow organizations to operate on a day-to-day basis.

Although we often regard the routine of organizational life as just that, routine, it does in fact rest on numerous skillful accomplishments. Being a factory or office worker calls on a depth of knowledge and cultural practice that, as members of an organizational society, we tend to take for granted.

For these reasons, some social scientists believe that it is often more useful to talk about the culture of industrial *society* rather than of industrial societies because the detailed differences between countries often mask more important commonalities. Many of the major cultural similarities and differences in the world today are occupational rather than national, the similarities and differences associated with being a factory worker, a janitor, a government official, a banker, a store assistant, or an agricultural worker being as significant as those associated with national identity. Important dimensions of modern culture are rooted in the structure of industrial society, the organization of which is itself a cultural phenomenon.

INTERNATIONAL DIFFERENCES IN ORGANIZATION AND MANAGEMENT

However, despite the commonalities, it would be a mistake to dismiss cross-national differences in culture as being of little significance. The course of history has fashioned many variations in national social characteristics, in views of the meaning of life, and in national styles and philosophies of organization and management. The recent success of Japan, the decline of industrial Great Britain, the fame of American enterprise, and the distinctive characteristics of many other organizational societies are all crucially linked with the cultural contexts in which they have evolved.

If we examine the Japanese concept of work and the relations between employees and their organizations, we find that they are very different from those prevailing in the West.

Japan: A culture of cooperation and service

The Japanese organization is viewed as a collectivity to which employees belong rather than just a workplace comprising separate individuals. The collaborative spirit of a village or commune often pervades work experience, and there is considerable emphasis on interdependence, shared concerns, and mutual help. Employees frequently make lifelong commitments to their organization, which they see as an extension of their family. Authority relations are often paternalistic and highly traditional and deferential. Strong links exist between the welfare of the individual, the corporation, and the nation. At Matsushita, one of Japan's largest and most successful corporations, these principles permeate company philosophy (exhibit 5.1).

Murray Sayle, an expert on Japan, offers an intriguing theory of the historical factors accounting for this solidarity. He believes that

MATSUSHITA'S BASIC BUSINESS PRINCIPLES

To recognize our responsibilities as industrialists, to foster progress, to promote the general welfare of society, and to devote ourselves to the further development of world culture.

EMPLOYEES' CREED

Progress and development can be realized only through the combined efforts and cooperation of each member of our Company. Each of us, therefore, shall keep this idea constantly in mind as we devote ourselves to the continuous improvement of our Company.

THE SEVEN "SPIRITUAL" VALUES

1. National Service through Industry

2. Fairness

3. Harmony and Cooperation

4. Struggle for Betterment

5. Courtesy and Humility

6. Adjustment and Assimilation

7. Gratitude

These values, taken to heart, provide a spiritual fabric of great resilience. They foster consistent expectations among employees in a workforce that reaches from continent to continent. They permit a highly complex and decentralized firm to evoke an enormous continuity that sustains it even when more operational guidance breaks down.

"It seems silly to Westerners," says one executive, "but every morning at 8:00 A.M., all across Japan, there are 87,000 people reciting the code of values and singing together. It's like we are all a community."

Exhibit 5.1. Company philosophy at Matsushita Electric Company, from R. Pascale and A. Athos, *The Art of Japanese Management*, pp. 73, 75–76. ©1981, Warner Books.

Japanese organizations combine the cultural values of the rice field with the spirit of service of the samurai. Whereas the former is crucial for understanding solidarity in the factory, the latter accounts for many characteristics of management and for the pattern of interorganizational relations that has played such a crucial role in Japan's economic success.

Rice growing in Japan has always been a precarious activity because of the scarcity of land and the short growing season. In retrospect, the process of building a civilization on this crop appears to be a prototype of the Japanese ability to take on projects that seem impossible. Above all else, traditional rice cultivation is a cooperative affair. There is no such thing as a solitary, independent, pioneering rice farmer. The growing process calls for intensive teamwork in short, back-breaking bursts of planting, transplanting, and harvest. Everyone is expected to perform to the best of his or her ability to ensure that the collective outcome is as good as it can be. If one family fails to maintain its irrigation ditches in good repair, the whole system suffers.

When the crop fails because of disastrous weather conditions, the whole group is punished. There are no individual winners or losers. Under such circumstances, conformity and tradition are favored over opportunism and individuality. Respect for and dependence on one another are central to the way of life. It is this rice culture that was originally transferred to the Japanese factory.

Rice farmers in Japan were always willing to share their crop with those who were able to look after them. Such was the case in relation to the samurai, the "men of service," who depended on the farmers for their rice and physical existence. They played an important role in Japanese military and bureaucratic history and are now paralleled in the managerial "clans" or elites that run Japanese society. Protection of one's employees, service to each other, and acceptance of one's place in and dependence on the overall system are dominant characteristics.

This service orientation extends to relations between organizations and the wider society, as reflected in the Matsushita philosophy. It is also crucial in explaining the close and collaborative relations between the banking system and Japanese industry. In contrast with the West, where the banks tend to act as independent judges and controllers of corporate investment, in Japan they assume a responsibility to provide help when and where it is needed.

Coupled with an amazing capacity to borrow and adapt ideas from elsewhere, first from China and later from the West, the cultures of rice field and samurai blended to create a hierarchical yet harmonious form of social organization within a modern industrial context. The managerial echelons were elitist and highly meritocratic, as they had been for centuries. Workers readily contributed to the material goals of their industrial masters and deferred to their authority because that had always been the traditional relationship between worker and samurai. It is no surprise, therefore, that so many people have been prepared to sing the company song and commit a lifetime to the corporate family.

The basic system of organization is feudal rather than modern, and from outside the culture seems distinctly oppressive, particularly as mobility between ranks is highly restricted, being determined for each individual from a very early age. However, it is important to realize that the kind of submissiveness and deference to authority found in Japan is not necessarily experienced as demeaning. Hierarchy in a Japanese corporation is as much a system of mutual service as one of top-down control.

It is difficult to judge a culture from the outside. What seems unacceptable from a Western viewpoint may be completely acceptable from within. That said, however, there is often a tendency in management reports of Japanese organizations to celebrate overall accomplishments while ignoring some of the more distasteful aspects of the work experience. Dazzling success stories tell of the way the Japanese arrive at work early or stay late to find ways of improving efficiency through the activities of voluntary "quality circles," or of how the dedicated Honda workman straightens the windshield-wiper blades on all the Hondas he passes on his way home each evening.

Far less attention is devoted to the disgruntlement with which many workers accept the burdens of factory life. The following first-hand account of work in a Toyota factory by Japanese journalist Satoshi Kamata helps provide a refreshing balance. Although perhaps untypical of Japanese industry as a whole, it shows how Toyota's relentless drive for success in the early 1970s was accompanied by much personal deprivation on the part of many workers, particularly those living hundreds of miles away from their families in camps rigidly policed by company guards.

> Although the workplace was characterized by the genuine spirit of cooperation found in the rice field, it was also characterized by constant pressures to achieve demanding work targets and fulfill the requirements of company values and norms. The exercise of company authority—whether in the form of an arbitrary transfer from one workplace to another, of a call for extra work effort, or of canceled leave—was often resented, even though accepted with a grumble and a joke as an inevitable feature of life.

Kamata's account suggests that day-to-day life in a Japanese factory can be at least as grueling as that in any Western manufacturing plant. The important difference is that the Japanese seem to have a greater capacity to grin and bear it!

Many discussions of Japanese management tend to ignore the cultural-historical circumstances that allow Japanese management to flourish as it does. They tend to overestimate the ease with which techniques and policies can be transplanted from one context to another, for it is the context that often makes the difference between success and failure.

Debates regarding the merits of the Japanese system continue. For some writers, it offers a model for practice throughout the world. For others, it represents the remnants of a feudal system that may be well on the verge of major transformation as a restless youth culture, exposed to Western rather than samurai and rice field values, exerts its influence on work and society. When people grow up in a city environment in a television and multimedia age, the rice field is an alien environment. The new experience is a transforming force.

Our focus on Japan is intended to be no more than illustrative. The point is that culture, whether Japanese, Arabian, British, Canadian, Chinese, French, or American, shapes the character of organization.

Great Britain: A culture shaped by deep division

In Great Britain, generations of social change and class conflict often perpetuate antagonistic divisions in the workplace that no amount of conciliation and management technique seems able to overcome. In contrast with the Japanese, British factory workers have traditionally defined themselves in opposition to a system they perceive as having exploited their ancestors as it now exploits them. Managerial elites assumed a basic right to rule "workers," who they saw as having a "duty to obey." Antagonism and strife rather than factory solidarity became the order of the day.

The antagonism that often runs throughout the British workplace is gently yet clearly illustrated in the following account offered by management writer Charles Handy in his book *Gods of Management:*

> My aunt by marriage is a splendid character, but from a bygone age. Her father never worked, nor his father before him, nor, of course, had she ever earned a penny in her life. Their capital worked for them, and they managed their capital. Work was done by workers. She sees all governments today as insanely prejudiced against capital, all workers as inherently greedy and

lazy, and most managements as incompetent. No wonder the world is in a mess and she getting [sic] poorer every day.

Tony is a friend from work. His father was a postman. He started life as a draftsman in a large engineering firm. He grew up believing that inherited capital was socially wrong. He had never met any man who did not or had not worked for his living.

They met, by chance, at my house over a meal. It started quietly, politely. Then she inquired what he did. It transpired that he had recently joined his staff union. Auntie had never met a union member.

"Good Heavens, how could you?" she said.

"It makes very good sense," said Tony, "to protect your rights."

"What rights? What poppycock is this? If people like you spent more time at their work and less looking after their own interests, this country wouldn't be in its present mess."

"Don't you," said Tony, "spend your time looking after your rights?"

"Of course," she said, "but then, I've rights. I provide the money that makes it possible for people like you to live."

"I provide the labor that keeps your money alive, although why I should work to preserve the capital of rich people whom I've never met is something that puzzles me."

"You talk like a Communist, young man, although you dress quite respectably. Do you know what you're saying?"

"You don't have to be a Communist to question the legitimacy of inherited wealth."

My aunt turned to me.

"You see why I'm worried about this country?" she said.

Each regarded the other as an example of an unnatural species. Given their opposed "core beliefs," no proper argument or dialogue was possible, only an exchange of slogans or abuse. It is a score that is replicated at negotiating tables as well as dinner tables.

The United States: A culture emphasizing competition

If we turn to the United States for illustrations of how culture shapes management, the ethic of competitive individualism is probably the one that stands out most clearly. Many American corporations and their employees are preoccupied with the desire to be "winners" and with the need to reward and punish successful and unsuccessful behavior. From an American perspective, industrial and economic performance is often understood as a kind of game, and the general orientation in many organizations is to play the game for all it's worth: set objectives, clarify accountability, and "kick ass" or reward success lavishly and conspicuously.

In an essay on the relation between morale and national character, Gregory Bateson drew attention to differences among parent-child relations in North America, England, and elsewhere. He noted the American practice of encouraging certain forms of boastful and exhibitionistic behavior on the part of children still in a dependent and subordinate position, whereas in England, children were encouraged to be submissive spectators in adult company and rewarded for being "seen but not heard."

Bateson suggests that these child-rearing practices have considerable implications for later life—in the American case, creating a great deal of room for self-appreciation and self-congratulation as a basis for independence and strength. We see this in the "We're Number 1" syndrome. We also find it in an organizational context in the opportunities created for conspicuous achievement on the part of those in subordinate roles combined with expressive congratulation from those in superior roles.

Consider some of the illustrations presented in Tom Peters and Robert Waterman's book *In Search of Excellence,* an American management response to the rise of Japan. The idea of rewarding and motivating employees so that they come to see themselves as winners is a dominant theme.

- Thomas Watson Sr. of IBM is reported to have made a practice of writing out a check on the spot for achievements he observed in wandering about the organization.

- At Tupperware, the process of positive reinforcement is ritualized every Monday night when all the saleswomen attend a rally for their distributorship. Everyone marches up on stage in the reverse order of the previous week's sales, a process known as "Count Up," while their peers celebrate them by joining in "All Rise." Almost anyone who has done anything at all receives a pin or badge or several pins and badges. The ceremony combines head-on competition with a positive tone that suggests that everyone wins. Applause and hoopla are reported to fill the entire event.

The above examples provide splendid illustrations of Gregory Bateson's point about how the culture of the United States re-creates patterns found in American parent-child relations.

However, the most colorful example emerging from the Peters and Waterman research is found in the early years of a company named Foxboro, where a technical advance was desperately needed for survival.

Late one evening, a scientist rushed into the president's office with a working prototype. Dumbfounded at the elegance of the solution and bemused about how to reward it, the president rummaged through the drawers in his desk, found something, and leaning toward the scientist, said "Here!" In his hand was a banana, the only reward he could immediately put his hands on. From that day on a small "gold banana" pin has been the highest accolade for scientific achievement at Foxboro.

Positive reinforcement is practiced in many Japanese, British, French, and other non-American corporations, often with considerable influence on employee motivation and performance. However, the United States stands supreme in the extent to which a concern for winning and direct reward for appropriate behavior have established themselves as important features of the culture and corporate life.

The value of recognizing cultural differences

While it is a mistake to talk about any country as if it has an integrated, homogeneous culture, especially when societies are becoming so culturally diverse, important cross-national differences definitely exist. By understanding these differences we are able to get a much better appreciation of "foreign" practice. At the same time, we are able to gain a much better appreciation of our own.

One of the interesting aspects of culture is that it creates a form of "blindness" and ethnocentrism. In providing taken-for-granted codes of action that we recognize as "normal," it leads us to see activities that do not conform with these codes as abnormal. A full awareness of the nature of culture, however, shows us that we are all equally abnormal in this regard. There is considerable value in adopting the standpoint of the cultural stranger because, in becoming aware of the stranger's point of view, we can see our own in a refreshingly new perspective.

CORPORATE CULTURES AND SUBCULTURES

The influence of a host culture is rarely uniform. Just as individuals in a culture can have different personalities while sharing much in common, so too with groups and organizations. It is this phenomenon that is now recognized as "corporate culture."

Organizations are minisocieties that have their own distinctive patterns of culture and subculture. One organization may see itself as a tight-knit team or family that believes in working together. Another may be permeated by the idea that "we're the best in the industry and intend to stay that way." Yet another may be highly fragmented, divided into groups that think about the world in very different ways or that have different aspirations as to what their organization should be. Such patterns of belief or shared meaning, fragmented or integrated and supported by various operating norms and rituals, can exert a decisive influence on the overall ability of the organization to deal with the challenges that it faces.

Observing cultural differences

One of the easiest ways of appreciating the nature of corporate culture and subculture is simply to observe the day-to-day functioning of a group or organization to which one belongs *as if one were an outsider*. Adopt the role of anthropologist. The characteristics of the culture will gradually become evident as one becomes aware of the patterns of interaction between individuals, the language that is used, the images and themes explored in conversation, and the various rituals of daily routine. As one explores the rationale for these aspects of culture, one usually finds that there are sound historical explanations for the way things are done.

Example 1: A fragmented culture in an insurance firm

Linda Smircich studied the top executive group of an American insurance company. The company was a division of a much larger organization offering a broad range of insurance services to agricultural organizations and to the general public. Sustained observation of day-to-day management generated two key conflicting impressions:

- On the one hand, the company seemed to emphasize cooperative values and an identity rooted in the world of agriculture rather than in that of competitive business. The staff were polite and gracious and always seemed prepared to give help and assistance wherever it was needed. This ethos was reflected in one of the company's mottoes: "We grow friends."

- On the other hand, a second dimension of organizational culture suggested that the cooperative ethos was at best superficial. Meetings and other public forums always seemed dominated by polite yet disinterested exchange. Staff rarely got involved in any real debate and seemed to take very little in-depth interest in what was being said. Hardly anyone took any notes, and the meetings were treated as ritual occasions. This superficiality was confirmed by observed differences between the public and private faces of the organization. Whereas in public the ethos of harmony and cooperation ruled, in private people often expressed considerable anger and dissatisfaction with various staff members and with the organization in general.

Many organizations have fragmented cultures of this kind, where people say one thing and do another. One of the interesting features of Linda Smircich's study was that she was able to identify the precise circumstances that had produced the fragmentation within the company and was able to show why it continued to operate in its somewhat schizophrenic fashion.

A fragmented history

Ten years earlier, when the organization was just four years old, it had passed through a particularly traumatic period that witnessed the demotion of its president, the hiring and firing of his successor, and the appointment of a group of professionals from the insurance industry at large. These events led to the development of separate subcultures. The first of these was represented by the original staff, or the "inside group" as they came to be known, and the second by the new professionals—the "outside group." Most of the outside group had been recruited from the same rival insurance company and brought with them very strong beliefs as to what was needed in their new organization. "This was how we did it at . . ." became a frequent stance taken in discussion. They wanted to model the new organization on the old.

The new president, appointed after the firing of the second, was a kind and peace-loving man. He set out to create a team atmosphere that would bind the organization together. However, rather than encourage a situation where organizational members could explore and resolve their differences in an open manner, he adopted a style of management that really required organizational members to put aside or repress their differences.

Unification attempts through rituals, images, and symbols

The desire for harmony was communicated in a variety of ways, particularly through the use of specific rituals. For example, at special management meetings the staff became an Indian tribe. Each member was given an Indian name and a headband with a feather. The aim was to forge unity between inside and outside groups. During this ritual, the practice of levying a 50-cent fine on anyone who mentioned the name of the rival insurance firm was introduced.

In both subtle and more obvious ways, the president continued to send messages about the need for harmony. He introduced regular staff meetings to review operations at which calm, polite cooperation quickly established itself as a norm. As some staff members reported:

"We sit in the same seats, like cows always go to the same stall."

"It's a real waste of time. It's a situation where you can say just about anything and no one will refute it."

"People are very hesitant to speak up, afraid to say too much. They say what everyone else wants to hear."

Harmony and teamwork were also sought through the use of imagery to define the desired company spirit—for example, the slogan "wheeling together." The logo of a wagon wheel was spread through the company. The idea of "putting one's shoulder to the wheel" or "wheeling together" was featured in many discussions and documents. An actual wagon wheel, mounted on a flat base, was moved from department to department.

An unhealthy suppression of conflict

The effect of this leadership style was to create a superficial appearance of harmony while driving conflict underground. This created the divergence between the public and private faces of the organization and led to a situation where the organization became increasingly unable to deal with real problems.

Because the identification of problems or concerns about company operation frequently created controversy the organization didn't really want to handle, the staff tended to confine their discussion of these issues to private places. In public, the impression that all was well gained the upper hand. When problematic issues were identified, they were always presented in the form of "challenges" to minimize the possibility of upsetting anyone. Driven underground by a style of management that effectively prevented the discussion of differences, genuine concerns were not given the attention they deserved. Not surprisingly, the organization no longer exists as a separate entity; the parent group eventually decided to reabsorb the insurance division into the main company.

In this case study, we see how corporate culture develops as an ethos (e.g., "let's bury our differences and keep the peace") created and sustained by social processes, images, symbols, and ritual.

Rituals are often embedded in the formal structure of the organization, as in the case of the president's weekly staff meeting, the real function of which was to affirm that senior members of the organization were at some form of peace with each other. The case illustrates the crucial role played by those in power in shaping the values that guide an organization: even though the president was perceived by the staff as being relatively weak, he managed to exert a decisive influence on the nature of the organization.

The study also shows how

- historical circumstances, i.e., the conflict between inside and outside groups, can shape the present, and
- the fundamental nature of an organization rests as much in its corporate culture as in the more formal organization chart and codes of procedure.

Indeed, it is probably no exaggeration to suggest that for this organization corporate culture may have been the single most important factor standing between success and failure.

The idea of building a team of integrated players is a powerful one, and the president of the insurance company was probably not at fault in choosing this metaphor. Rather, the problems lay in the way it was coupled with norms favoring passivity. Had the metaphor been linked with an ethos favoring openness and innovation and had team players been encouraged to make active contributions, the company's fortunes could have turned out very differently indeed.

Example 2: Team commitment at Hewlett-Packard

Hewlett-Packard (H-P) was started in the 1940s by Bill Hewlett and Dave Packard and has established a corporate culture famed for strong team commitment coupled with a philosophy of innovation through people. The company decided to put the team ethos on the line early in its history, adopting a policy that it would not be "a hire and fire company." This principle was severely tested on a couple of occasions in the 1970s, as it has been many times since then, when declines in business forced the company to adopt the policy of a "nine-day fortnight," whereby staff took a 10 percent pay cut and worked 10 percent fewer hours. Whereas other companies resorted to layoffs, H-P kept its full complement of staff, emphasizing that all members of the

H-P team shared the same fortune and that a measure of job security was possible even in unfavorable times.

Being a member of this team carried a set of obligations. Enthusiasm for work and an ethos of sharing problems and ideas in an atmosphere of free and open exchange were values the organization actively encouraged. Much of this ethos stemmed from the day-to-day example set by the founding heroes, who established a reputation for hands-on management throughout the company. The ethos was also fostered by ritual "beer busts" and "coffee klatches" and by numerous ad hoc meetings that created regular opportunities for informal interaction.

Promoting culture through stories, legends, and myths

Stories, legends, and myths about corporate heroes circulated through the organization and did much to communicate and sustain the cultural values underlying H-P's success. New recruits were treated to slide presentations that showed how "Bill and Dave" started the company in Bill's garage and used the Hewlett oven for making some of the first products. On another occasion they learned that when Bill Hewlett visited a plant one Saturday and found the lab stock area locked he immediately cut the padlock, leaving a note saying "Don't ever lock this door again. Thanks, Bill."

Along with more formal statements of company philosophy, the message soon hits home: At H-P we trust and value you. You're free to be enthusiastic about your job even if it's Saturday and to innovate and contribute in whatever way you can. Even though Hewlett-Packard is now spread across many continents, the founding spirit of "Bill and Dave" still pervades the company.

Example 3: A corporate jungle at ITT

For a very different example of the development of corporate culture, let us now turn to the development of ITT under the tough and uncompromising leadership of Harold Geneen. The story here is one of success built on a ruthless style of management that converted a medium-sized communications business with sales of $765 million in 1959 into one of the world's largest, most powerful, and diversified conglomerates, operating in over ninety countries with revenues of almost $12 billion in 1978.

Under Geneen's twenty-year reign, the company established a reputation as one of the fastest-growing and most profitable American companies—and, following its role in overseas bribery and the downfall of the Allende government in Chile, as one of the most corrupt and controversial.

Geneen's managerial style was simple and straightforward:

- He sought to keep his staff on top of their work by creating an intensely competitive atmosphere based on confrontation and intimidation.

- The foundation of his approach rested in his quest for what were known as "unshakable facts."

- He insisted that all managerial reports, decisions, and business plans be based on irrefutable premises, and he developed a complete information system, a network of special task forces, and a method of cross-examination that allowed him to check virtually every statement put forward.

Geneen possessed an extraordinary memory and an ability to absorb vast amounts of information in a relatively short time. This made it possible for him to keep his executives on their toes by demonstrating that he knew their situations as well as, if not better than, they did. His interrogation sessions at policy review meetings have become legendary.

Motivation through intimidation and fear

These meetings, described as "show trials," were held around an enormous table capable of seating over fifty people, each executive being provided with a microphone into which to speak. It is reported that Geneen's approach was to pose a question to a specific executive or to sit back listening to the reports being offered while specially appointed staff people cross-examined what was being said. As soon as the executive being questioned showed evasiveness or lack of certainty, Geneen would move in to probe the weakness. In complete command of the facts and equipped with a razor-sharp ability to cut to the center of an issue, he would invariably also cut the floundering executive and his argument to shreds. It is said that these experiences were so grueling that many executives were known to break down and cry under the pressure.

Geneen's approach motivated people through fear. If an executive was making a presentation, there was every incentive to stay up preparing throughout the night to ensure that all possible questions and angles were covered. This intimidating style was set by Geneen from the very beginning of his tenure: early in his career with ITT he would call executives at all hours, perhaps in the middle of the night, to inquire about the validity of some fact or obscure point in a written report.

The message was clear: ITT executives were expected to be company men and women on top of their jobs at all times. The idea that loyalty to the goals of the organization should take precedence over loyalty to colleagues was established as a key principle.

ITT under Geneen was a successful corporate jungle. High executive performance was undoubtedly achieved but at considerable cost in terms of staff stress and the kind of actions that this sometimes produced, such as the company's notorious activities in Chile. The pressure on ITT executives was above all to perform and deliver the goods they had promised. Their corporate necks were always on the line. Geneen's approach typifies the managerial style that psychoanalyst Michael Maccoby has characterized as that of the "jungle fighter": the power-hungry manager who experiences life and work as a jungle where it is eat or be eaten and where winners destroy losers.

COMPARING CORPORATE CULTURES
The influence of values and leadership style

The "cut and thrust" corporate culture of ITT under Geneen stands poles apart from the "let's bury our differences" culture of the humble insurance company. It also stands poles apart from the successful team atmosphere created at Hewlett-Packard. As in the case of our cross-cultural comparisons between Japan, Great Britain, and the United States, the examples are just illustrative. They show how different organizations can have different cultures. Extending the principle, we see that IBM is very different from Microsoft. Both are unlike Compaq, Apple, Coca-Cola, or Boeing.

A focus on the links between leadership style and corporate culture often provides key insights on why organizations work the way they do. However, there are other factors that need to be considered.

For example, gender may also be a powerful cultural force.

The influence of gender

"Macho" case studies such as that of Harold Geneen do an excellent job in bringing the influence of gender to light in an extreme way. But this influence is even more pervasive.

Male-dominated value systems. Traditional forms of organization are often dominated and shaped by male value systems. For example, the emphasis on logical, linear modes of thought and action and the drive for results at the expense of network and community building, from a gender standpoint, express values and approaches to life that are much more "male" than "female."

We have a lot more to say on this in the chapters on politics and psychic prisons because a strong case can be made for the idea that many aspects of the corporate world have been trapped within a male archetype. Until recently, it has been a man's world where women and associated gender styles were physically and psychologically marginalized or excluded from the male-dominated reality.

Male domination has led to the creation of organizations that often have strong female subcultures standing in tension with and, at times, in opposition to male power structures. Often, this unleashes powerful forces that can politicize a corporate culture along gender lines, a point further discussed in the politics chapter.

The female influence: Balancing rational and organic styles. From a cultural standpoint, organizations shaped around female values are more likely to balance and integrate the rational-analytic mode with values that emphasize more empathic, intuitive, organic forms of behavior. Interestingly, the new flat network forms of organization that are emerging to cope with the uncertainty and turbulence of modern environments require managerial competencies that have more in common with the female archetype than the male. As this develops, we can expect to see the transformation of many corporate cultures and subcultures away from the dominant influence of male values and associated modes of behavior.

The trend is already evident in the way that new-style corporate leaders such as Anita Roddick of the Body Shop are forging different styles of management and creating very different niches for their organizations. As Roddick puts it, "I run my company according to feminine principles— principles of caring, making intuitive decisions, not getting hung up on hierarchy or all those dreadfully boring business-school management ideas; having a sense of work as being part of your life, not separate from it; putting your labor where your love is; being responsible to the world in how you use your profits; recognizing the bottom line should stay at the bottom."

Sally Helgesen, in her book *Female Advantage,* shows how women like Frances Hesselbein of the Girl Scouts of the USA, Barbara Grogan of Western Industrial Contractors, Nancy Badore of Ford Motor Company's Executive Development Center, and Dorothy Brunson of Brunson Communications, like Anita Roddick, bring distinctively female styles of management to the workplace.

They help create cultures where hierarchy gives way to "webs of inclusion." They manage in a way that puts them "in the middle of things," building communities based on inclusive relationships characterized by trust, support, encouragement, and mutual respect. They help to produce organizations that are truly "networked," where the *process* of doing things is as important as the end result or product. Through their actions and successes they are modeling ways of producing corporate cultures that seem to have a lot in common with the brainlike forms of organization explored in the previous chapter.

The identification of gender values returns us to the links between leadership and corporate culture. Powerful leaders seem to symbolize so many aspects of their organization. But it is really important to recognize that formal leaders do not have any monopoly on the ability to create shared meaning.

The leader's position of power may lend him or her a special advantage in developing corporate value systems and codes of behavior because formal leaders often have important sources of power through which they can encourage, reward, or punish those who follow their lead. However, others are also able to influence the process by acting as informal opinion leaders or simply by acting as the people they are.

Other influences

Culture is not something that can be imposed on a social setting. Rather, it develops during the course of social interaction. In any organization there may be different and competing value systems that create a mosaic of organizational realities rather than a uniform corporate culture. Besides gender, race, language, and ethnicity, religious, socioeconomic, friendship, and professional groups can have a decisive impact on the cultural mosaic.

Professional groups. Different professional groups may each have a different view of the world and of the nature of their organization's business. Accountants may subscribe to one kind of philosophy and marketing people to another. The frame of reference guiding development engineers may be different from the perspective of members of the production department, marketing, and sales. Each group may have developed its own specialized language and set of favored concepts for formulating business priorities.

Subcultures: Social and ethnic groups. Social or ethnic groupings may also give rise to different norms and patterns of behavior with a crucial impact on day-to-day functioning, especially when the ethnic groupings coincide with different organizational activities.

W. F. Whyte in his studies of restaurants found status and other social differences between kitchen staff and those waiting on tables often create many operational problems. When a high-status group interacts with a low-status group or when groups with very different occupational attitudes are placed in a relation of dependence, organizations can become plagued by a kind of subcultural warfare. Different norms, beliefs, and attitudes to time, efficiency, or service can combine to create all kinds of contradictions and dysfunctions. These can be extremely difficult to tackle in a rational manner because they are intertwined with all kinds of deep-seated personal issues that in effect *define* the human beings involved.

Coalitions and countercultures. Subcultural divisions may also arise because organization members have divided loyalties. Not everyone is fully committed to the organization. People may develop specific subcultural practices as a way of adding meaning to their lives (e.g., by getting involved with friendship and other social groupings at work) or by developing norms and values that advance personal rather than organizational ends.

The politicking through which organizational members sometimes advance careers or specific interests can result in the development of coalitions sustained by specific sets of values. These coalitions sometimes develop into forms of counterculture in opposition to the organizational values espoused by those formally in control.

Many organizations are characterized by informal divisions of opinion within the top management group and sometimes in the organization at large. Typically, these divisions usually result in a struggle for control, which in certain important respects can be understood as a struggle for the right to shape corporate culture. As in politics, such struggles are often closely linked to questions of ideology.

Foremost among all organizational countercultures are those fostered by trade unions. It is here that the battle for ideological control is often most clearly defined, for trade unions are in effect counterorganizations in the sense that their existence stems from the fact that the interests of employee and employer may not be synonymous.

Trade unions have their own specific cultural histories, which vary from industry to industry and from organization to organization within an industry. The philosophy, values, and norms of union culture usually exert an important impact on the mosaic of culture, subculture, and counterculture that characterizes life in any organization.

CREATING ORGANIZATIONAL REALITY

Shared values, shared beliefs, shared meaning, shared understanding, and shared sense making are all different ways of describing culture.

In talking about culture we are really talking about a process of reality construction that allows people to see and understand particular events, actions, objects, utterances, or situations in distinctive ways. These patterns of understanding help us to cope with the situations being encountered and also provide a basis for making our own behavior sensible and meaningful.

But how does this occur?

- How is culture created and sustained?

- How do we construct our realities?

We have already begun to answer these questions in general terms, but it is useful to take a closer and more systematic look at the process involved.

CULTURE: RULE FOLLOWING OR ENACTMENT?

Sociologist Harold Garfinkel illustrates how the most routine and taken-for-granted aspects of social reality are in fact skillful *accomplishments*.

When we travel on a subway car, visit a neighbor, or act as a normal person walking down the street, we employ numerous social skills of which we are only dimly aware, just as a tightrope walker might think nothing of running across a high wire to collect his or her possessions at the end of rehearsal, oblivious to the skill that this involves.

Garfinkel elucidates our taken-for-granted skills by showing us what happens if we deliberately attempt to disrupt normal patterns of life.

- Look a fellow subway passenger in the eye for a prolonged period of time. He or she will no doubt look away at first but get increasingly uncomfortable as your gaze continues. Perhaps he or she will eventually inquire what's wrong, change seats, or get off at the next stop.

- Behave in your neighbor's house as if you live there.

- Disrupt the smooth and continuous line of your walk down a crowded street with a series of random stops and turns or with the shifty manner of a suspicious character.

In each case, you will gradually discover how life within a given culture flows smoothly only insofar as one's behavior conforms with unwritten codes. Disrupt these norms and the ordered reality of life inevitably breaks down.

The influence of social norms and customs

In one sense, then, we can say that the nature of a culture is found in its social norms and customs and that if one adheres to these rules of behavior one will be successful in constructing an appropriate social reality. As many business travelers have learned the hard way, in visiting overseas or even visiting a client or another organization at home, it is advisable to learn the norms that will allow them to "go native."

In visiting an Arab state it is important to understand the different roles played by men and women in Arab society and the local rules regarding the flexible nature of time. In general, Arabs in their home country have reservations about conducting business with women. Also, they like to take their time in building business trust and sound relationships before they make decisions, refuse to be hurried, and do not necessarily see a 2:00 P.M. appointment as meaning 2:00 P.M.

People who unwittingly break these rules and attempt to keep a fixed schedule or to rush their business will frequently get nowhere. Their actions are likely to be as disruptive as those of the norm-breaking passenger on the subway car.

The influence of the situational context

However, there seems to be more to culture than rule following. Several important studies show that the ability to apply a rule calls for much more than a knowledge of the rule itself, as rules are invariably incomplete.

Consider the legal system and the administration of justice, an area of human activity where action is supposed to be determined by clearly defined rules. The application of a specific law calls upon background knowledge on the part of the legal officer or judge that goes well beyond what is stated in the law itself. Studies show that cases of child molesting or burglary are typically assigned to legal categories on the basis of images and judgments as to what constitutes a "normal crime" in these areas. So a series of subjective decisions is made on the nature of the case before any rule is applied.

Lawyers and judges do not follow the rules. Rather, they invoke rules as a means of making a particular activity or particular judgment sensible and meaningful to themselves and to others. In effect, the parties are involved in a definition of the rules that are to be applied. The process often involves negotiation—for example, among the defendant and his or her lawyer, the public prosecutor, and the judge, all of whom may subscribe to competing definitions of the situation being considered.

If we return to consider how we accomplish the everyday realities of riding a subway car, visiting a neighbor, or walking down the street, we find the same process at work. As in judgments within the legal system, our constructions of the situation influence what rules and codes of behavior are to be summoned as appropriate to the situation.

Suppose we are visiting a neighbor to party and drink beer. Our understanding of the nature of the situation will lead us to invoke certain rules (e.g., that it is all right to go to the refrigerator to fetch another beer or to search for a bottle opener in the kitchen drawers), even though these rules might be considered quite inappropriate on another occasion.

The norms operating in different situations have to be invoked and defined in the light of our understanding of the context. We implicitly make many decisions and assumptions about a situation before any norm or rule is applied. Many of these decisions and assumptions are made quite unconsciously, as a result of our previous socialization and taken-for-granted knowledge, so that action appears quite spontaneous. And in most circumstances, the sense-making process or justification for action will occur only if the behavior is challenged.

Enacting reality

Karl Weick described the process through which we shape and structure our realities as a process of *enactment*. Like Garfinkel's concept of accomplishment, Weick's concept stresses the proactive role that we unconsciously play in creating our world. Although we often see ourselves as living in a reality with objective characteristics, life actually demands much more of us. It requires that we take an active role in bringing our realities into being through various interpretive schemes, even though these realities may then have a habit of imposing themselves on us as "the way things are."

The point of enactment is well illustrated in a wonderful tale related by Charles Hampden-Turner about a man whose wife's portrait was being painted by Picasso.

> One day the man called at the artist's studio. "What do you think?" asked Picasso, indicating the nearly finished picture. "Well . . . ," said the husband, trying to be polite, "it isn't how she really looks." "Oh," said the artist, "and how does she really look?" The husband decided not to be intimidated. "Like this!" said he, producing a photograph from his wallet. Picasso studied the photograph.
> "Mmm . . . ," he said, "small, isn't she?"

In recognizing that we accomplish or enact the reality of our everyday world, we have a powerful way of thinking about culture. It means that we must attempt to understand culture as an ongoing, proactive process of reality construction. Culture can no longer just be viewed as a simple variable that societies or organizations possess or something that a leader brings to his or her organization. Rather, it must be understood as an active, living phenomenon through which people jointly create and re-create the worlds in which they live.

ORGANIZATION: THE ENACTMENT OF A SHARED REALITY
Organizations as social constructions

The enactment view of culture has enormous implications for how we understand organizations as cultural phenomena, for it emphasizes that we must root our understanding of organization in the processes that produce systems of shared meaning.

- What are the shared frames of reference that make organization possible?
- Where do they come from?
- How are they created, communicated, and sustained?

These questions now become central to the task of organizational analysis and effective management. They help us see that organizations are socially constructed realities that are as much in the minds of their members as they are in concrete structures, rules, and relations.

The power of this insight has been mobilized with great effect by management writers like Tom Peters and Robert Waterman, who emphasize that successful organizations build cohesive cultures around common sets of norms, values, and ideas that create an appropriate focus for doing business. In their book *In Search of Excellence,* they showed how America's leading companies built around core values and ideas such as

- "IBM means service."
- "Never kill a new product idea." (3M)
- "Sell it to the sales staff." (Hewlett-Packard)

The focus at IBM was to create a service-driven organization where staff at every level made the needs of the customer a core priority. The focus at 3M was on the need for constant innovation as a means of creating a flow of new products. At Hewlett-Packard, a company operating in a sector where technical innovation can easily run away with itself, the focus was on marketability. In each case, the core ideas helped create a corporate culture that diffused fundamental values and operating principles throughout the organization to create a basis for success.

Cultural change and core values

The total quality and customer service movements that dominated managerial thinking and practice in the 1980s and 1990s have sought to create a cultural change in management at large. The various theories and techniques advocated by these movements offered new mindsets and new values for doing business, backed by a detailed "language" and protocol through which organizational members could begin to think, talk, and act in new ways. Their implicit aims were to create a kind of "cultural revolution" that would replace the old bureaucratic way of life with a focus on a new "customer and quality driven" business logic.

To the extent that the new cultural values were able to replace the bureaucratic ones, initiatives spawned by these movements were extremely successful. Many organizations succeeded in revolutionizing and reinventing themselves through the values of quality and customer service. But as many as 70 percent of the firms that set off on this new path were unsuccessful, largely because they failed to replace the bureaucratic logic governing the old mode of operation. Their quality and service programs became no more than programs. Despite all the money and effort that was spent, they failed to dent the dominant culture and the political dynamic that often supports it.

The reengineering and empowerment movements have encountered a similar experience. To be effective they needed to transform prevailing organizational mindsets and political patterns. But in the majority of cases, they failed to do so.

Cultural change as transformation of mindsets, values, and shared meanings

There can be little doubt that the culture metaphor offers a fresh way of thinking about organization. It shows that the challenge of creating new forms of organization and management is very much a challenge of cultural change. It is a challenge of transforming the mindsets, visions, paradigms, images, metaphors, beliefs, and shared meanings that sustain existing business realities, and of creating a detailed language and code of behavior through which the desired new reality can be lived on a daily basis. Viewed in this way, the creation of a particular corporate culture is not just about inventing new slogans or acquiring a new leader. It is about inventing what amounts to a new way of life.

Those who understand the challenge of cultural change recognize that the task is enormous because it involves the creation of shared systems of meaning that are accepted, internalized, and acted on at every level of the organization. In the most fundamental sense, culture has a holographic quality. Characteristics of the whole must be encoded in all the parts. Otherwise, the parts fail to express and act on the character of the whole. The best teams and the free-flowing organizations that have discarded bureaucratic forms of management constantly reflect this quality. They are organized through core meanings that people own and share. It is this quality that allows them to be flexible, adaptive, and nonbureaucratic.

Organizationally, shared meanings provide alternatives to control through external procedures and rules.

The hidden depth of culture

There is much more to culture and corporate culture than meets the eye. Many management theorists and practitioners influenced by the metaphor fail to recognize this. As a result, they think and talk about culture as what may be described as "the level of slogans," and their methods and techniques of cultural change usually do little more than dent surface reality.

To come to grips with an organization's culture, it is necessary to uncover the mundane as well as the more vivid aspects of the reality-construction process. Sometimes these are so subtle and all-pervasive that they are very difficult to identify.

Recall our discussion of how Japanese organizations are shaped by the values of the rice field or of how some British organizations reproduce attitudes rooted in a long history of class conflict. These values may have very little to do with the actual organizations in which they are found, being imported in an invisible way. Yet they can play a crucial role in upsetting all attempts at cultural change.

Or take the way in which financial considerations may be allowed to shape the reality of an organization through the routine operation of financial information systems. Under the influence of these kinds of controls, people or organizational units, whether they be pupils in schools, patients in hospitals, or work teams in manufacturing plants, may be translated into profit centers generating costs and revenues. These systems may not be seen as cultural in nature. But they definitely are. Their influence may be far more pervasive than other policies and programs that are explicitly designed to create cultural change, for example, in relation to the enhancement of "quality production" or the "empowerment of staff."

Although it is not usual to regard accountants as "reality constructors" exerting a decisive influence on an organization's culture, this is exactly the role that they play. They can shape the reality of an organization by persuading people that the interpretive lens of "financial performance" should be given priority in determining the way that the organization is to be run. This, of course, is not to say that financial considerations are unimportant.

The point is that thinking about an organization in financial terms is but one way of thinking about that organization. There are always others, and these are usually forced into the background as financial considerations gain a major hold on the definition of organizational reality.

Organizational structure, rules, policies, goals, missions, job descriptions, and standardized operating procedures perform a similar interpretive function, for they act as primary points of reference for the way people think about and make sense of the contexts in which they work. Although typically viewed as among the more objective characteristics of an organization, an enactment view emphasizes that they are cultural artifacts shaping the ongoing reality.

Just as a tribal society's values, beliefs, and traditions may be embedded in kinship and other social structures, many aspects of an organization's culture are embedded in routine aspects of everyday practice. They define the socially constructed stage on which organizational members lend their culture living form. More mundane than the vivid ritual and ceremony that decorated meetings at the insurance company discussed earlier, the weekly rally at Tupperware, the gold banana awards at Foxboro, or the new corporate philosophies and programs through which an organization is trying to improve quality or customer service, routines are incredibly important in understanding how organizations work when no one is really looking and why established practice may be so resistant to change.

As we explore corporate culture with this frame of reference in mind, it is amazing to see the extent to which *every* aspect of organization is rich in symbolic meaning and how the familiar often appears in a new light. That weekly meeting or annual planning cycle that everyone knows is a waste of time assumes a new significance: as a ritual serving various kinds of hidden functions.

Meetings are more than just meetings. They carry important aspects of organizational culture: norms of passivity in the insurance company, and fear and respect for unshakable facts in Geneen's intimidation rituals. Even the nature of an empty meeting room conveys something about the general organizational culture, for these rooms generally reflect and reproduce the structures of interaction expected in the organization.

Straight lines of chairs and note pads, each guarded by a water glass, communicate a sense of conformity and order. The friendly chaos and casualness of more informal meeting rooms extend a more open invitation to self-organization.

- The everyday language of bureaucracy is understood as one of the means through which the organization actually creates its bureaucratic characteristics.

- The aggressive character of an organization is understood in terms of the implicit military mentality that leads it to shape aggressive relations with its environment and the local labor union.

Organizations end up being what they think and say, as their ideas and visions realize themselves.

As we look at the everyday relations between people in an organization with an eye on the reality-construction process, new insights on group functioning and leadership also emerge:

- We find that the formation of a group or the process of becoming a leader ultimately hinges on an ability to create a shared sense of reality.

- We find that cohesive groups are those that arise around shared understandings, while fragmented groups tend to be those characterized by multiple realities.

As we deepen our view of corporate culture to embrace even the most bedrock assumptions about organizational reality, we find ourselves confronting some of the basic myths shaping organizational life. For example, Ely Devons has drawn parallels between decision-making processes in formal organizations and magic and divination in tribal societies. In primitive society, magic decides whether hunting should proceed in one direction or another, whether the tribe should go to war, or who should marry whom, giving clear-cut decisions in situations that might otherwise be open to endless wrangling.

In formal organizations, techniques of quantitative analysis seem to perform a similar role. They are used to forecast the future and analyze the consequences of different courses of action in a way that lends decision making a semblance of rationality. The use of such techniques does not, of course, reduce risks. The uncertainties surrounding a situation still exist, hidden in the assumptions underlying the technical analysis.

The function of such analysis is to increase the credibility of action in situations that would otherwise have to be managed through guesswork and hunch. Like the magician who consults a chicken's entrails, many organizational decision makers insist that the facts and figures be examined before a policy decision is made, even though the statistics provide unreliable guides as to what is likely to happen in the future. And, as with the magician, they or their magic are not discredited when events prove them wrong.

Just as the magician may attribute failure to imperfect execution or the unanticipated intervention of some hostile force, the technical expert is allowed to blame the model used or the turn of events as a means of explaining why forecasts are inaccurate. The analysis is never discredited. The appearance of rationality is preserved.

Modern organizations are sustained by belief systems that emphasize the importance of rationality, and their legitimacy in the public eye usually depends on their ability to demonstrate rationality and objectivity in action. It is for this reason that anthropologists often refer to rationality as the myth of modern society, for, like primitive myth, it provides us with a comprehensive frame of reference, or structure of belief, through which we can negotiate day-to-day experience and help to make it intelligible. The myth of rationality helps us see certain patterns of action as legitimate, credible, and normal. It helps us avoid the wrangling and debate that would arise if we were to recognize the basic uncertainty and ambiguity underlying many of our values and the situations with which we have to deal.

STRENGTHS AND LIMITATIONS OF THE CULTURE METAPHOR

In seeing organizations as cultures, we can see almost every aspect in a new way.

STRENGTHS

- **The metaphor emphasizes the symbolic significance of almost everything we do.**

Even the most concrete and rational aspects of organization—whether structures, hierarchies, rules, or organizational routines—embody social constructions and meanings that are crucial for understanding how organization functions day by day. In highlighting this, the culture metaphor focuses attention on a human side that other metaphors ignore or gloss over.

- **We learn that organization and shared meaning are one and the same.**

A second major strength of the metaphor is that it shows how organization ultimately rests in shared systems of meaning, hence in the actions and interpretive schemes that create and re-create that meaning. Under mechanical and organismic metaphors, primary emphasis tends to be placed on the importance of organizational *design:* the design of organizational structures or the design of adaptive processes.

The culture metaphor points toward another means of creating and shaping organized activity: by influencing the ideologies, values, beliefs, language, norms, ceremonies, and other social practices that ultimately shape and guide organized action.

- **Leaders and managers see how their success hinges on the creation of shared meaning.**

This is the aspect of the culture metaphor that has had the greatest impact on organizational practice to date. Since the 1980s, there has been a growing realization that the fundamental task facing leaders and managers rests in creating appropriate systems of shared meaning that can mobilize the efforts of people in pursuit of desired aims and objectives.

The two key words here are "appropriate" and "shared."

The shared vision that "IBM means service" served the company extremely well in an era dominated by mainframe computers. The company had an industry dominance that allowed it to lavish high-priced attention on key customers through its service philosophy. However, under different circumstances, the very same vision became a liability. As the result of the meteoric rise of the personal computer, networked computing, a rapidly developing software industry, an era of global communication systems, plus dozens of competitors with high-quality, state-of-the-art, low-priced products, the core values that helped IBM achieve dominance were no longer enough. Like other once-successful corporations, the organization was faced with the challenge of reinventing and repositioning itself through new visions and shared values that could help mobilize a new-style corporate culture capable of dealing with the new reality.

The challenge of change is enormous because corporate culture is not a simple phenomenon. It is not something that can be mandated, designed, or made. It is a living, evolving, self-organizing reality that can be shaped and reshaped but not in an absolute way. But a broad understanding of the nature of the metaphor can offer important insights in approaching this task.

- **Leaders and managers gain a new understanding of their impacts and roles.**

Under the influence of the culture metaphor, leaders and managers come to see themselves as people who ultimately help to create and shape the meanings that are to guide organized action. This involves a major reframing of their roles.

When leaders and managers ask themselves "What impact am I having on the social construction of reality in my organization?" and "What can I do to have a different and more positive impact?" they penetrate to a new level of understanding about the significance of what they are truly doing.

This approach contrasts with the traditional views of management in which managers may use their formal authority, function, and role as a kind of protective device that insulates them from many of the realities of organizational life. They could persuade themselves that, so long as they were doing what was mandated, they were doing the right thing: "To hell with what others think. I'm doing my job."

But the culture metaphor responds "No you're not!" You are what you are *seen and experienced as being,* not what you think you are or what your job title or job description says you are. This obliges the leader and manager to understand their roles and significance in terms of actual impacts on the reality construction process.

This is a major strength of the metaphor because it makes people own their impact on the way things are and shows that it is their responsibility to change when appropriate. They can no longer hide behind formal structures and roles or excuse themselves for having unfortunate personality traits. From a cultural standpoint, the impact on shared meaning is all important.

■ **We see that organizations and their environments are enacted domains.**

Organizations are a social enactment; their relations with the environment are also socially constructed. The people who bring organizations to life choose and structure internal and external relationships through a host of interpretive decisions that are extensions of corporate culture.

This has profound implications for how we understand organization-environment relations and strategic management, for in stressing the fundamental interconnection between these phenomena we recognize that our environments are extensions of ourselves. (This idea is explored in some detail in the chapter on flux and transformation.) We choose and operate in environmental domains according to how we construct conceptions of what we are and what we are trying to do (e.g., "be an organization in the computer industry," "produce and sell automobiles," "be a leader in our field," "whip the competition"). And we act in relation to these domains through the definitions that we impose on them.

For example, firms in an industry typically develop a language for making sense of their market, technology, and relations with other segments of the economy, aligning their actions in relation to the pattern of threats and opportunities that this set of interpretations makes visible. Firms organize their environments exactly as they organize their internal operations, enacting the realities with which they have to deal.

Of course, the environment may not be so easily controlled as internal operations. Other organizations also inhabit this domain, shaping action in accordance with *their* favorite interpretive schemes and influencing the environment to which others are trying to adapt and react.

Environmental turbulence and change is a product of this ongoing process of enactment. Environments are enacted by hosts of individuals and organizations each acting on the basis of their interpretations of a world that is in effect mutually defined. A competitive ethos produces competitive environments. Visions of recession produce recession. The beliefs and ideas that organizations hold about who they are, what they are trying to do, and what their environment is like have a much greater tendency to realize themselves than is usually believed.

■ **Strategic management is understood as an enactment process.**

All the above points have considerable relevance for the way organizations should approach strategy formulation. By appreciating that strategy making is a process of enactment that *produces* a large element of the future with which the organization will have to deal, it is possible to overcome the false impression that organizations are adapting or reacting to a world that is independent of their own making. This can help empower organizations to take responsibility for the future in an active way and help them appreciate that they themselves often create the constraints, barriers, and situations that cause them problems.

For example, in the 1970s, the American automobile industry saw the Japanese challenge as lying at the heart of their problems and tried to deflect the challenge through import restrictions and regulation. A closer look at the situation would have led them to see that members of their industry had enacted the conditions that helped to make the Japanese challenge successful (e.g., by ignoring the possibility that the American market might be amenable to the idea of buying smaller cars). Strategy enacts problems as well as solutions.

■ **The metaphor offers a fresh perspective on organizational change.**

Traditionally, the organizational change process has been conceptualized as a problem of changing technologies, structures, and the abilities and motivations of employees. This is partly correct. But effective change also depends on changing the images and values that are to guide action.

Without this support it is unlikely that technical and structural changes will have the desired effect. The message of the culture metaphor is that change programs must give attention to the kind of corporate ethos required in the new situation and find how this can be developed. Since organization ultimately resides in the heads of the people involved, effective organizational change always implies cultural change. Changes in technology, rules, systems, procedures, and policies are just not enough.

LIMITATIONS

The insights generated by the culture metaphor have encouraged many managers and management theorists to find ways of managing corporate culture. Most are now aware of the symbolic consequences of organizational values, and many organizations have started to explore the pattern of culture and subculture that shapes day-to-day action. On the one hand, this can be seen as a positive development since it recognizes the truly human nature of organizations and the need to build organization around people rather than techniques. On the other hand, there are a number of potentially negative consequences.

- **The metaphor can be used to support ideological manipulation and control.**

Persuaded by the ideas that there are good and bad cultures, that a strong organizational culture is essential for success, or that modifications to an existing culture will lead employees to work harder and feel more content, many managers and management consultants have begun to adopt new roles as change agents attempting to create new forms of corporate consciousness. Although many managers approach this task on the assumption that what's good for the organization will inevitably be in the interests of its employees, critics feel that this trend is a potentially dangerous one, developing the art of management into a process of ideological control or what is sometimes described as "values engineering."

Management has always been to some extent an ideological practice, promoting appropriate attitudes, values, and norms as means of motivating and controlling employees. What is new in many recent developments is the not-so-subtle way in which ideological manipulation and control is being advocated as an essential managerial strategy. There is often an ideological blindness in much of the writing about corporate culture, especially by those who advocate that managers attempt to become folk heroes shaping and reshaping the culture of their organizations. The fact that such manipulation may well be accompanied by resistance, resentment, and mistrust and that employees may react against being manipulated in this way receives scant attention.

There is an important distinction to be drawn between attempts to create networks of shared meaning that link key members of an organization around visions, values, and codes of practice so essential to the holographic self-organization described in the brain chapter, and the use of culture as a manipulative tool. To the extent that the insights of the culture metaphor are used to create an Orwellian world of "corporate newspeak," where the culture controls rather than expresses human character, the metaphor may prove quite manipulative and totalitarian in its influence.

When we observe a culture, whether in an organization or in society at large, we are observing an evolved form of social practice that has been influenced by many complex interactions between people, events, situations, actions, and general circumstance. Culture is self-organizing and is always evolving. Although at any given time it can be seen as having a discernible pattern (e.g., reflecting an ethos of competition or cooperation), this pattern tends to be a snapshot abstraction imposed on the culture from the outside. It is a pattern that helps the observer to make sense of what is happening in the culture. But it is not synonymous with experience in the culture itself.

Recall the earlier discussion of Western interpretations versus Japanese experience of hierarchical relationships. From the Western standpoint, Japanese hierarchy may be seen as a pattern of domination. Internally, it may be experienced as a process of mutual service.

The message: Observer beware. There is often more to culture than meets the eye, and our understandings are usually much more fragmented and superficial than the reality itself.

■ **Culture is holographic and cannot really be managed.**

This is an important point because many management theorists view culture as a phenomenon with clearly defined attributes. Like organizational structure, culture is often reduced to a set of discrete variables such as values, beliefs, stories, norms, and rituals that can be documented and manipulated in an instrumental way.

It is this kind of mechanistic attitude that underlies many perspectives advocating the management of culture. But culture seems more holographic than mechanistic. Where corporate culture is strong and robust, a distinctive ethos pervades the whole organization: employees exude the characteristics that define the mission or ethos of the whole; for example, outstanding commitment to service, perseverance against the odds, a commitment to innovation, or in less fortunate circumstances, lethargy or a sense of helplessness or futility.

Corporate culture rests in distinctive capacities and incapacities that are built into the attitudes and approaches of organizational members. Culture is not something that can be measured on a scale because it is a form of lived experience. Managers can influence that experience by being aware of the symbolic consequences of their actions and by attempting to foster desired values. But they can never control culture in the sense that many management writers advocate.

The holographic diffusion of culture means that it pervades activity in a way that is not amenable to direct control by any single group of individuals. An understanding of organizations as cultures opens our eyes to many crucial insights that elude other metaphors, but these insights do not always provide the easy recipe for solving managerial problems that many managers and management writers hope for.

■ **Like an iceberg, important dimensions of culture are always invisible, and what is easily seen can be relatively unimportant.**

When anthropologist Franz Boas entertained a Kwakiutl from the Pacific Northwest in New York City in the early twentieth century, his visitor reserved most of his intellectual curiosity for the brass balls on hotel banisters and the bearded ladies then exhibited in Times Square. His attention was caught by the bizarre rather than the fundamental aspects of the culture. This experience contains a valuable caution for those interested in understanding organizational culture, for in this sphere too, attention may be captured by the hoopla and ritual that decorate the surface of organizational life rather than by the deeper and more fundamental structures that sustain these visible aspects. To grasp the full implications of the culture metaphor we have to learn to go beneath the surface, and this can be an extremely difficult task.

■ **Culture usually has a deep political dimension, making it impossible to grasp the full significance of culture through the culture metaphor.**

In studies of organizational culture, the process of enacting organizational reality is usually seen as a voluntary process under the direct influence of the actors involved. This view can be important in empowering people to take greater responsibility for their world by recognizing that they play an important part in the construction of their realities. But it can be misleading to the extent that it ignores the stage on which the enactment occurs. We all construct or enact our realities but not necessarily under circumstances of our own choosing. There is an important power dimension underlying the enactment process that the culture metaphor does not always highlight to the degree possible. When this is taken into account, the culture metaphor becomes infused with a political flavor that has close links with the perspectives to be explored in subsequent chapters.

6 Interests, Conflict, and Power: Organizations As Political Systems

WHEN WE SEE ORGANIZATIONS THROUGH THE
LENS OF POLITICS, patterns of competing interests, conflicts, and power
plays dominate the scene.

- We view organization and management as a political process.
- We can identify different styles of government.
- We see how organization becomes politicized because of divergent interests of individuals and groups.
- We appreciate the fact that conflict is a natural property of every organization.
- We observe many different sources of power and learn how they can be used to our advantage.

Understanding organizations in political terms allows us to accept politics as an inevitable feature of corporate life. We learn that effective managers are skilled political actors who recognize the continuous interplay between competing interests and who use conflict as a positive force.

> I live in a democratic society. Why should I have to obey the
> orders of my boss eight hours a day? He acts like a bloody dictator,
> ordering us around and telling us what we should be thinking and
> doing. What right does he have to act in this way? The company pays
> our wages, but does this mean it has the right to command all our
> beliefs and feelings? It certainly has no right to reduce us to robots who
> must obey every command.

THIS RATHER ANGRY COMMENT OF A FACTORY WORKER EXASPER-
ATED BY THE GRINDING AND OPPRESSIVE EXPERIENCE OF DAILY
WORK LIFE captures an aspect of organization that has escaped us up to
now. He recognizes that his rights as a citizen and as a paid employee are in
conflict with each other. As a citizen in a democratic society he is theoreti-
cally free to hold his own opinions, make his own decisions, and be treated
as an equal. As an employee he is denied all these rights. He is expected to
keep his mouth shut, do what he is told, and submit to the will of his superior. For eight hours a day, five days a week, he is expected to forget about
democracy and get on with his work. His only democratic right rests in the
freedom to find another job and move on. Or as his manager put it, "You
can vote with your feet. If you don't like it here, you don't have to stay."

The situation described is an extreme one. Not all organizations are
characterized by such entrenched relations between managers and workers
or by such dictatorial modes of rule. But the situation is more common than
we often like to think, especially in industrial organizations where battle
lines have developed between labor and management. Typical or not, the
point of our illustration is that it invites us to understand organizations as
political systems.

Managers frequently talk about authority, power, and superior-
subordinate relations. It takes but a small step to recognize these as political issues involving the activities of rulers and ruled. If we develop this idea,
it is clear that we can understand organizations as systems of government
that vary according to the political principles employed.

Some organizations, like the one considered above, may be highly
authoritarian while others may be model democracies. By recognizing that
organization is intrinsically political, in the sense that ways must be found
to create order and direction among people with potentially diverse and
conflicting interests, much can be learned about the problems and legitimacy of management as a process of government and about the relation
between organization and society.

The political metaphor can also be used to unravel the politics of day-
to-day organizational life. Most people working in an organization readily

admit in private that they are surrounded by forms of "wheeling and deal-ing" through which different people attempt to advance specific interests. However, this kind of activity is rarely discussed in public. The idea that organizations are supposed to be rational enterprises in which their mem-bers seek common goals tends to discourage discussion of political motive. Politics, in short, is seen as a dirty word. This is unfortunate because it can prevent us from recognizing that politics and politicking may be an essen-tial aspect of organizational life and not necessarily an optional and dys-functional extra.

In its original meaning the idea of politics stems from the view that, where interests are divergent, society should provide a means of allowing individuals to reconcile their differences through consultation and negoti-ation. In ancient Greece, Aristotle advocated politics as a means of recon-ciling the need for unity in the Greek *polis* (city-state) with the fact that the *polis* was an "aggregate of many members." Politics, for him, provided a means of creating order out of diversity while avoiding forms of totalitar-ian rule. Political science and many systems of government have built on this basic idea, advocating politics and the recognition and interplay of competing interests as a means of creating a noncoercive form of social order.

By attempting to understand organizations as systems of government and by attempting to unravel the detailed politics of organizational life, we can grasp important qualities of organization that are often glossed over or ignored.

ORGANIZATIONS AS SYSTEMS OF GOVERNMENT

In April 1979, *Business Week* ran a cover story on the Ford Motor Company. The cover featured a cartoon of Henry Ford II sitting in a throne-like driving seat with a steering wheel between his hands. Behind the throne stands a shadowy figure—we are left to guess who. The prominent Ford-like nose suggests that it may be Henry Ford I, founder of the Ford dynasty, scrutinizing the way his grandson is driving the company.

The focus of the story is on the problem of succession. After thirty-four years as chief executive officer, Henry II was contemplating retirement, but there was no obvious successor capable of taking the wheel. Until his demotion and dismissal in summer 1978, the popular candidate had been Lee Iacocca, the highly successful Ford executive who later became head of Chrysler. The firing of Iacocca added depth to the imagery conveyed in the cartoon, for it symbolized the authoritarian nature of Ford under the two Henrys.

Iacocca's dismissal was merely the most recent and controversial in a list of firings that had included the names of seven company presidents since 1960. Iacocca was a popular and powerful figure at the Ford company but obviously not popular where it mattered most: His dismissal was solely linked to the fact that he did not have Henry II's approval. Henry II is reported as having presented an "it's him or me" ultimatum to his board's Organization Review Committee and won. The formal reason given by Henry II to *Business Week* was that Iacocca did not fit into his way of looking at things. Informally, it is speculated that Iacocca's fate was sealed by the fact that he had become too powerful within the company. Although the guiding philosophy of Ford was reported to be moving toward a General Motors style of "group management," *Business Week* stated that it believed Henry had found it difficult to reconcile himself with the loss of personal power that this kind of decentralization involved.

The story is by no means unique. Many organizations are ruled by authoritarian managers who wield considerable power as a result of their personal characteristics, family ties, or skill in building influence and prestige within the organization. Obvious examples are the owner-operated firm where the principle that "It's my business and I'll do as I like" holds sway; the family business ruled through "iron hands" that respect family interest and tradition above all else; and large corporations, business firms, labor unions, and even voluntary organizations or clubs dominated by self-perpetuating oligarchies. The basis of day-to-day order in these organizations tends to be autocratic rather than democratic in that the ultimate power to shape action rests in the hands of a single individual or group who typically makes all the important decisions. Although it is rare in practice to find an organization that is completely autocratic, many organizations have strong autocratic tendencies and characteristics.

DIFFERENTIATING BETWEEN TYPES OF POWER AND RULE

When we summon terms like autocracy and democracy to describe the nature of an organization, we are implicitly drawing parallels between organizations and political systems. We do the same when we talk about organizations as bureaucracies or technocracies because in each case we are characterizing the organization in terms of a particular style of political rule. In each of these words the suffix -*cracy*, meaning power or rule, is coupled with a prefix that indicates the precise nature of the power or rule employed:

- In *auto*cracies, such as many paternalistic organizational or family firms, the rule of "one" individual or a small group is characterized by absolute and often dictatorial power.

- In *bureau*cracies, such as many government and regulatory organizations, rule is associated with use of the written word and is exercised by bureaucrats who sit behind their "bureaux," or desks, making and administering the rules that guide organizational activity. Power and accountability in such organizations are intimately connected with one's knowledge and use of the rules and the related lawlike form of administration.

- In *techno*cracies, such as the flexible and ever-changing firms that thrive in the electronics industry and other turbulent environments, power and accountability are directly linked to one's "technical" knowledge and expertise. Power and influence often tend to follow the "whiz kids" and other knowledgeable people who seem capable of addressing dominant concerns or of opening new paths to corporate fame and fortune.

- In *demo*cracies, the power to rule rests with the *demos*, or populace. This power may be exercised through representative forms of management, where different stakeholders are formally represented in decision-making processes, as in systems of "codetermination" or coalition government and in forms of worker or shareholder control. Democratic power may also be exercised directly through participative forms of rule where everyone shares in the management process, such as in cooperatives and kibbutzim.

Whereas in autocracies and bureaucracies the pattern of power and authority is fairly stable and clearly defined, in technocracies it is often in flux as different individuals and groups rise and decline in power along with the value of their technical contributions. In democracies, power and authority are usually rooted in the culture and ideologies shaping the political history of the enterprise.

It is rare to find organizations that use just one kind of rule. One of the tasks of political—and organizational—analysis is to discover which principles are in evidence, as well as where, when, why, and how.

Many people hold the belief that business and politics should be kept apart, and the idea that workers should sit on boards of directors or that employees should control a particular organization or industry is viewed as taking an unwarranted political stand. But the person advocating the case of employee rights or industrial democracy is not introducing a political issue so much as arguing for a different approach to a situation that is already political. Organizations that are autocratic, bureaucratic, or technocratic have as much political significance as joint labor-management schemes, such as those used in Germany's system of codetermination or in more fully developed systems of worker control. Their political nature is simply of a different kind, drawing on different principles of legitimacy.

Whether we are discussing the management of the Ford Motor Company under a member of the Ford dynasty or the management of a worker-controlled cooperative, it is clear that organizational choice always implies political choice. Although the language of organization theory often presents ideas relating to the management and motivation of people at work in relatively neutral terms—for example, as issues of leadership style, autonomy, participation, and employer-employee relations—they are by no means as neutral as they seem. In understanding organizations as political systems we have a means of exploring the political significance of these issues and the general relation between politics and organization.

ORGANIZATIONS AS SYSTEMS OF POLITICAL ACTIVITY

To understand the day-to-day political dynamics of organization, it is necessary to explore the detailed processes through which people engage in politics. Let's return to Aristotle's idea that politics stems from a diversity of interests and trace how this diversity gives rise to the "wheeling and dealing," negotiation, and other processes of coalition building and mutual influence that shape so much of organizational life.

An organization's politics is most clearly manifest in conflicts and power plays and in the interpersonal intrigues that divert the flow of organizational activity. More fundamentally, however, politics occurs on an ongoing basis, often in a way that is invisible to all but those directly involved.

We can analyze organizational politics in a systematic way by focusing on relations among *interests, conflict,* and *power.* Organizational politics arise when people think differently and want to act differently when confronted with alternative paths of action. This diversity creates a tension that must be resolved through political means. As we have already seen, there are many ways in which the tension can be resolved:

- autocratically ("We'll do it this way."),
- bureaucratically ("We're supposed to do it this way."),
- technocratically ("It's best to do it this way."), and
- democratically ("How shall we do it?").

In each case the choice between alternative paths of action hinges on the power relations between the actors involved. Their divergent interests give rise to conflicts, visible and invisible, that are resolved or perpetuated by various kinds of power plays.

UNDERSTANDING TASK, CAREER, AND PERSONAL INTERESTS

In talking about "interests" we are talking about predispositions that embrace goals, values, desires, expectations, and other orientations and inclinations that lead a person to act in one way rather than another. In everyday life we tend to think of interests in a spatial way, as areas of concern that we wish to preserve or enlarge or as positions that we wish to protect or achieve. We live "in" our interests, often see others as "encroaching" on them, and readily engage in defenses or attacks designed to sustain or improve our position. The flow of politics is intimately connected with this way of positioning ourselves.

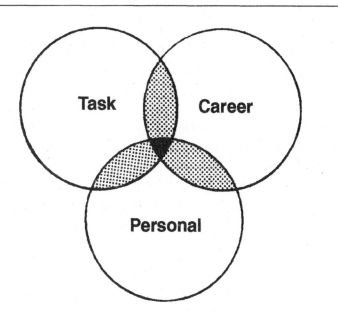

The above diagram illustrates the relationship and tension that often exist between one's job (task), career aspirations, and personal values and lifestyle (personal interests). The three domains can interact (the shaded areas) and also remain separate. In working in an organization we try to strike a balance between the three sets of interests. Most often, the balance is an uneasy and ever-changing one, creating tensions that lie at the center of political activity. The fact that the area of complete convergence of interests is often small (the darkest area) is one reason why organizational (or task) rationality is such a rare phenomenon. The degree of overlap varies from situation to situation.

Exhibit 6.1. Organizational interests: task, career, and personal

There are many ways in which we can define and analyze the pursuit and defense of interests. One way that has particular relevance to understanding organizational politics is to conceive interests in terms of three interconnected domains relating to one's organizational task, career, and personal life (exhibit 6.1).

Task interests are connected with the work one has to perform. The manager of a production plant must ensure that products are produced in a timely and efficient manner. A salesperson must sell his or her quota of goods and sustain customer relations. An accountant must maintain appropriate records and produce regular accounts. However, work life always involves more than just doing one's job.

Employees bring to the workplace aspirations and visions as to what their futures may hold, providing the basis for *career interests* that may be independent of the jobs being performed.

Employees also bring *personal interests,* their personalities, private attitudes, values, preferences, beliefs, and sets of commitments from outside work, allowing these to shape the way they act in relation to both job and career.

The relations among the three sets of interests will become more apparent when we examine the following situation:

> A corporate executive works in a large organization. He may be highly committed to his job, ambitious, and also highly involved with family life. In his work experience, he may desire to manage all three: to do a good job, move ahead in the organization, and strike a reasonable balance between work and leisure so that he can spend weekends and most evenings with his family. In some situations, all three spheres of interest may coincide; in others, two spheres may be compatible; whereas in others, the different interests may have no relation with each other.
>
> Life runs very smoothly for the executive in the area of work and family interests—he gets a great idea that contributes to his job performance and promotion prospects and gives him more leisure time as well. But it gets difficult in the two situations of partial overlaps—for example, if his great idea improves performance and career prospects, it could mean more work and less leisure; or if it enables him to reduce his workload, it could make him less visible and hence a less obvious candidate for promotion; or, in the final case, the idea may be great for getting on with his job but have no other significance at all.

The executive's attitude and relation to tasks, ideas, or other suggestions from the workplace are all likely to be crucially affected by where they fall on the diagram of interests depicted in exhibit 6.1.

The tensions existing between the different interests that the executive wishes to pursue make his relation to work inherently "political," even before we take into account the existence and actions of other organizational members. These tensions are inherent in work life in Western society because of the latent contradictions between the demands of work and leisure, on the one hand, and the demands of present and future, on the other.

The orientation of different people toward these tensions varies from situation to situation, producing a great variety in styles of behavior. Some people are committed to doing their jobs as an end in itself; others are more careerist. Yet others spend most of their energy attempting to make work life less onerous or as comfortable and consistent with their personal preferences as possible. Many people manage to achieve considerable degrees of overlap between competing aims and aspirations, shaping their general tasks or missions in a way that allows them to achieve all their aims at once. Others have to content themselves with compromise positions.

Analyzing the relationships between different kinds of interests provides us with a means of decoding the personal agendas underlying specific actions and activities. We can begin to understand how people relate to their work through their personal concerns and detect the motivating factors that underpin the varied styles of careerism, gamesmanship, task commitment, rigidity, "turf protection," zealousness, detachment, and freewheeling that lend the politics of organizational life its detailed character.

Every individual's personal interests may be viewed in a political context, and the politicization increases manyfold when we recognize the existence of other players, each with interest-based agendas to pursue. This is particularly true in transitional situations that involve choices between different avenues for personal development, the influx of new people, or the succession of one person by another.

For the purpose of illustration, consider the following case:

> Mr. X was the flamboyant marketing vice president in a medium-sized cosmetics firm. After five years, he had a solid reputation within his firm, having steered many successful campaigns designed to establish the firm's products as premier brands available in up-market retail outlets. Although he had encountered difficult times in persuading his colleagues that it was preferable to concentrate on relatively low-volume, high-quality products rather than to go for the mass market, over the years they had come to accept his viewpoint.

His marketing philosophy and vision were in keeping with his personality, reflecting an interest and involvement with the social elites with whom he felt at home.

The settings and themes of the firm's ads were selected by Mr. X and, as noted by many of his colleagues, were very much a reflection of his personal lifestyle. Crucial to the adoption of this marketing strategy and the line of corporate development it involved was the support of key members of the board who shared family connections and a taste for the style of life symbolized by Mr. X and his marketing philosophy.

Other, less well connected members who were appointed for their professional knowledge and links with the industry at large, along with the chief executive officer and a number of vice presidents, felt that many opportunities were being lost by the need to preserve an elite image. Whenever possible, they tried to mobilize an awareness of the need to consider other policy options, but the success of the company muted their inclination to press their concerns too far. So long as Mr. X's charismatic influence remained an important driving force, the firm was committed to preserving and developing its elite status.

An opportunity for change dropped by chance in the mailbox of Mr. Y, vice president for corporate planning and one of those most concerned about the lost opportunities. A friend and former colleague, now chief of a prestigious "head-hunting" firm, had written asking if he could recommend possible candidates for the position of marketing vice president in the new North American branch of a European firm dealing in high-society fashion. A vision of Mr. X smiling in the midst of furs, diamonds, and Paris fashions immediately floated into Mr. Y's mind. Within the hour he had made an off-the-record call to his friend suggesting that Mr. X might well be approached. Within two months, Mr. X had been offered and had accepted the job.

Mr. X's successor at the cosmetics firm, Ms. Z, was a relatively young and ambitious woman with a liking for the glossy life. She had been a compromise selection, the board having been split on two other candidates. Ms. Z seemed to strike the balance between the dashing style to which Mr. X's allies had become accustomed and the promise of new initiative favored by those who had felt constrained by the direction set by Mr. X's philosophy. Even though neither group was delighted with the appointment, they both felt that Ms. Z was eminently capable of handling the job, especially since she would inherit a successful operation.

For Ms. Z, the job was a great opportunity. She felt that the time was right to make her mark in the industry and saw in the steady direction steered by Mr. X a base on which to launch new initiatives. In her interview discussions with Mr. X's former supporters, she had made much of the need to conserve what had been achieved. In her discussions with those less committed to this philosophy, she had stressed the promise of new markets.

Her first year in the new job was spent developing an initiative that would bring these goals together, by retaining the up-market image but broadening marketing outlets to include selected chains of retail drug and department stores. She knew that she had to come up with a philosophy that set her apart from Mr. X but that she must retain the support of the board and the senior executives who were essential for ensuring success.

Her colleagues ready for a change were willing partners, and excellent working relations soon developed through a give-and-take approach that helped define ideas and opportunities where all seemed to gain. Her task in relation to those who still equated the style and personality of Mr. X with what the company stood for was much more difficult. Resistance and heated exchange became a feature of boardroom discussion. Over a period of three years, however, most came to accept the idea that the broadening of the market was still consistent with the image of a high-status product, particularly since the changing strategy was sweetened by its obvious financial success. As one board member put it while looking at the latest returns, "I think I'll be able to live with even more ads in those dreadful magazines if I think about these figures."

Our case sketches only the dynamics of the situation in broadest outline, but it serves to illustrate the politics intrinsic to any situation where people wish to pursue divergent interests. Mr. X had a vision that others were persuaded to share. His charismatic personality allowed him to use the organization to express himself through a strategy that combined task, career, and personal interests in a coherent way. The colleagues who bought into his strategy did so to the extent that their aims were achieved as well. Those opposed to the strategy had other aspirations. They wanted to see the organization go elsewhere. For this reason, Mr. Y took advantage of a chance opportunity to change the situation.

The state of transition opened up new opportunities. Rival coalitions formed around the candidates who people thought would be able to advance their interests. Ms. Z, the very able compromise candidate, read and played the situation well. She saw a convergence between personal and corporate opportunity and used her new job to further both. Given her ambitions, there was no way that she could accept the status quo. Her personal style and career aspirations required her to "be a mover" and "make her mark." So Mr. X's philosophy, although solidly successful, had to change.

Others were prepared to join Ms. Z in shaping a new corporate direction in return for prizes of their own. The confidence of the rival coalitions, although doubtful at times, was retained because the new situation resulted in a transformation that most could identify with.

Even though our discussion glosses over the power relations and other aspects of this case, the interactions between these few key actors and their supporters illustrate the thick and rich political dynamic of organizational life. The diversity of interests that Aristotle observed in the Greek city-state is evident in every organization and can be analyzed by tracing how the ideas and actions of people collide or coincide.

Organizations as coalitions

In contrast with the view that organizations are integrated rational enterprises whose members pursue a common goal, the political metaphor encourages us to see organizations as loose networks of people with divergent interests who gather together for the sake of expediency (e.g., making a living, developing a career, or pursuing a desired goal or objective). Organizations are coalitions and are made up of coalitions, and coalition building is an important dimension of almost all organizational life.

Coalitions arise when groups of individuals get together to cooperate on specific issues, events, or decisions or to advance specific values and ideologies. Organizations are comprised of groups of managers, workers, shareholders, customers, suppliers, lawyers, governmental agents, and other formal and informal groups with an interest or stake in the organization but whose goals and preferences differ. The organization as a coalition of diverse stakeholders is a coalition with multiple goals.

Some organization theorists draw a distinction between cliques that become aware of common goals and coalitions of two or more such groups who unite to pursue a joint interest, often working against a rival network. Clearly, people in organizations can pursue their interests as individuals, specific interest groups, or more generalized coalitions, so this distinction is often a useful one.

In many organizations, there is often a dominant coalition that controls important areas of policy. Such coalitions usually build around the chief executive or other key actors in the organization, each participant making demands on and contributions to the coalition as a price of participation. All coalitions have to strike some kind of balance between the rewards and contributions necessary to sustain membership—a balance usually influenced by factors such as age, organizational position, education, time spent in the organization, and values and attitudes.

Many approaches to organization actually foster the development of cliques and coalitions, as functional and other divisions fragment interests—for example, allocating different goals and activities to subunits such as departments or project teams. As a result, salespeople become preoccupied with sales objectives, production people with production, and project teams with their group projects, often requiring the organization to function with a minimal degree of consensus. This influences its effectiveness and ability to survive, forcing it to accept satisfactory rather than optimal solutions to problems, with negotiation and compromise overruling technical rationality.

Coalition development offers a strategy for advancing interests, power, and influence in an organization. Sometimes, coalitions are initiated by less powerful actors who seek the support of others. At other times, they may be developed by the powerful to consolidate their power: for example, an executive may promote people to key positions where they can serve as loyal lieutenants. Whether formal or informal, confined to the organization or extended to include key interests outside, coalitions and interest groups often provide important means of securing desired ends.

UNDERSTANDING CONFLICT

Conflict arises whenever interests collide. The natural reaction to conflict in organizational contexts is usually to view it as a dysfunctional force that can be attributed to some regrettable set of circumstances or causes: "It's a personality problem." "They're rivals who always meet head on." "Production people and marketing people never get along." "Everyone hates auditors and accountants." Conflict is regarded as an unfortunate state that in more favorable circumstances would disappear.

But conflict is normal and will always be present in organizations. Conflict may be personal, interpersonal, or between rival groups or coalitions. It may be built into organizational structures, roles, attitudes, and stereotypes or arise over a scarcity of resources. It may be explicit or covert. Whatever the reason, and whatever the form it takes, its source rests in some perceived or real divergence of interests.

Most modern organizations actually encourage organizational politics because they are designed as systems of simultaneous competition and collaboration. People must collaborate in pursuit of a common task, yet they are often pitted against each other in competition for limited resources, status, and career advancement.

Conflicting dimensions of organization are symbolized in the hierarchical organization chart, which is both a system of cooperation, in that it reflects a rational subdivision of tasks, *and* a career ladder that people are motivated to climb. The fact that there are more jobs at the bottom than at the top means that competition for the top places is likely to be keen and that in any career race there are likely to be far fewer winners than losers. The system more or less ensures the kinds of competitive struggle on which organizational politics thrives.

One does not have to be consciously cunning or deviously political to end up playing organizational politics. The corporate Machiavellis who systematically wheel and deal their way through organizational affairs merely illustrate the most extreme and fully developed form of a latent tendency present in most aspects of organizational life.

The literature on organization theory is full of examples of how everyday organizational life produces political forms of behavior. Some of the most vivid of these are found in reports by sociologists who have infiltrated the workplace in the role of participant-observers. The setting of budgets and work standards, the day-to-day supervision and control of work, and the pursuit of opportunity and career are often characterized by sophisticated forms of gamesmanship.

Conflicting interests in factories and offices

W. F. Whyte in his classic study *Money and Motivation* reveals the guile with which factory workers are able to control their pace of work and level of earnings, even when under the close eye of their supervisors or efficiency experts trying to find ways of increasing productivity. The workers know that to maintain their positions they have to find ways of beating the system and do so with great skill and ingenuity.

- Starkey, an experienced factory worker, builds extra movements into his job when work standards are being set so that the job can be made easier under normal circumstances. He also finds completely new ways of working at high speeds when his supervisor is not around, allowing him to create slack time elsewhere in his day.

- Ray, famed among his fellow workers for his skill in outthinking and outperforming his controllers, gets his machine to destroy the product on which he is working when he is asked to work at too fast a pace. He also has a great ability to look as if he is working harder than he is, generating a profuse sweat to impress and deceive his observers.

- Workers share ideas on how to get better work standards, to restrict output, to cash in on "gravy" jobs, or to land their competitors with the "stinkers." Such collaboration is often used against management and at other times against other workers or work teams.

Management, of course, often knows about this subterfuge but is frequently powerless to do anything about it, particularly where plants are unionized. Sometimes, management gains control of one problem, only to find another one arising. The relationship is essentially combative. The status and self-respect of both groups rest on their ability to outwit or control the other.

Similar relations are found in office settings, where staff manage impressions and schedules in a way that makes them seem busier and more productive than they actually are. Also, in budget-setting and other decision-making sessions, managers often attempt to outwit their own managers by padding their estimates to create slack resources or by negotiating easy work targets to allow room for error or to allow them to look good when the next salary review comes around.

Politicking is also latent in the horizontal relations between specialist units and within multidisciplinary teams. People may identify with the responsibilities and objectives associated with their specific role, work group, department, or project team in a way that leads them to value achievement of these responsibilities and objectives over and above the achievement of wider organizational goals, especially when reward systems, status and success are linked with performance at the level of one's specialized responsibilities.

Even when people recognize the importance of working together, the nature of any given job often combines contradictory elements that create various kinds of role conflict.

The politicized interactions so often observed between production and marketing staff or between accountants and the users of financial services often rest in part on the fact that they are being asked to engage in activities that impinge on each other in a negative way. The product modification requested by marketing creates problems in the design and sequencing of production. The accountant's concern for firm control over expenditure proves an unwelcome constraint for executives in the spending department. Similar conflicts are often observed between line managers responsible for day-to-day results and staff people such as planners, lawyers, accountants, and other experts who perform an advisory role; between professionals seeking to extend their sphere of autonomy and bureaucrats seeking to reduce it in the interests of improving control; and so on.

The potential complexity of organizational politics is mind-boggling, even before we take account of the personalities and personality clashes that usually bring roles and their conflicts to life. Sometimes, the conflicts generated are quite explicit and open for all to see. At other times, they lie beneath the surface.

Relationships in meetings may be governed by various hidden agendas. Disputes may have a long history, decisions and actions in the present being shaped by conflicts, grudges, or differences that others believe long forgotten or settled. The manager of a production department may align with the marketing manager to block a proposal from the production engineer not because he disagrees with the basic ideas but because of resentments associated with the fact that he and the production engineer have never gotten along.

Although such resentments may seem petty, they are often powerful forces in organizational life.

Many organizational conflicts become institutionalized in the attitudes, stereotypes, values, beliefs, rituals, and other aspects of organizational culture. The underlying conflicts can be extremely difficult to identify and break down, and history can shape the present in subtle ways. However, by remembering Aristotle's injunction to understand the source of politics in the diversity of interests, organizational analysts have a means of penetrating beneath the surface of any conflict situation to understand its genesis.

EXPLORING POWER

Power is the medium through which conflicts of interest are ultimately resolved.

Power influences who gets what, when, and how.

In recent years, organization and management theorists have become increasingly aware of the need to recognize the importance of power in explaining organizational affairs. However, no really clear and consistent definition of power has emerged. While some view power as a resource (i.e., as something one possesses), others view it as a social relation characterized by some kind of dependency (i.e., as an influence *over* something or someone). Most organization theorists tend to take their point of departure from the definition of power offered by Robert Dahl, who suggests power involves an ability to get another person to do something that he or she would not otherwise have done.

For some theorists, this definition leads to a study of the "here and now" conditions under which one person, group, or organization becomes dependent on another, whereas for others it leads to an examination of the historical forces that shape the stage of action on which contemporary power relations are set. In the following discussion we will examine briefly how sources of power (exhibit 6.2) are used to shape the dynamics of organizational life. In so doing we will better understand the power dynamics within an organization and identify the ways in which organizational members can attempt to exert their influence.

THE FOLLOWING ARE AMONG THE MOST IMPORTANT SOURCES OF POWER:

1. Formal authority
2. Control of scarce resources
3. Use of organizational structure, rules, and regulations
4. Control of decision processes
5. Control of knowledge and information
6. Control of boundaries
7. Ability to cope with uncertainty
8. Control of technology
9. Interpersonal alliances, networks, and control of "informal organization"
10. Control of counterorganizations
11. Symbolism and the management of meaning
12. Gender and the management of gender relations
13. Structural factors that define the stage of action
14. The power one already has

The sources of power provide organizational members with a variety of means for enhancing their interests and resolving or perpetuating organizational conflict.

Exhibit 6.2. Sources of power in organizations

Formal authority

Formal authority is a form of legitimized power that is respected and acknowledged by those with whom one interacts. Legitimacy arises when people recognize that a person has a right to rule some area of human life and that it is their duty to obey. If claimed (or espoused) authority is not respected, the authority becomes vacuous, and power depends on other sources.

The most obvious type of *formal* authority is associated with the position one holds in an organization, whether as sales manager, accountant, project coordinator, secretary, factory supervisor, or machine operator.

These different organizational positions are usually defined in terms of rights and obligations, which create a field of influence within which one can legitimately operate with the formal support of those with whom one works. For example, a sales manager may be given the "right" to influence policy on sales campaigns—but not on financial accounting. Positions on an organization chart can create a valuable power base.

Control of scarce resources

All organizations depend for their continued existence on an adequate flow of resources, such as money, materials, technology, personnel, and support from customers, suppliers, and the community at large. An ability to exercise control over any of these resources can provide an important source of power within and between organizations. Access to funds, possession of a crucial skill or raw material, control of access to some valued computer program or new technology, or even access to a special customer or supplier can lend individuals considerable organizational power. If the resource is in scarce supply and someone is dependent on its availability, then it can almost certainly be translated into power. Scarcity and dependence are the keys to resource power!

Whether we are talking about the control of finance, skills, materials, or personnel, or even the provision of emotional support to a key decision maker who has come to value one's support and friendship, the principles remain the same. The more Machiavellian among us will quickly see how these principles point the way to a strategy for increasing power by *creating* dependence through the planned control of critical resources. One doesn't have to have full control over these resources—just an ability to influence key decisions that influence their availability and allocation.

We can also increase our power by reducing our own dependence on others. This is why many managers and organizational units like to have their own pockets of resources. The seemingly needless duplication of resources where each unit has the same underemployed machines, technical experts, or reserve of staff that can be used in rush periods is often a result of attempts to reduce dependence on the resources of others. The idea of stockpiling staff and expertise used to be a very familiar sign of organizational power. With the streamlining that comes with cost cutting and efficiency drives and the possibility of gaining the required flexibility through outsourcing or subcontracting, it has now become less common.

Use of organizational structure, rules, regulations, and procedures

Most often, organizational structure, rules, regulations, and procedures are viewed as rational instruments intended to aid task performance. A political view of these arrangements, however, suggests that in many situations they are often best understood as products and reflections of a struggle for political control. Organizational structure can be used to divide or marginalize one's perceived opponents. Rules and regulations can provide powerful weapons in gaining an advantage.

Take the case of the old state-owned British Rail. Rather than going on strike to further a claim or address a grievance, a process that is costly to employees because they forfeit their pay, the union acquired the habit of declaring a "work to rule," whereby employees did exactly what was required by the regulations developed by the railway authorities. The result was that hardly any train left on time. Schedules went haywire, and the whole railway system quickly slowed to a snail's pace, if not a halt, because normal functioning required that employees find shortcuts or at least streamline procedures.

Many organizations have comprehensive systems of rules that, as almost every employee knows, can never be applied if the system is to achieve any degree of operational effectiveness. Although their formal purpose may be to protect employees, customers, or the public at large, the real significance of rules is that they also protect their creators.

Rules and regulations are often created, invoked, and used in either a proactive or retrospective fashion as part of a power play. All bureaucratic regulations, decision-making criteria, plans and schedules, promotion and job-evaluation requirements, and other rules that guide organizational functioning give potential power to both the controllers and those controlled. Rules designed to guide and streamline activities can almost always be used to block activities. Just as lawyers make a profession out of finding a new angle on what appears to be a clear-cut rule, many organizational members are able to invoke rules in ways that no one ever imagined possible. An ability to use the rules to one's advantage is an important source of organizational power and, as in the case of organizational structures, defines a contested terrain that is forever being negotiated, preserved, or changed.

Control of decision processes

In discussing control of decision processes, it is useful to distinguish between control of three interrelated elements:

- decision premises,
- decision processes, and
- decision issues and objectives.

By influencing decision *premises* one can control the foundations of decision making—preventing crucial decisions from being made and fostering those that one actually desires. To influence premises, we control decision agendas and strategies that help to force or guide others' attention to our point of view.

Control of decision-making *processes* is usually more visible than the control of decision premises. How should a decision be made? Who should be involved? When will the decision be made? By determining whether a decision can be taken and then reported to appropriate quarters, whether it must go before a committee and which committee, whether it must be supported by a full report, whether it will appear on an agenda where it is likely to receive a rough ride (or an easy passage), the order of an agenda, and even whether the decision should be discussed at the beginning or end of a meeting, a manager can have a considerable impact on decision outcomes.

A final way of controlling decision making is to influence the *issues and objectives* to be addressed and the evaluative criteria to be employed. An individual can shape issues and objectives most directly through preparing the reports and contributing to the discussion on which the decision will be based, or by getting others to do so on his or her behalf. By emphasizing the importance of particular constraints, selecting and evaluating the alternatives on which a decision will be made, and highlighting the importance of certain values or outcomes, decision makers can exert considerable influence on the decision that emerges from discussion. Eloquence, command of the facts, passionate commitment, or sheer tenacity or endurance can in the end win the day, adding to a person's power to influence the decisions with which he or she is involved.

Control of knowledge and information

By controlling knowledge and information, a person can systematically influence the definition of organizational situations and can create patterns of dependency. Both these activities deserve attention on their own account.

Many skillful organizational politicians control information flows and the knowledge that is made available to different people, thereby influencing their perception of situations and hence the ways they act in relation to those situations. These politicians are often known as "gatekeepers," opening and closing channels of communication and filtering, summarizing, analyzing, and shaping knowledge in accordance with a view of the world that favors their interests.

Besides shaping definitions of organizational realities, knowledge and information can weave patterns of dependency. By possessing the right information at the right time, by having exclusive access to key data, or by simply demonstrating the ability to marshal and synthesize facts in an effective manner, organizational members can increase the power they wield within an organization. Many people jealously guard or block access to crucial knowledge to enhance their indispensability and "expert" status. Other organizational members have an interest in breaking such exclusivity and widening access, creating a tendency in organizations to routinize valued skills and abilities whenever possible. Some members also try to break down dependencies on specific individuals and departments by acquiring their own experts, which is why departments often prefer to have their own specialist skills on hand, even if this involves duplication and some redundancy of specialisms within the organization as a whole.

A final aspect of expert power relates to the use of knowledge and expertise as a means of legitimizing what one wishes to do. "The expert" often carries an aura of authority and power that can add considerable weight to a decision that rests in the balance, or that needs further support of justification.

Control of boundaries

A boundary refers to the interface between different elements of an organization such as the boundary between different work groups or departments or between an organization and its environment. By monitoring and controlling boundary transactions, people build up considerable power. They can acquire knowledge of critical interdependencies over which they may be able to secure a degree of control, or gain access to critical information that places them in a particularly powerful position to interpret what is happening in the outside world. They can also control transactions across boundaries by performing a buffering function that allows or even encourages certain transactions while blocking others.

Boundary management can also help integrate a unit with the outside world, or it can be used to isolate that unit so that it can function in an autonomous way. The quest for autonomy—by individuals, groups, and even departments—is a powerful feature of organizational life because many people like to be in full control over their lives. Boundary management aids this quest, for it often shows ways in which a unit can acquire the resources necessary to create autonomy and points to strategies that can be used to fend off threats to autonomy.

The quest for autonomy is, however, often countered by opposing strategies initiated by managers elsewhere in the system. They may attempt to break down the cohesiveness of the group by nominating their own representatives or allies to key positions, find ways of minimizing the slack resources available to the group, develop information systems that make activities transparent to outsiders, or encourage organizational redesigns that increase interdependence and minimize the consequences of autonomous actions. Boundary transactions are, therefore, often characterized by competing strategies for control and countercontrol. Many groups and departments are successful in acquiring considerable degrees of autonomy and in defending their position in a way that makes the organization a system of loosely coupled groups and departments rather than a highly integrated unit.

Ability to cope with uncertainty

Organization implies a certain degree of interdependence—discontinuous or unpredictable situations in one part of an organization have considerable implications for operations elsewhere. An ability to deal with these uncertainties gives an individual, group, or subunit considerable power in the organization as a whole.

The ability to cope with uncertainty is often intimately connected with one's place in the overall division of labor in an organization. Generally speaking, there are two kinds of uncertainty. First, environmental uncertainties (e.g., with regard to markets, sources of raw materials, or finance) can provide great opportunities for those with the contacts or skills to tackle the problems and who can therefore minimize the effects of uncertainty on the organization as a whole. Second, operational uncertainties (e.g., the breakdown of critical machinery used in factory production or data processing) can help troubleshooters, maintenance staff, or others with the requisite skills and abilities acquire power and status as a result of their ability to restore normal operations. The degree of power that accrues to people who can tackle either kind of uncertainty depends primarily on two factors: (1) the degree to which their skills are substitutable, i.e., the ease with which they can be replaced; and (2) the centrality of their functions to the operations of the organization as a whole.

In understanding the impact of uncertainty on the way an organization operates, we have an important means of understanding the power relations between different groups and departments. We also get a better understanding of the conditions under which the power of the expert or troubleshooter comes into play and of the importance of the various kinds of power deriving from the control of resources. The existence of uncertainty and an ability to cope with uncertainty are often reasons explaining why and when these other kinds of power become so critical in shaping organizational affairs.

Control of technology

Organizations usually become vitally dependent on some form of core technology as a means of converting organizational inputs into outputs. This technology may be a factory assembly line, a telephone switchboard, a centralized computer or record-keeping system, or perhaps a capital-intensive plant like those used in oil refining. The kind of technology employed influences the patterns of interdependence within an organization and hence the power relations between different individuals and departments. For example, in organizations where the technology creates patterns of sequential interdependence, as in a mass-production assembly line where task A must be completed before B, which must be completed before C, the people controlling any one part of the technology possess considerable power to disrupt the whole. In organizations where the technology involves more autonomous systems of production, the ability of one individual or group to influence the operation of the whole is much more limited.

The fact that technology has a major impact on power relations is an important reason why attempts to change technology often create major conflicts between managers and employees and between different groups within an organization, for the introduction of a new technology can alter the balance of power. The introduction of assembly-line production into industry, designed to increase managerial control over the work process, may also have the unintended effect of increasing the power of factory workers and their unions. "Cellular" or "team-based" production tends to shift power in the opposite direction, fragmenting worker control—one of the main reasons it has been resisted by unionized workforces.

The power associated with the control of technology becomes most visible in confrontations and negotiations surrounding organizational change or when groups are attempting to improve their lot within the organization. It also operates in more subtle ways. In working with a particular machine or work system, employees learn the ins and outs of its operation in a way that often lends them considerable power. They can control the use of their technology to improve their wages and control their pace of work. Technology designed to direct and control the work of employees frequently becomes a tool of workers' control!

Interpersonal alliances, networks, and control of "informal organization"

Friends in high places, sponsors, mentors, ethnic or cultural affiliations, coalitions of people prepared to trade support and favors to further their individual ends, and informal networks for touching base, sounding out, or merely shooting the breeze—all provide sources of power. The skilled organizational politician systematically builds and cultivates interpersonal alliances and networks, incorporating whenever possible the help and influence of all those who have common interests. Successful networking or coalition building involves an awareness that it is necessary to incorporate and pacify potential enemies, as well as to win friends. The successful alliance and coalition builder recognizes that the currency is one of mutual dependency and exchange.

Besides drawing power from networking and coalition building, many members of an organization may draw power from social networks known as the "informal organization." All organizations have informal networks where people interact in ways that meet social needs. Groups of coworkers go to lunch together or go drinking on Fridays after work or may evolve means of enhancing the quality of their life at work. They may share similar ethnic or cultural backgrounds and have affiliations that extend beyond the workplace. Informal group leaders may become as powerful an influence on their network or group as any rule, regulation, or manager. In a culturally diverse workforce, such leaders can acquire enormous power as "gatekeepers," "boundary managers," and representatives and interpreters of reality for the groups they lead.

One other variant of informal organization arises in situations where one member of an organization develops a psychological or emotional dependency on another. The history of corporate and public life is full of examples of a key decision maker who becomes critically dependent on his or her spouse, lover, secretary, or trusted aide or even on a self-proclaimed prophet or mystic. In the power-behind-the-throne syndrome that results, the informal collaborator exerts a critical influence on how the decision maker's power is used. Such relations often develop by chance, but it is by no means uncommon for people to rise to power by cultivating such dependencies in a Machiavellian way.

Control of counterorganizations

Counterorganizations consist of individuals who coordinate their actions to create a rival power bloc. For example, unions develop as a check on management in industries where there is a high degree of industrial concentration; government and other regulatory agencies develop as a check on the abuse of monopoly power; and the concentration of production is often balanced by the development of large organizations in the field of distribution as when chain stores balance the power exercised by large producers and suppliers.

The strategy of exercising countervailing power provides a way of influencing organizations where one is not part of the established power structure. By joining and working for a trade union, consumers' association, social movement, cooperative, or lobby group—or by exercising citizens' rights and pressuring the media, a political representative, or a government agency—people have a way of balancing power relations.

Many socially conscious lawyers, journalists, academics, and members of other professional groups find that criticizing is a more effective route to influence than joining the organizations that are the object of their concern.

The principle of countervailing power is also often employed by the leaders of large conglomerates, who in effect play a form of chess with their environment, buying and selling organizations as corporate pawns. More than one multinational has attempted to counter the power of its competitors or bargain with its host government with the principle of countervailing power in mind.

Symbolism and the management of meaning

Leadership ultimately involves an ability to define the reality of others. While the authoritarian leader attempts to "sell," "tell," or force a reality on his or her subordinates, more democratic leaders allow definitions of a situation to evolve from the views of others. The democratic leader's influence is far more subtle and symbolic. He or she spends time listening, summarizing, integrating, and guiding what is being said, making key interventions and summoning images, ideas, and values that help those involved to make sense of the situation with which they are dealing. In managing the meanings and interpretations assigned to a situation, the leader in effect wields a form of symbolic power that exerts a decisive influence on how people perceive their realities and hence on the way they act.

Many successful managers and leaders are aware of the power of evocative imagery and instinctively give a great deal of attention to the impact their words and actions have on those around them.

Many organizational members are also keenly aware of the way in which theater—including physical settings, appearances, and styles of behavior—can add to their power. An executive's office is the stage on which that person performs and is often carefully organized in ways that help that performance. In some organizations, it is possible to distinguish marketing people, accountants, or even those who work on a certain floor according to their choice of fashion and general demeanor. Style also counts. It is amazing how someone can symbolize power by being a couple of minutes late for an all-important meeting where everyone depends on his or her presence or how visibility in certain situations can enhance status.

Finally, we note "gamesmanship." Sometimes the organizational game player is reckless and ruthless, "shooting from the hip," engaging in boardroom brawls, and never missing an opportunity to intimidate others. Others may be more crafty and low profile, shaping key impressions at every turn. Game players see organization—with its rewards of success, status, power, and influence—as a game to be played according to their own sets of unwritten rules.

Gender and the management of gender relations

As many feminist writers have emphasized, organizations often segment opportunity structures and job markets in ways that enable men to achieve positions of prestige and power more easily than women. It is sometimes called the "glass ceiling" effect. Women can see opportunities at the top of their organizations, but the path is often blocked by gender bias. This bias also shapes how organizational reality is created and sustained on a day-to-day basis. This is most obvious in situations of open discrimination and various forms of sexual harassment but often pervades the culture of an organization in a way that is much less visible.

The gender balance in many organizations is changing rapidly as gender and equal opportunity continue to become politically hot issues. The shift from hierarchical to flat, networked forms of organization is creating a major political shift that favors what have been traditionally seen as female styles of management. The ability to weave "webs of inclusion," build consensus, mobilize insight and intuition, and pay more attention to "process" rather than "product" are all part of the shifting balance.

As recently as the 1980s, the best advice to women wishing to succeed in organizational life was "fit in" and beat men at their own game. Now, a lot of the advice given women is to change the rules of the game. Switch the archetype. In a networked as opposed to hierarchical world, new skills and competencies are needed. The characteristics of the female archetype have much to offer here.

Gender politics are in a state of flux. Everyone's power is shaped to some degree by his or her position on the gender continuum, whether male, female, or somewhere in between. We shall have much more to say about the nature of gender issues in the psychic prisons chapter, where we discuss the role of sexuality and the patriarchal family in corporate life.

Structural factors that define the stage of action

One of the surprising things one discovers in talking with members of an organization is that hardly anyone admits to having any real power. Everyone usually feels in some degree hemmed in either by forces within the organization or by requirements posed by the environment. How is it that there can be so many sources of power, yet so many feelings of powerlessness?

One possible answer rests in the "pluralist" view that access to power is so open, wide, and varied that to a large extent power relations become more or less balanced.

Another explanation rests in the "deep structural" view that while organizations and society may at any one time comprise a variety of political actors drawing on a variety of power bases, the stage on which they engage in their various kinds of power play is defined by economics, race, class relationships, and other deep-structural factors shaping the social epoch in which they live. A manager may control an important budget, have access to key information, be excellent at impression management, and be powerful for all these reasons. But her ability to draw on and use these sources of power may be neutralized by structural factors such as intercorporate power plays or an impending merger that will eliminate her job. Similarly, a factory worker may possess considerable power to disrupt production as a result of his or her role on an assembly line. Knowing the way in which production can be disrupted is the immediate source of power, but the ultimate source is the structure of productive activity that makes such power significant. A black manager may be extremely skilled in mobilizing ideas and valued resources, only to find himself blocked by racial prejudice.

These considerations encourage us to see people as agents or carriers of power relations embedded in the wider structure of society. As such, people may be no more than semiautonomous pawns moving themselves around in a game where they can learn to understand the rules but have no power to change them. This phenomenon may explain why even the powerful often feel that they have little real choice as to how they should behave.

The power one already has

Power is a route to power, and one can often use power to acquire more. For example a manager may use his or her power to support X in a struggle with Y, knowing that when X is successful it will be possible to call upon similar (if not more) support from X: "Remember last July? Your future was on the line, and I risked everything to help out. Surely you'll now do a small favor for me?"

It is also possible to take advantage of the honeypot characteristic of power. The presence of power attracts and sustains people who wish to feed off that power and serves to increase the power holder's power. In the hope of gaining favor, people may begin to lend the power holder uninvited support or buy into that person's way of thinking to show that they're on the same side. When the time comes for the power holder to recognize this interest with active support, people then actually become indebted to the power holder, with all kinds of IOUs coming into play. Power, like honey, is a perpetual source of sustenance and attraction among fellow bees.

Finally, there is the empowering aspect of power. When people experience progress or success, they are often energized to achieve further progress and success. Knowing that a sense of power can lead to more power emphasizes the importance of developing proactive can-do mindsets that lead people to see and act on their world in a way that will produce the results they desire. The process is most evident in situations where people who believe that they have absolutely no power or ability fight and win a small victory or achieve unbelievable things, like running over hot coals or bungee-cord jumping from the top of a cliff. The experience of success becomes a transforming force as they realize that one victory can lead to another. Many organizations and communities have been transformed by this kind of experience in quite unexpected ways.

STRENGTHS AND LIMITATIONS OF THE POLITICAL METAPHOR

One of the curious features of organizational life is that although many people know they are surrounded by organizational politics they rarely come out and say so. They ponder politics in private moments or discuss it off the record with close confidants and friends or in the context of their own political maneuverings with members of their coalition. They know that manager A is pushing for a particular project because it will serve her own aims or that B got a particular job because of his associations with C, but they can rarely say so. It breaks all the rules of organizational etiquette to impute private motive to organizational acts, which are supposed to serve the organization's interests above all else. For these and other reasons, including the fact that secrecy can serve political ends, organizational politics becomes a taboo subject, which at times makes it extremely difficult for organization members to deal with this crucially important aspect of organizational reality.

STRENGTHS

- The political metaphor encourages us to see how *all* organizational activity is interest based and to evaluate organizational functioning with this in mind.

The discussion presented in this chapter helps us accept the reality of politics as an inevitable feature of organizational life and, following the Aristotelian view, to recognize its constructive role in the creation of social order. Organizational goals, structure, technology, job design, leadership style, and other seemingly formal aspects of organizational functioning have a political dimension as well as the more obvious political power plays and conflicts.

■ **The role of power is placed center stage.**

The model of interests, conflict, and power developed in this chapter provides a practical and systematic means of understanding the relationship between politics and organization and emphasizes the key role of power in determining many features of organizational life. The metaphors considered in earlier chapters tend to underplay the relation between power and organization. The political metaphor overcomes this deficiency, encouraging us to use our understanding of corporate politics in a positive way.

■ **Conflict management becomes a key activity.**

The political metaphor encourages managers to recognize that since individuals have different interests, aims, and objectives, employees are likely to use their membership in an organization for their own ends. Management is focused on balancing and coordinating these interests so that people can work together within the constraints set by the organization's formal goals. Managers are encouraged to recognize that conflict and power plays can serve both positive and negative functions and to find ways of using conflict as an energizing force.

Conflict can encourage self-evaluation and challenge conventional wisdom. It may cause a certain degree of pain within an organization but can also do much to stimulate learning and change. It can help an organization keep abreast of a changing environment and be a source of constant innovation. This is particularly true in group decision-making situations where the absence of conflict often produces conformity and staleness.

Conflict can also serve as an important release valve that gets rid of pent-up pressures. It facilitates processes of mutual accommodation through the exploration and resolution of differences, often in a way that preempts more subversive or explosive resolutions. Somewhat paradoxically, conflict can at times serve to stimulate change and at other times help maintain the status quo.

One of the main tasks of the political manager is to find ways of maintaining just the right level of conflict. Too much conflict can immobilize an organization by channeling the efforts of its members into unproductive activities, but too little conflict may encourage complacency and lethargy. In the former case, the manager may need to employ conflict resolution techniques or reorient conflict in more productive directions. In the latter, he or she may need to find ways of promoting appropriate conflicts, often by making hidden conflicts overt, or perhaps by actually creating conflict. Although this may at times help to enliven the atmosphere and performance of an organization, it can also be perceived as a form of unwarranted manipulation with disastrous results for relations between managers and their employees.

■ **The myth of organizational rationality is debunked.**

Organizations may pursue goals and stress the importance of rational, efficient, and effective management. But rational, efficient, and effective for whom? Whose goals are being pursued? What interests are being served? Who benefits? The political metaphor emphasizes that organizational goals may be rational for some people's interest but not for others. An organization embraces many rationalities because rationality is always interest based and changes according to the perspective adopted.

Rationality is always political. No one is neutral in the management of organizations—even managers! They, like others, use the organization as a legitimizing umbrella under which to pursue a variety of task, career, and personal interests. Like others, they often use the idea of rationality as a resource for pursuing political agendas—justifying actions that suit their personal aspirations in terms that appear rational from an organizational standpoint.

From a political perspective, rationality emerges as a societal myth that people use to mask or overcome the contradiction that an organization is simultaneously a system of competition and a system of cooperation. The emphasis on rationality attempts to bind together a political system that, because of the diversity of interests on which it builds, always has a latent tendency to move in diverse directions, and sometimes, to fall apart.

■ **Organizational integration becomes problematic.**

As we saw in the organism chapter, much organization theory has built on the assumption that organizations, like machines or organisms, are unified systems that bind part and whole in a quest for survival. The political metaphor suggests otherwise, pointing to the disintegrative strains and tensions that stem from the diverse sets of interests on which organization builds.

The strains have become increasingly apparent with the organizational downsizing movement of the 1990s. Organizations that have promoted the ideology that "we're a family" or "we're a team" have found themselves firing team members in order to cut costs. If team members are so dispensable, is the organization really a team? Or is the team idea merely used to promote a sense of unity?

If the basic reality is that of diverse and often incompatible interests where a high degree of commitment is problematic, interaction ultimately depends on the degree to which people *really* need each other. In such circumstances it is much better to think about the organization as a coalition of changing interests and manage it that way than to pretend that it has more integrated properties.

Many organizations are more likely to have the characteristics of loosely coupled systems—where semiautonomous parts strive to maintain a degree of independence while working under the name and framework provided by the organization—than the characteristics of a completely integrated organism. In organizations where a desire for autonomy or subunit goals becomes more important than the aims of the wider organization, schismatic tendencies may be a constant feature and transforming force. Such organizations usually spawn new organizations when key members or subunits spin off into entities of their own. Or different elements may end up fighting and destroying each other. An analysis of organizational politics in terms of the interplay among rival interests, conflicts, and sources of power can help us understand and manage these forces.

- **Politics is a natural feature of organization.**

Tensions between private and organizational interests provide an incentive for individuals to act politically. Whereas some people view such action as a manifestation of the selfish or "dark" side of human personality, the analysis presented here suggests that there is usually a structural as well as a motivational basis. Even the most altruistic persons may find their actions following a political script in the sense that their orientation to organizational life is influenced by the conflicting sets of interests that they bring to issues of immediate concern.

Although some people are no doubt more political in orientation than others, employing gamesmanship and other forms of wheeling and dealing as a basic strategy, the enactments of everyone are, at least in part, of a political nature. The political metaphor encourages us to recognize how and why the organizational actor is a political actor and to understand the political significance of the patterns of meaning enacted in corporate culture and subculture.

- **The political metaphor raises fundamental questions about power and control in society.**

Finally, the metaphor also encourages us to recognize the sociopolitical implications of different kinds of organization and their societal roles.

Recall the quotation that opened this chapter. Should people be prepared to surrender their democratic rights when they begin work each morning? Is it possible to have a democratic society if most people spend their working lives obeying the commands of others? Should organizations be allowed to play politics by lobbying in an attempt to influence legislation and other government policies? Should there be closer or more distant relations between business and government?

The political metaphor brings questions such as these to the center of our attention. Although it is common to draw strict divisions between organization theory and political science, it is clear that business and organization are always to some extent political and that the political implications of organization need to be systematically explored.

LIMITATIONS

■ Politics can breed more politics!

When we analyze organizations in terms of the political metaphor it is almost always possible to see signs of political activity. The danger is that this can lead to an increased politicization of the organization, for when we understand organizations as political systems, we are more likely to behave politically in relation to what we see. We begin to see politics everywhere and to look for hidden agendas even where there are none. For this reason, the metaphor must be used with caution. Otherwise, its use may generate cynicism and mistrust in situations where there were none before.

Under the influence of a political mode of understanding, everything becomes political. The analysis of interests, conflicts, and power easily gives rise to a Machiavellian interpretation that suggests everyone is trying to outwit and outmaneuver everyone else. Rather than use the political metaphor to generate new insights and understandings that can help us deal with divergent interests, we often reduce the metaphor to a tool to be used to advance our own personal interests.

This Machiavellianism is reflected in many contemporary writings on the politics of organization, which have a tendency to emphasize the cynical, selfish, ruthless, get-ahead-at-all-costs mentality that so often turns organizations into corporate jungles. These writings "sell" the insights of the metaphor through statements such as "Find out where the real power is and use it," "Understand and harvest the grapevine," "Win through intimidation," "Protect your job by knowing your enemies," or "Seize power and wield clout."

This use of the metaphor breeds mistrust and encourages the idea that organization involves a zero-sum game where there must be winners and losers. There may be a measure of truth in this, in that many organizations are dominated by competitive relations, yet the effect is to reduce the scope for genuine openness and collaboration. The approach loses sight of the more general implications of the political metaphor, such as the Aristotelian vision of politics as a constructive force in the creation of social order, and the possibility of using political principles to examine and restructure the relationship between organization and society.

- **From certain standpoints, the political metaphor can seem too friendly because it underplays gross inequalities in power and influence.**

Is it realistic to presume a plurality of interests and a plurality of power holders?

Or are more radical organization theorists correct in seeing class, racial, and other social divisions as primary forces defining unequal and antagonistic structures of interest and power?

As Marxian theorists have argued, a strong case can be made for the idea that the interests of individuals or small coalitions are best served if they recognize affinities of a "class" kind and act in a unified manner. Such is the logic of trade unionism and other class-based movements that have encouraged people to understand the deep structure that underpins their situation. Unionists have long called on workers of the world to unite. Feminists have invited women and men to unite against the oppressive force of patriarchical hierarchies. Racial groups have pointed to various forms of systemic discrimination. And Third World movements have led other attacks on capitalistic or Western-controlled organizations.

From these points of view a strong case can be made for the idea that, although everyone has access to sources of power, ultimate power rests with the people or forces that are able to define the stage of action on which the game of politics is played.

From this standpoint, multiple forms of power may be more apparent than real. Ultimately, some people have much more power than others. These considerations, which will be examined in more detail in the flux and transformation and domination chapters, suggest that pluralist politics may be restricted to the resolution of marginal, narrow, and superficial issues and may fail to take account of the structural forces that shape the nature of those issues. As a result, the political metaphor may overstate the power and importance of the individual and underplay the system dynamics that determine what becomes political and how politics occurs.

7 Exploring Plato's Cave: Organizations As Psychic Prisons

WHAT IF WE VIEW ORGANIZATIONS AS SYSTEMS
THAT GET TRAPPED IN THEIR OWN THOUGHTS AND ACTIONS?
Obsessions, mind traps, latent sexuality, narcissism, fear of death, strong emotions, illusions of control, anxieties, and defense mechanisms become the focus of attention.

- We see that organization *always* has unconscious significance.

- We learn how psychic forces can act as hidden dimensions of organization that encourage or block innovation.

- We pay particular attention to how frozen mindsets and unconscious forces can make people resist organizational change.

- We recognize the power and significance of what, on the surface, seems irrational.

- We recognize how we can become imprisoned by our ways of thinking and how, if desired, this pattern can be changed.

By exploring the psychoanalytic theories that underpin this perspective, we gain detailed insights about the links between organization, the unconscious, and behavior that are usually ignored by traditional management theory.

HUMAN BEINGS HAVE A KNACK FOR GETTING TRAPPED IN WEBS OF THEIR OWN CREATION. In this chapter we will examine some of the ways this occurs by exploring the idea of organizations as psychic prisons. This metaphor joins the idea that organizations are ultimately created and sustained by conscious and unconscious processes, with the notion that people can actually become imprisoned in or confined by the images, ideas, thoughts, and actions to which these processes give rise. The metaphor encourages us to understand that while organizations may be socially constructed realities, these constructions often have attributed to them an existence and power of their own that allow them to exercise a measure of control over their creators.

The idea of a psychic prison was first explored in Plato's *The Republic* in the famous allegory of the cave in which Socrates addresses the relations among appearance, reality, and knowledge:

> The allegory pictures an underground cave with its mouth open toward the light of a blazing fire. Within the cave are people chained so that they cannot move. They can see only the cave wall directly in front of them. This is illuminated by the light of the fire, which throws shadows of people and objects onto the wall. The cave dwellers equate the shadows with reality, naming them, talking about them, and even linking sounds from outside the cave with the movements on the wall. Truth and reality for the prisoners rest in this shadowy world, because they have no knowledge of any other.
>
> However, if one of the inhabitants were allowed to leave the cave, he would realize that the shadows are just reflections of a more complex reality and that the knowledge and perceptions of his fellow cave dwellers are distorted and flawed. If he were then to return to the cave, he would never be able to live in the old way, since for him the world would be a very different place. No doubt he would find difficulty in accepting his confinement and would pity the plight of his fellows. And if he were to try and share his new knowledge with them, he would probably be ridiculed for his views. For the prisoners, the familiar images of the cave would be much more meaningful than a world they had never seen. Moreover, as the person espousing the new knowledge would now no longer be able to function with conviction in relation to the shadows, his fellow inmates would likely view the world outside as a dangerous place, something to be avoided. The experience could actually lead them to tighten their grip on their familiar way of seeing.

In this chapter we will use this image of a psychic prison to explore some of the ways in which organizations and their members become trapped by constructions of reality that, at best, give an imperfect grasp on the world:

- We start by examining how people in organizations can become trapped by favored ways of thinking.
- We then explore how organizations can become trapped by unconscious processes that lend organization a hidden significance.

As we shall see, the perspective puts familiar patterns in a fresh light and contributes much to our understanding of why people and organizations often find it so difficult to change.

THE TRAP OF FAVORED WAYS OF THINKING

WAYS OF SEEING BECOME WAYS OF NOT SEEING

Consider the following examples:

Following the OPEC oil crisis of 1973 the Japanese automobile industry began to make massive inroads on the North American market. Caught up in the mindset of the American way of producing cars, the large U.S. manufacturers were completely ill equipped to meet the Japanese challenge. For years they had taken their superior resources, technical competence, and skills in engineering and marketing as a given. Oriented to the large-car market and kept alive by annual model changes, the large firms ignored the potential of small, fuel-efficient cars. The myopia allowed the Japanese to capture a stronghold on their traditional market base.

A similar pattern can be observed in the computer industry where IBM established a dominant position in the 1970s and early 1980s. The IBM view of the world was dominated by "hardware" and the development of large powerful computer systems. It was a view that blocked out the possibility of a computer industry driven by software and networks of personal computers. The myopia created the opportunity for Bill Gates's Microsoft and other organizations to create a world completely at odds with the one in which IBM wanted to live.

In times of change, it is possible to look at almost any industry and find once-successful firms struggling to survive. In 1982, Tom Peters and Robert Waterman wrote about excellent companies such as IBM. By the 1990s, many were struggling. Their particular style of excellence had become a trap that prevented them from thinking in new ways and from transforming themselves to meet new challenges.

In his book *The Icarus Paradox,* Danny Miller offers some of the reasons why this occurs, arguing that organizations can get caught in vicious circles in which victories and strengths become weaknesses leading to their downfall. Icarus was the figure in Greek mythology who, flying with his artificial wax wings, soared so close to the sun that the wings melted, plunging him to his death. The power created through the wings ultimately led to his downfall. In a similar way, strong corporate cultures can become pathological. Powerful visions of the future can lead to blind spots. Ways of seeing become ways of not seeing. All the forces that help people and their organizations create the shared systems of meaning that allow them to negotiate their world in an orderly way can become constraints that prevent them from acting in other ways.

Marshall McLuhan noted that the last thing a fish is likely to discover is the water it is swimming in. The water is so fundamental to the fish's way of life that it is not seen or questioned. The organizational world is full of similar examples.

Consider how manufacturing systems perfected throughout the twentieth century locked thousands of North American and European organizations into modes of industrialized inefficiency. Their mechanistic design required the creation of certainty. Assembly lines and other modes of mass manufacture were typically designed to prevent errors or unacceptable variances from traveling throughout a system. Buffer stocks of inventory or work in progress were typically held at different stages of the production process to "protect" one part from another. The procedure seemed inevitable and quickly became adopted as a foundation for effective production design.

However, these very same buffer stocks that guaranteed the continuous operation of the system perpetuated inefficiency. Buffer stocks create "slack" in a system. They represent unused resources. They allow one part of the manufacturing process to become separate from another. They create the kind of autonomy and space on which politics and empire building thrive. People are able to struggle for control over their particular part of the system. The existence of adequate stocks of high-quality work in process also institutionalizes errors and sloppy work. If a person or machine produces a defective product, production can still continue at its regular pace. Traditional systems of quality control institutionalized the error-producing process further by accepting a certain percentage of damaged products, waste, and inefficiency as the norm.

The challenge to this mechanistic approach to manufacturing came from outside the system: in the form of "just-in-time" methods of production where parts and raw materials are delivered just before they are needed, and in the related concept of "zero inventory." Both were pioneered in Japan. From the Japanese perspective, buffer stocks represented costs that could be eliminated. By building systems of production that relied on high-quality work being performed at every stage, the Japanese were able to develop production systems that resulted in high-quality, high-volume, low-cost production every time:

- When there are no buffer stocks to absorb error, there is no room for error, and systems of production must become error free.

- When people are no longer buffered from each other they must recognize the nature of their interdependence. Collaboration and mutual problem solving are encouraged. Activities have to be synchronized. Root problems must be confronted and eliminated.

Just-in-time manufacturing systems were unthinkable from a Western point of view. They contradicted all that seemed logical in designing manufacturing systems that could cope with the inevitable uncertainties of our uncertain world. The Western response was to try to eliminate and protect against uncertainty. The Japanese response was to learn from uncertainty and flow with it.

Of course, just-in-time systems are now widely used in Western manufacturing. But until they were demonstrated in reality by the Japanese, they remained an unthinkable or crazy ideal.

Such is the nature of psychic prisons. Favored ways of thinking and acting become traps that confine individuals within socially constructed worlds and prevent the emergence of other worlds. As in the case of Plato's allegory of the cave, disruption usually comes from the outside. But the hold of favored ways of thinking can be so strong that even the disruption is often transformed into a view consistent with the reality of the cave.

BLINDED BY GROUPTHINK

Sometimes, this process is described as *groupthink,* a term coined by Irving Janis that characterizes situations where people are carried along by group illusions and perceptions that have a self-sealing quality. One of the most famous examples is the abortive invasion of Cuba at the Bay of Pigs by 1,200 anti-Castro exiles. Launched on April 17, 1961, by the Kennedy administration, it almost led to nuclear war. "How could we have been so stupid?" President Kennedy later remarked. In retrospect, the plan looked completely misguided. Yet it had never seriously been questioned or challenged.

Kennedy and his advisers had unwittingly developed shared illusions and operating norms that interfered with their ability to think critically and to engage in the required reality testing. The president's charisma and a sense of invulnerability set the momentum for all kinds of self-affirming processes that produced conformity among key decision makers and advisers. Strong rationalizing tendencies mobilized support for favored opinions. A strong sense of "assumed consensus" inhibited people from expressing their doubts. Self-appointed people worked informally to protect the president from information that might damage his confidence. As a result, the CIA-planned invasion went ahead with a minimum of debate about the core assumptions on which its success depended.

The groupthink phenomenon has been reproduced in thousands of decision-making situations in organizations of all kinds. It may seem overly dramatic to describe the phenomenon as reflecting a kind of psychic prison. Many people would prefer to describe it through the culture metaphor, seeing the pathologies described in all the above examples as the product of particular cultural beliefs and norms. But there is great merit in recognizing the prisonlike qualities of culture.

Yes, culture gives us our world, but it traps us in that world! The psychic prison metaphor alerts us to pathologies that may accompany our ways of thinking and it encourages us to question the fundamental premises on which we enact everyday reality. Plato's allegory draws attention to blind spots in *conscious* awareness. But, as we shall see, there are also many *unconscious* dimensions to how we construct the reality of organizational life. When we explore this realm, the image of a psychic prison takes on a new quality.

ORGANIZATION AND THE UNCONSCIOUS

According to psychoanalytic theory, much of the rational and taken-for-granted reality of everyday life expresses preoccupations and concerns that lie beneath the level of conscious awareness. This places the study of organization and management in an interesting perspective, suggesting that much of what happens at a surface level must take account of the hidden structure and dynamics of the human psyche.

As is well known, the basis for this kind of thinking was laid by Sigmund Freud, who argued that the unconscious is created as humans repress their innermost desires and private thoughts. He believed that in order to live in harmony with one another humans must moderate and control their impulses, and that the unconscious and culture are really two sides of the same coin. He saw culture as the visible surface of the "repression" that accompanied the development of human sociability. It was in this sense that he talked about the essence of society being the repression of the individual, and about the essence of the individual being the repression of himself or herself.

Since Freud's early work, the whole field of psychoanalysis has become a battleground between rival theories of the origin and nature of the unconscious. While Freud placed importance on its links with various forms of repressed sexuality, others have stressed its links with the structure of the patriarchal family, fear of death, anxieties associated with early infancy, the collective unconscious, and so on.

Common to all these different interpretations is the idea that humans live their lives as prisoners or products of their individual and collective psychic history. The past is seen as living in the present through the unconscious, often in ways that create distorted and uncomfortable relations with the external world. Whereas Plato saw the route to enlightenment in the pursuit of objective knowledge and the activities of philosopher-kings, the psychoanalysts seek it in forms of self-understanding that show how in encounters with the external world, people are really meeting hidden dimensions of themselves.

As we shall see, the detailed images and ideas that have shaped the field of psychoanalysis have great relevance for how we understand organizational life.

ORGANIZATION AND REPRESSED SEXUALITY
The case of Frederick Taylor

Frederick Taylor, the creator of "scientific management," was a man totally preoccupied with control. He was an obsessive-compulsive character, driven by a relentless need to tie down and master almost every aspect of his life. His activities at home, in the garden, and on the golf course, as well as at work, were dominated by programs and schedules, which were planned in detail and rigidly followed. Even his afternoon walks were carefully laid out in advance; it was not unknown for him to observe his motions, to measure the time taken over different phases, and even to count his steps.

These traits were evident in Taylor's personality from an early age. Living in a well-to-do household dominated by strong puritan values (emphasizing work, discipline, and the ability to keep one's emotions decently in check), Taylor quickly learned how to regiment himself. Childhood friends described the meticulous "scientific" approach that he brought to their games. Taylor insisted that all be subjected to strict rules and exact formulas. Before playing a game of baseball he would often insist that accurate measurements be made of the field so that everything would be in perfect relation, even though most of a sunny morning was spent ensuring that measurements were correct to the inch. Even a game of croquet was subject to careful analysis, with Fred working on the angles of the various strokes and calculating the force of impact and the advantages and disadvantages of understroke and overstroke. On cross-country walks, the young Fred would constantly experiment with his legs to discover how to cover the greatest distance with a minimum of energy or the easiest method of vaulting a fence or the ideal length of a walking stick. As an adolescent, before going to a dance he would be sure to make lists of the attractive and unattractive girls likely to be present so that he could spend equal time with each.

Even during sleep this same meticulous regulation was brought into operation. From about the age of twelve, Taylor suffered from fearful nightmares and insomnia. Noticing that his worst dreams occurred while he was lying on his back, he constructed a harness of straps and wooden points that would wake him whenever he was in danger of getting into this position. He experimented with other means of overcoming his nightmares, constructing a canvas sheet hung between two poles so that he could keep his brain cool. The insomnia and sleeping devices stayed with him in one way or another throughout his life. In later years, he preferred to sleep in an upright position propped by numerous pillows. This made spending nights away from home a rather difficult business, and in hotels where pillows were in short supply he would sometimes spend the night propped up by bureau drawers.

Taylor's life provides a splendid illustration of how unconscious concerns and preoccupations can have an effect on organization. In psychoanalytic terms, his theory of scientific management was the product of the inner struggles of a disturbed and neurotic personality. His attempt to organize and control the world, whether in childhood games or in systems of scientific management, was really an attempt to organize and control himself.

From a Freudian perspective, Taylor's case presents a classic illustration of the anal-compulsive type of personality in which various forms of repression surface in later life. As explained in exhibit 7.1, repression may set the basis for all kinds of defense mechanisms that displace and redirect unconscious strivings so that they appear in other less threatening and more controlled forms. For example, excessive concerns with parsimony, order, regularity, correctness, tidiness, obedience, duty, and punctuality may be direct corollaries of what is learned and repressed as a child. Taylor's life is permeated with many of these preoccupations and with "reaction formations" (see exhibit 7.1) that manifest the opposite.

Much of Taylor's life reflects an inner struggle with the puritanical discipline and authority relations of his childhood. There is good reason to believe that the relations that his scientific management struck between

Freudian psychology emphasizes how human personality is shaped as the human mind learns to cope with raw impulses and desires. Freud believed that in the process of maturation these are brought under control or banished to the unconscious. The unconscious thus becomes a reservoir of repressed impulses. The adult person deals with this reservoir in a variety of ways, engaging in various defense mechanisms to keep them in check. Here are some of the important defenses that have been identified by Freud and his followers:

Repression: "Pushing down" unwanted impulses and ideas into the unconscious

Denial: Refusal to acknowledge an impulse-evoking fact, feeling, or memory

Displacement: Shifting impulses aroused by one person or situation to a safer target

Fixation: Rigid commitment to a particular attitude or behavior

Projection: Attribution of one's own feelings and impulses to others

Introduction: Internalizing aspects of the external world in one's psyche

Rationalization: Creation of elaborate schemes of justification that disguise underlying motives and intentions

Reaction formation: Converting an attitude or feeling into its opposite

Regression: Adoption of behavior patterns found satisfying in childhood in order to reduce present demands on one's ego

Sublimation: Channeling basic impulses into socially acceptable forms

Idealization: Playing up the good aspects of a situation to protect oneself from the bad

Splitting: Isolating different elements of experience, often to protect the good from the bad

Exhibit 7.1. Glossary of some Freudian and neo-Freudian defense mechanisms, adapted from C. Hampden-Turner, *Maps of the Mind*, pp. 40-42. © 1981, Macmillan; and M. Klein, *Envy, Gratitude, and Other Works*, pp. 1-24. © 1980, Hogarth.

managers and working men were rooted in the disciplinary structure under which he grew up. His relish in the dirt and grime of factories and his identification with the workers (he always claimed that he was one of them) can be understood as reactions against the same family situation. Amid all the conflict surrounding the introduction of scientific management, including direct insults, threats on his life, and his appearance before a special U.S. House of Representatives subcommittee on Taylorism, where he was presented as the "enemy of the working man," Taylor clung to the view that he had the friendship of those whom he sought to control. Within Taylor's mind, the aggression of scientific management was turned into its opposite: the idea that it promoted harmony. It was this view that allowed him to see himself as an industrial peacemaker at the very same time that scientific management was one of the major forces creating industrial unrest.

Taylor had a productive neurosis! His preoccupations and ideas dovetailed perfectly with the concerns of the organizations of his day, so rather than be dismissed as a crank he became a kind of infamous hero. The resolution of his own internal struggle resulted in productive innovations, ideas, and methods of control that had wide social impact.

The relationship between Taylor's anal-compulsive approach to life and the mode of organization embraced by scientific management raises a number of intriguing questions about styles of organization generally:

- To what extent is it possible to understand organization as an external reflection of unconscious strivings?
- What are the detailed links between the rise of formal organization and libidinal repression?
- To what extent do modes of organization institutionalize defense mechanisms? Is there a pattern?
- Do tightly controlled bureaucratic forms reflect the influence of compulsive preoccupations?
- Do they attract and reward people who share these characteristics?
- Do organic and other forms of organization reflect and institutionalize preoccupations concerned with Freud's other personality types?

These questions may seem rather far-fetched. But interesting links can be drawn. For example, it is clear that there has always been a highly visible connection between the rise of formal organization and the control of sexuality.

Organization and control of the body

If we return to the Middle Ages, we find a libidinal society where few distinctions were drawn between public and private life. Open displays of sexual behavior were common. As Gibson Burrell has shown, even in medieval monasteries, convents, and churches outrageous sexual behaviors presented a major problem. Manuscripts from the seventh and eighth centuries reveal that punishments for different classes of sexual misconduct were calculated in elaborate detail. Some of the most extreme offenses called for castration; others required extensive penitentials. A monk found guilty of simple fornication with unmarried persons could expect to fast for a year on bread and water, whereas a nun could expect three to seven years of fasting, and a bishop twelve years. The punishment for masturbation in church was forty days' fasting (sixty days' psalm singing for monks and nuns). A bishop caught fornicating with cattle could expect eight years' fasting for a first offense and ten years' fasting for each subsequent offense.

The very fact that these schedules existed indicates the extent to which sexual behaviors posed an ever-present problem to the order and routine of monastic life: one of the earliest modes of formal organization. They provide a graphic illustration of Freud's point that to promote social order and "civilized" behavior the libido has to be brought under control.

In the view of Michel Foucault, this conflict between organization and sexuality should come as no surprise, for mastery and control of the body are fundamental for control over social and political life. Parallels between the rise of formal organization and the routinization and regimentation of the human body are evident not only in Taylor's scientific form of management and the need to control sexuality in monastic life but also in how Frederick the Great made a disciplined Prussian army out of an unruly mob (discussed in the machine chapter), and in early forms of industrial organization. For example, the British Factory Acts of 1833 gave much attention to the problem of controlling sexual behavior at work, just as modern legislation on sexual harassment seeks to tackle the residue of this problem. Virtues of abstinence, restraint, and clean living were actively promoted in the Industrial Revolution of the eighteenth and nineteenth centuries. Many of the early industrialists in Europe and North America had Quaker and Puritan affiliations, the background against which Frederick Taylor later emerged.

In Freudian terms, this process of acquiring control over the body hinges on a social process in which the kind of organization and discipline of the anal personality becomes dominant. This sublimation has provided much of the energy underlying the development of industrial society.

A psychoanalytic organization theory

As we examine the bureaucratic form of organization, we should be alert to the hidden meaning of the close regulation and supervision of human activity, the relentless planning and scheduling of work, and the emphasis on productivity, rule following, discipline, duty, and obedience. The bureaucracy is a mechanistic form of organization but an anal one, too. Not surprisingly, some people are able to work in this kind of organization more effectively than others.

Historically, a strong case can be made for the idea that anality has been the major form of repressed sexuality shaping the nature of organizations. However, as we look around the organizational world, it is easy to see signs of other forms. Take the more flamboyant, flexible, organic, innovative firms now making such an impact on the corporate world. These organizations often call for a creative looseness of style that is quite alien to the bureaucratic personality. Freudian theory would suggest that the corporate cultures of these organizations often institutionalize various combinations of repressed oral, phallic, and genital sexuality.

Consider the driving ambition behind boardroom conquests, acquisitions, and mergers or the exhibitionistic "me-oriented" behaviors through which managers and organizations may lavish attention on themselves. In aggressive, individualistic organizations the corporate culture is often characterized by a phallic-narcissistic ethos, where satisfaction is derived from being visible, adored, and "a winner." Such organizations regard and encourage this narcissistic behavior exactly as rigid bureaucracies institutionalize anality.

Freudian theory provides an interesting twist to the kind of exhibitionistic behavior found in some of the corporate cultures discussed in the culture chapter. It suggests a new kind of contingency theory. Organizations are shaped not just by their environments. They are also shaped by the unconscious concerns of their members and the unconscious forces shaping the societies in which they exist.

ORGANIZATION AND THE PATRIARCHAL FAMILY

While the Freudian perspective creates many novel interpretations of organizational life, in the view of many critics Freud was too hung up on sexuality and took the argument too far. Notable among these critics are members of the contemporary women's movement who see Freud as a man espousing male values and trapped in his own unconscious sexual preoccupations, especially as they interacted with the Victorian morality of his day. Rather than place emphasis on repressed sexuality as a driving force behind modern organization, these critics suggest that we try to understand organization as an expression of partriarchy. From their standpoint, patriarchy operates as a kind of conceptual prison, producing and reproducing organizational structures that give dominance to males and traditional male values.

The dominance of male values and roles

The evidence for a patriarchal view of organization is easy to see. Formal organizations typically build upon characteristics associated with Western male values and, historically, have been dominated by males, except in those jobs where the function is to support, serve, flatter, please, and entertain.

Men have tended to dominate organizational roles and functions where there is a need for aggressive and forthright behavior, whereas women have, until fairly recently, been socialized to accept roles placing them in a subordinate position, as in nursing, clerical, and secretarial work or roles designed to satisfy various kinds of male narcissism.

The bureaucratic approach to organization tends to foster the rational, analytic, and instrumental characteristics associated with the Western stereotype of maleness, while downplaying abilities traditionally viewed as "female," such as intuition, nurturing, and empathic support. In the process, it has created organizations that in more ways than one define "a man's world," where men, and the women who have entered the fray, joust and jostle for positions of dominance.

In the view of many writers on the relationship between gender and organization, the dominant influence of the male is rooted in the hierarchical relations found in the patriarchal family, which, as Wilhelm Reich has observed, serves as "a factory for authoritarian ideologies." In many formal organizations, one person defers to the authority of another exactly as the child defers to parental rule. The prolonged dependency of the child upon the parents facilitates the kind of dependency institutionalized in the relationship between leaders and followers and in the practice where people look to others to initiate action in response to problematic issues. In organizations, as in the patriarchal family, fortitude, courage, and heroism, flavored by narcissistic self-admiration, are often valued qualities, as is the determination and sense of duty that a father expects from his son. Key organizational members also often cultivate fatherly roles by acting as mentors to those in need of help and protection.

Critics of patriarchy suggest that in contrast with matriarchal values, which emphasize unconditional love, optimism, trust, compassion, and a capacity for intuition, creativity, and happiness, the psychic structure of the male-dominated family tends to create a feeling of impotence accompanied by a fear of and dependence on authority. These critics argue that under the influence of matriarchal values organizational life would be far less hierarchical, be more compassionate and holistic, value means over ends, and be far more tolerant of diversity and open to creativity. Many of these traditionally female values are evident in nonbureaucratic forms of organization where nurturing and networking replace authority and hierarchy as the dominant modes of integration.

In viewing organizations as unconscious extensions of family relations, we have a powerful means of understanding key features of the corporate world. We are also given a clue as to how organizations are likely to change along with contemporary changes in family structure and parenting relations. We see the major role that women and gender-related values can play in transforming the corporate world. So long as organizations are dominated by patriarchal values, the roles of women in organizations will always be played out on male terms. Hence, the view of many feminist critics of the modern corporation: The real challenge facing women who want to succeed in the organizational world is to change organizational values in the most fundamental sense.

ORGANIZATION, DEATH, AND IMMORTALITY

In his book *The Denial of Death,* Ernest Becker suggests that human beings are "Gods with anuses." Among all the animals, we alone are conscious of the fact that we will die, and we are obliged to spend our lives with knowledge of the paradox that while we may be capable of spiritual transcendence beyond our bodies, our existence is dependent on a finite structure of flesh and bone that will ultimately wither away. In Becker's view, humans spend much of their lives attempting to deny the oncoming reality of death by pushing their morbid fears deep into the recesses of their unconscious. He in effect reinterprets the Freudian theory of repressed sexuality, linking childhood fears associated with birth and the development of sexuality with fears relating to our own inadequacies, vulnerability, and mortality.

These views lead us to understand culture and organization in a novel way. They encourage us to understand many of our symbolic acts and constructions as flights from our own mortality. In joining with others in the creation of culture as a set of shared norms, beliefs, ideas, and social practices, we attempt to locate ourselves in something larger and more enduring than ourselves. In creating a world that can be perceived as objective and real, we reaffirm the concrete and real nature of our own existence. In creating symbol systems that allow us to engage in meaningful exchanges with others, we also help to find meaning in our own lives. Although we may in quiet times confront the fact that we are going to die, much of our daily life is lived in the artificial realness created through culture.

This perspective suggests that we can understand organizations and much of the behavior within organizations in terms of a quest for immortality.

- In creating organizations, we create structures of activity that are larger than life and that often survive for generations.

- In becoming identified with such organizations, we ourselves find meaning and permanence.

- As we invest ourselves in our work, our roles become our realities, and as we objectify ourselves in the goods we produce or the money we make, we make ourselves visible and real to ourselves.

No wonder that questions of survival are such a high priority in organizations, for there is often much more than the survival of the organization at stake.

Organization and illusions of control

In understanding the unconscious significance of the relationship between immortality and organization, we realize that in attempting to manage and organize our world we are really attempting to manage and organize ourselves. Of particular importance here is the fact that many of our most basic conceptions of organization hinge on the idea of making the complex simple, as in the bureaucratic approach to organization where activities and functions are broken into clearly defined component parts. As in much of science and everyday life, we manage our world by simplifying it. For in making it simple, we create the illusion that it can be controlled and that we are more powerful than we really are. Much of the knowledge through which we organize our world can be seen as protecting us from the idea that, ultimately, we probably understand and control very little. Arrogance often hides weakness. The idea that human beings can organize and boast mastery of nature is a sign of their own vulnerability.

At a practical level, people use detailed myths and rituals to shield their vulnerability. Consider, for example, how jokes and humor are used to cope with difficult working conditions. In many hazardous situations, it is well known that workers will often make the situation even more dangerous by engaging in exhibitionist behavior or by playing practical jokes on their colleagues. Paradoxically, the practices give a feeling of greater control.

In other organizational contexts, processes of goal setting, planning, and other kinds of ritual activity perform similar functions. In setting personal or organizational goals, we reassert confidence in our future. In investing our time and energy in a favored project, we convert the flight of time into something concrete and enduring.

Whereas Freudian analysis would view excessive concerns with productivity, planning, and control as expressions of sublimated anal concerns, the work of Becker leads us to understand them as an attempt to preserve and tie down life in the face of death.

ORGANIZATION AND ANXIETY

In his later work, Freud came to place increasing emphasis on the struggle between life and death instincts within the individual. This relationship became a special focus for study by Melanie Klein and the so-called English school of psychoanalysis based at the Tavistock Institute in London, who have spent a great deal of time tracing the impact of childhood defenses against anxiety on the adult personality.

Klein's work builds on the premise that from the beginning of life the human child experiences unease associated with the death instinct and fear of annihilation and that this fear becomes internalized in the form of "persecutory anxiety." To cope with this anxiety, the child develops defense mechanisms, including splitting, introjection, and projection (see exhibit 7.1). From Klein's perspective, it is possible to understand the structure, process, culture, and even the environment of an organization in terms of the unconscious defense mechanisms developed by its members to cope with individual and collective anxiety.

Defense mechanisms in groups

This approach to organizational analysis has been systematically developed by many members of the Tavistock Institute. In his analysis of group behavior, Wilfred Bion suggested that groups often regress to childhood patterns of behavior to protect themselves from uncomfortable aspects of the real world. When a group is fully engaged with a task, its energies tend to be occupied and directed in ways that keep the group in touch with an external reality of some kind. However, when problems that challenge the group's functioning arise, the group tends to withdraw its energies from task performance and use them to defend itself against the anxieties associated with the new situation. Bion described how in such anxiety-provoking situations groups tend to revert to one of three styles of operation that employ different kinds of defense against anxiety: dependency, pairing, or fight-flight.

- *Dependency.* In anxious times, some groups assume they need some form of leadership to resolve their predicament. The group's attention is split from the problems at hand and projected onto a particular individual. Group members often proclaim helplessness in coping with the situation and idealize the characteristics of the chosen leader. Sometimes, the group projects its energies onto an attractive symbol of its past, celebrating the way things used to be instead of coping with the current reality. Such a climate makes it easy for a potential leader to step in and take charge of the group's affairs. However, he or she often inherits an extremely difficult situation, as the very existence of a leader will provide an excuse for personal inaction on the part of others. The leader will also have to embody traits fantasized by people in the group who project desired aspects of their own egos onto the leader figure. As a result, the leader often fails to live up to expectations and is soon replaced by another person, often one of the least able members of the group. He or she in turn usually fails, and so the problems continue, perhaps leading to fragmentation and infighting within the group. Group functioning may become immobilized as all kinds of petty wrangling and divisionary issues serve as substitutes for real action.

- *Pairing.* In another pattern of response, a group may attempt to deal with its problems through *pairing.* This involves a fantasy where members of the group come to believe that a messiah figure will emerge to deliver the group from its fear and anxiety. The group's dependence on the emergence of such a figure again paralyzes its ability to take effective action.

- *Fight-flight.* A third pattern of response is *fight-flight,* in which the group tends to project its fears on an enemy of some kind. This enemy embodies the unconscious persecutory anxiety experienced by the group. The enemy may take the form of a competitor in the environment, a government regulation, a public attitude, or a particular person or organization that appears to be "out to get us." While uniting the group and making a strong form of leadership possible, the fight-flight process tends to distort the group's appreciation of reality and hence its ability to cope. Time and energy tend to be devoted to fighting or protecting the group from the perceived danger rather than taking a more balanced look at the problems that are evident in the situation.

A good example of fight-flight is the way automobile manufacturers and many other branches of the manufacturing industry in North America first reacted to the challenge posed by the import of goods from Japan and other parts of Asia. While this new source of competition was very real in its effects, preoccupation with "the enemy" and the need to fight or protect oneself through legislation and import quotas diverted attention from an equally important aspect of the situation: the need to reexamine the nature of one's own products to find how they might be modified or improved to compete in the new market conditions. The fight-flight response illustrated in this example tapped an unconscious paranoia that is common to many group situations.

Defense mechanisms in organizations

Defense mechanisms contribute to understanding the dynamics of leadership, group processes, the enactment of organizational culture, relations between organization and environment, and other day-to-day aspects of organizational functioning. They pervade almost every aspect of organizational activity as people—operating as individuals or through unconscious collusion as groups—construct realities wherein threats and concerns within the unconscious mind become embodied in their understanding of the wider world. Corporate culture and understandings of the external environment become an extension of this internal domain.

Defense mechanisms can also help explain many of the more formal aspects of organization. For example, Eliott Jaques and Isobel Menzies, former members of the Tavistock Institute, have described how aspects of organizational structure can be understood as social defenses. Jaques illustrates how many organizational roles may be the focus of various kinds of paranoid or persecutory anxiety. The first officer on a ship is typically held responsible for many things that go wrong, even if he is not responsible. By common unconscious consent, he is usually blamed as the source of all trouble, allowing the crew to find relief from their own internal persecutors. Or the captain may be idealized as a good protective figure.

All kinds of organizational scapegoats serve similar functions—people in roles that everyone "loves to hate," convenient "troublemakers" and "misfits," and people who are "just not playing the game." They provide a focus for unconscious anger and sadistic tendencies, relieving tension in the wider organization and binding it together.

Jaques suggests defense against paranoid anxiety is often a feature of labor-management relations, where bad impulses are projected onto different groups who are then perceived as villains or sources of trouble. They often become the objects of vengeful attitudes and actions. The process also occurs in many patterns of interorganizational relations:

- Many of the relations between government and business reflect what Robert Chatov has described as "regulatory sadism," as regulators inflict burdensome and superfluous requirements on regulatees.
- Organizations in competitive environments often attempt to dominate, punish, and control their rivals or others with whom they work.

- One part of an organization may set out to create punishing problems for another or build various kinds of punishment into its general policies and procedures.

- In economic recessions, key people often take pleasure in tightening up organizational practices and privileges established in the preceding "fat" years.

- In the field of labor-management relations, a weakened position of trade unions can open the door to aggressive "union bashing."

- Major restructurings may be motivated as much by desires to take revenge and punish individuals and groups as by the genuine rationalization of work practices.

In another domain, Isobel Menzies describes how defenses against anxiety underpin many aspects of the way nursing work is organized. As is well known, nurses often have to deal with distressing tasks that can arouse mixed feelings of pity, compassion, love, guilt, fear, hatred, envy, and resentment. So the splitting up of the nurse-patient relation into discrete tasks distributed among different nurses; the depersonalization, categorization, and denial of the significance of the patient as an individual in favor of the patient as a "case"; and the detachment and denial of personal feelings often have unconscious as well as bureaucratic significance. They are coping mechanisms. Sometimes, they contribute to efficient health care. At other times, they get in the way. In both cases, they may be extremely difficult to remove or change.

Abraham Zaleznik suggests that patterns of unconscious anxiety often exert a decisive influence on coalition building and the politics of organizational life. In some situations, leaders may be unable to develop close relations with their colleagues and subordinates because of unconscious fears or because some form of unconscious anger or envy leads them to resent any trace of rivalry. Such concerns may motivate the leaders to maintain control by dividing and ruling subordinates in ways that ensure that they are "kept in place." Often, the unconscious fears prevent them from being able to accept genuine help and advice. For example, policy suggestions put forward by subordinates may be interpreted as rivalry and hence dismissed or suppressed regardless of their substantive merit. Ironically, these leaders frequently isolate themselves, providing an ideal situation for subordinates to club together in a way that may lead to the leaders' demise. Unconscious projections often have self-realizing effects.

The unconscious and corporate culture

The patterns of meaning that shape corporate culture and subculture may also have unconscious significance. The common values that bind an organization often have their origin in shared concerns that lurk below the surface of conscious awareness.

In organizations that project a team image, various kinds of splitting mechanisms are often in operation, idealizing the qualities of team members while projecting fears, anger, envy, and other bad impulses onto persons and objects that are not part of the team. As in war, the ability to create unity and a feeling of purpose often depends upon the ability to deflect destructive impulses onto the enemy. These impulses then confront the team as "real" threats.

In organizations characterized by internal strife or an ethos of cutthroat competition, these destructive impulses are often unleashed within, creating a culture that thrives on various kinds of sadism rather than by projecting its sadism elsewhere. Deep-seated envy may lead people to block the success of their colleagues because they fear that they will be unable to match that success. This hidden process may undermine the ability to develop teamlike cooperation, which requires organizational members to enjoy success through affiliation with successful others as well as through their own achievements. Again, unresolved persecutory anxieties, which invariably inhibit learning because they prevent people from accepting criticism and correcting their mistakes, may lead to a culture characterized by all kinds of tension and defensiveness.

Considerations such as these suggest there may be much more to corporate culture than is evident in the popular idea that it is possible to "manage culture." Culture, like organization, may not be what it seems to be. Culture may be of as much significance in helping us avoid an inner reality as in helping us cope with the external reality of our day-to-day lives.

ORGANIZATION AND TEDDY BEARS

As children, most of us had a favorite soft toy, blanket, piece of clothing, or other special object on which we lavished attention and from which we were virtually inseparable. Psychoanalyst Donald Winnicott suggests that these objects are critical in developing distinctions between the "me" and the "not me," creating what he calls an "area of illusion" that helps the child develop relations with the outside world. In effect, these objects provide a bridge between the child's internal and external worlds. If the favored object or phenomenon is modified (e.g., Teddy is washed), then the child may feel that his or her own existence is being threatened in some way.

The theory of transitional objects

The relationship with such "transitional objects" continues throughout life, the doll, teddy bear, or blanket gradually being replaced by other objects and experiences that mediate relations with one's world to help maintain a sense of identity. In later life, a valued possession, a collection of letters, a cherished dream, or perhaps a valued attribute, skill, or ability may come to act as a substitute for our lost doll or teddy, symbolizing and reassuring us about who we actually are and where we stand in the wider world. While they play a crucial role in linking us with our reality, on occasion these objects and experiences may also acquire the status of a fetish or fixation that we are unable to relinquish. In such cases, adult development becomes stuck and distorted, a rigid commitment to a particular aspect of our world making it difficult for us to move on and deal with the changing nature of our surroundings.

Theories of transitional phenomena and associated areas of illusion add to our understanding of how we engage and construct organizational reality. They also provide a powerful perspective on the role of the unconscious in shaping and resisting change.

Unconscious blocks to innovation and change

Harold Bridger of the Tavistock Institute has held numerous seminars exploring the unconscious significance of transitional phenomena in organizational life. His perspective leads us to understand that many organizational arrangements can themselves serve as transitional phenomena: they play a critical role in defining the nature and identity of organizations and their members and in shaping attitudes that can block creativity, innovation, and change.

- A particular aspect of organizational structure or corporate culture may come to assume special significance and be preserved and retained even in the face of great pressure to change.

- A family firm may cling to a particular aspect of its history and mission, even though it is now operating in new conditions where this aspect is no longer relevant.

- Trade-union officials or a group of employees may want to fight to the death to defend a particular principle or a set of concessions won in previous battles, even though they are no longer of any real value to their members.

- Managers or work groups may insist that they have the right and discretion to make particular decisions or that work must be performed in a specific manner, even though when pressed they recognize that their requirements are ritualistic rather than substantive in nature.

In each of these cases, the phenomenon to be preserved may be of transitional significance to those involved. Just as children may rely on the presence of the doll or teddy bear as a means of reaffirming who and where they are, managers and workers may rely on equivalent phenomena for defining their sense of identity. When these phenomena are challenged, basic identities are challenged. The fear of loss that this entails often generates a reaction that may be out of all proportion to the importance of the issue when viewed from a more detached point of view. This unconscious dynamic may help explain why some organizations have been unable to cope with the changing demands of their environment and why there is often so much unconscious resistance to change in organizations.

The process is well illustrated in the case of an engineering company that, like many others in its industry, experienced difficulties in adapting to changes being created by new developments in computer technology. One of the interesting features of the culture of the company was its commitment to the use of slide rules. Even though the new computer technology offered a radically new and vastly more efficient way of making engineering calculations, many of the engineers insisted on continuing to use their "slides." The theory of transitional phenomena leads us to understand this in terms of an unconscious process where the use of slide rules was associated with a past that was fast disappearing and a reluctance to relinquish an old identity and move on with the changing times. As might be expected, the firm lost its position in the industry and eventually was taken over by another firm.

The theory of transitional phenomena contributes important insights to the practice of organizational change and development. It suggests that change will occur spontaneously only when people are prepared to relinquish what they hold dear for the purpose of acquiring something new or can find ways of carrying what they value in the old into the new. The engineering firm in the above example was committed to a symbolic object that could not perform transitional functions in the current situation. Some new object, insight, or experience was needed to aid in the transition to microprocessing. Interestingly, consultants and other change agents often become transitional objects for their client firms: the client refuses to let go and becomes crucially dependent on the change agent's advice in relation to every move.

Helping people move on

In helping facilitate any kind of social change, it may be necessary for the change agent to create transitional phenomena when they do not exist naturally. Just as a father or mother may have to help his or her child find a substitute for Teddy, a change agent—whether a social revolutionary or a paid consultant—must usually help his or her target group to relinquish what is held dear before they can move on. Significantly, this can rarely be done effectively by "selling" or imposing a "change package," an ideology, or a set of techniques. The theory of transitional phenomena suggests that in situations of voluntary change the person doing the changing must be in control of the process, for change ultimately hinges on questions of identity and the problematic relation between me and not-me. People frequently need time to reflect, think over, feel out, and mull through action if a change is to be effective and long-lasting. If the change agent tries to bypass or suppress what is valued, it is almost sure to resurface at a later date.

The theory of transitional phenomena provides a way of understanding the dynamics of change and offers important ideas that can help individuals and groups make effective transitions from one state to another.

ORGANIZATION, SHADOW, AND ARCHETYPE

In the above analysis, we have focused on Freudian and neo-Freudian interpretations of the unconscious. It is now time to turn to the implications of the work of Carl Jung. Whereas Freud was preoccupied with the demands that the body, as carrier of the psyche, placed on the unconscious, Jung broke away from this constraint, viewing the psyche as part of a universal and transcendental reality. As his thinking developed, he came to place increasing emphasis on the idea that the human psyche is part of a "collective unconscious" that transcends the limits of space and time.

Jung's work has major implications for understanding how people enact organizational reality. We will focus here on two of the more important considerations:

- the way Jung encourages us to understand the general relations between internal and external life, and

- the role that archetypes play in shaping our understanding of the external world.

Organization and shadow

The first theme has been explored in some detail by Robert Denhardt. In his book *In the Shadow of Organization,* he invites us to examine the repressed human side of organization lying beneath the surface of formal rationality. Jung used the term "shadow" to refer to unrecognized or unwanted drives and desires. In his view, neurosis and human maladaption stem from an inability to recognize and deal with the repressed shadow, which typically contains both constructive and destructive forces. Like the other theorists we have considered in this chapter, he also believed that many of these unresolved tensions in ourselves are projected onto other people and external situations and that to understand our external reality we must first understand what he called "the other within."

In the shadow of organization, we find all the repressed opposites of rationality struggling to surface and change the nature of rationality in practice. Sociologist Max Weber noted that the more the bureaucratic form of organization advances, the more perfectly it succeeds in eliminating all human qualities that escape technical calculation. However, Jung's work suggests that irrational qualities can never be eliminated, only banished or submerged. His work also leads us to understand that irrational qualities never accept their banishment idly and are always looking for a way to modify their rational other side. We see this in much of the unofficial politicking that shapes organizational life and also in stress, lying, cheating, depression, and acts of sabotage. From a Jungian standpoint, such factors reflect inevitable yet neglected or suppressed tensions in a two-sided process. Just as the unconscious of the individual strives to achieve completeness with the ego, the shadowy unconscious in an organization can also be seen as crying for recognition, warning us that the development of one side of our humanness (e.g., the capacity to exercise technical reason) often does violence to other sides. The pathologies and alienations we find in organizational contexts can, from a Jungian standpoint, be interpreted as a manifestation of this essential wholeness of the psyche.

Jung's work shows that the repressed shadow of organization acts as a reservoir not only of forces that are unwanted and hence repressed, but of forces that have been lost or undervalued. For example, as the male archetype asserts itself, values associated with the female are submerged. By recognizing the resources of this reservoir, we can tap submerged sources of energy and creativity and make our institutions much more human, vibrant, and morally responsive and responsible than they are now.

Organization and archetype

Jung's analysis of personality in terms of the way people relate to their world conveniently brings us to consider the role of archetypes in shaping the details of our reality. Archetypes are recurring themes of thought and experience that seem to have universal significance. For example, mythology and literature are dominated by a small number of basic themes—apocalyptic, demonic, romantic, tragic, comic, and ironic. The characters, situations, and actions may change, but the stories remain much the same. In other aspects of life, too, powerful themes that help people make sense of their experience are used time and again to create patterns of meaning. These archetypal structures give people a sense of place in their own lives and in history, thereby helping them to make sense of who and where they are in the grand order of things.

Jung devoted great time and energy to demonstrating the universal and timeless character of these archetypal structures, showing how they are found in the dreams, myths, and ideas of primitive, ancient, and modern man. For Jung, these archetypes shape the way we "meet ourselves" in encounters with the external world and are crucial for understanding links between conscious and unconscious aspects of the psyche.

According to Jung's theory, we would expect the pattern of organizational life to be created and re-created in accordance with the structures found in the history of myth and literature. Unfortunately, very little research has been conducted on this topic.

THE UNCONSCIOUS: A CREATIVE AND DESTRUCTIVE FORCE

Our exploration of organization and the unconscious has drawn on many images of the psychic prison, tracing relations between our conscious and unconscious life in terms of repressed sexuality, patriarchy, fear of death, defense mechanisms, teddy bears, and shadows and archetypes—the list is by no means exhaustive. These metaphors encourage us to become more sensitive about the hidden meaning of our everyday actions and preoccupations and to learn how we can process and transform our unconscious energy in constructive ways. They lead us to see how aggression, envy, anger, resentment, and numerous other dimensions of our hidden life may be built into work and organization. These hidden concerns influence whether we attempt to design work to avoid or to deal with problematic aspects of our reality and how we enact our organizational world. They lie at the center of many issues associated with group dynamics, effective leadership, and innovation and change.

Frances Delahanty and Gary Gemmill suggest that we should understand the role of the unconscious in organizational life as a kind of "black hole." This metaphor has been used in physics to characterize invisible yet intense gravitational fields that capture all passing matter. In a similar way, the invisible dimension of organization that we have described as the unconscious can swallow and trap the rich energies of people involved in the organizing process.

The challenge of understanding the significance of the unconscious in organization also carries a promise: that it is possible to release trapped energy in ways that may promote creative transformation and change and create more integrated relations among individuals, groups, organizations, and their environments. This promise is in perfect harmony with the metaphor of the psychic prison, for a vision of confinement is invariably accompanied by a vision of freedom. For Plato, this freedom rests in the pursuit of knowledge about the world. For the psychoanalysts, it has rested in knowledge of the unconscious and in the capacity of humans to create a better world through an improved understanding of how we construct and interpret our realities.

STRENGTHS AND LIMITATIONS OF THE PSYCHIC PRISON METAPHOR

The psychic prison metaphor offers a powerful set of perspectives for exploring the hidden meaning of our taken-for-granted worlds. It encourages us to dig below the surface to uncover the processes and patterns of control that trap people in unsatisfactory modes of existence and to find ways through which they can be transformed.

STRENGTHS

- **The metaphor encourages us to challenge basic assumptions about how we see and experience our world.**

Why do we get trapped by favored ways of thinking? Why do we protect our illusions? Why do we find it so difficult to change established and even uncomfortable modes of behavior? Why do we create so many problems for each other? The ideas that we have explored point toward some answers and offer some interesting ways of gaining new perspective on critical problems.

The image of a psychic prison is itself a powerful image for approaching this task because it encourages us to recognize how we may be caught in a self-sealing environment. We see each other, and we see the world around us. But what are we really seeing? Are we seeing an independent world? Or are we just seeing and experiencing projections of ourselves? Are we imprisoned by the language, concepts, beliefs, and a general culture through which we enact our world?

Paradoxically, by posing these kinds of questions we take the first steps in finding an escape. We are encouraged to look for messages coming from outside our particular "cave" and to use them for gaining new leverage on our world. This can bring enormous benefits to individuals and organizations, offering a way out of the groupthink and psychic traps that may lock us into ineffective and undesirable patterns of behavior.

- **We gain important insights into the challenges of organizational innovation and change.**

All the perspectives considered in this chapter show that in seeking to change organizational practice we are usually trying to change much, much more.

Structures, rules, behaviors, beliefs, and the patterns of culture that define an organization are not just corporate phenomena. They are personal in the most profound sense. Any attempt to change these aspects of the organizational world can mobilize all kinds of opposition as individuals and groups defend the status quo in an attempt to defend their very selves. Structures and rules may be crucial in *creating* boundaries and rigidities that help to symbolize a manager's sense of who he or she really is; an outdated practice may reflect an effort to cling to a cherished experience or mode of life; high regard for a particular person or leader may be carrying all kinds of unconscious anxieties, aggressions, and energies of those being led; bloody mergers, acquisitions, downsizings, or combative relations with competitors or the world at large may veil all kinds of individual and group fears and inadequacies; a corporate group's understanding of its external environment may be dominated by the unconscious projections of a few key managers; a strong corporate subculture may be mobilizing neglected aspects of a corporate "shadow" that are truly worthy of attention and of being brought to light.

In understanding these hidden dimensions of everyday reality, managers and change agents can open the way to modes of practice that respect and cope with organizational challenges in a new way. They can learn the art of carrying valuable dimensions of old ways into the new. They can begin to untangle sources of scapegoating, victimization, and blame and find ways of addressing the deeper anxieties to which they are giving form. They can approach the resistance and defensive routines that tend to sabotage and block change with a new sensitivity, and find constructive ways of dealing with them.

- **The "irrational" is put in a new perspective.**

The psychic prison metaphor shows us that we have over-rationalized our understanding of organization. As we saw in earlier chapters, the drive to create tightly controlled rational organizations has been a major feature of the twentieth century. Organization theory has sought to provide managers with perspectives and techniques that try to eliminate or control uncertainty and put management on a rational, objective basis. The ideas presented in this chapter reveal the imbalance and suggest that instead of trying to enhance the rationality of organizations as an end in itself, more attention should be devoted to understanding and developing the links between the rational and irrational (a term for human forces that we cannot order and control), because they are part of the very same phenomenon.

Both in our behavior in organizations and in our explanations of organizations, factors such as aggression, greed, fear, hate, and libidinal drives have no official status. When they do break into the open, they are usually quickly banished through apologies, rationalizations, and punishments designed to restore a more neutered state of affairs. An outburst of anger may be interpreted as a sign that someone is under pressure, an emotional breakdown treated with a few days' leave, and an act of sabotage punished with further controls. Yet apologize, rationalize, punish, and control as we may, we do not rid organizations of these repressed forces lurking in the shadow of rationality. This human underside will always exist and has to be taken into account if organization is to develop in a holistic and convivial way.

It is pointless to talk about creating "learning organizations" or trying to develop corporate cultures that thrive on change if the unconscious human dimension is ignored. If underlying preoccupations and concerns are not addressed, the rhetoric of creating a new organization is almost sure to fall on deaf ears—even in situations where change may seem beneficial and logical for all concerned.

The psychic prison metaphor heightens our awareness of the relationship between "the rational" and what *seems* "irrational," and warns of the dangers of dismissing or downplaying the significance of the latter, because the irrational can be an incredibly powerful force for the people involved. The metaphor also encourages us to recognize that rationality is often irrationality in disguise. We have seen this in how the rationality of a Frederick Taylor can disguise an extreme form of compulsiveness, just as a manager's workaholism, excessive concern for clear-cut targets and goals, or aggressive manner in dealing with colleagues or external competitors can disguise all kinds of personal insecurities. Rationality and irrationality are flip sides of each other, and when one is overemphasized, distortions and dysfunctions inevitably arise.

■ **We are encouraged to integrate and manage competing tensions rather than allow one side to dominate.**

The ideas presented in this chapter encourage us to understand the tensions between the rational and irrational and to find ways of achieving better integration and balance. This has enormous implications for dealing with the challenges of a turbulent world because it is clear that current conceptions and beliefs about organization and management over-assert the importance of "being rational" and "in control." If management is to rise to the challenge of encouraging emergent, self-organizing forms, these traditional concerns for control need to be tempered by a comfort in dealing with uncertainty, flux, and change as a norm. Similarly, the qualities of the male archetype that have dominated so much contemporary management need to be supplemented with those of the female. Rational decision processes need to make more room for intuitive creative leaps. The ethos of cutthroat competition needs to make more room for a gentler counterpart.

Interestingly, the forces that can help create the required integration are often present in most organizations: in the repressed "shadow side." If one examines the relationship between the dominant corporate culture and patterns of subculture within an organization, one can often see the tensions discussed above struggling for attention. Many subcultural groups provide rallying points for positive ideas and developments that cannot find formal expression elsewhere, or for counterbalancing negative aspects of the dominant culture. As such they offer a hidden reservoir of energy and ideas for mobilizing constructive change. It is vitally important for managers to recognize the constructive and reparative side of forces that may at first sight seem to be opposing their policies, especially in circumstances of high interdependence. In recognizing that the shadow side of our organizations sends us messages about "the good" and "the bad," we can find ways of organizing and managing in a much more integrated way.

■ **Ethical management acquires a new dimension.**

There is nothing neutral about the way we organize. It is always human in the fullest sense, and an increased awareness of the human dimension needs to be built into everything we do. While the metaphor offers obvious guidance on the management of change, it also warns us that we may be walking on dangerous ethical ground, especially when we systematically use our knowledge of archetypal feelings or social defense mechanisms to achieve corporate objectives. In the culture chapter we mentioned the ideological implications of attempts to shape and mold corporate culture for instrumental ends. The psychic prison metaphor adds depth to this insight, warning that cultural patterns may carry all kinds of unconscious significance of a deeply personal nature.

LIMITATIONS

■ **A focus on the unconscious may deflect attention from other forces of control.**

Our discussion has placed considerable emphasis on understanding and dealing with unconscious patterns of behavior and control. But what about the more explicit ideological factors that control and shape organizational life? People are often locked into unconscious traps because it is in the interests of certain individuals and groups to sustain one pattern of belief rather than another. An understanding of the psychic prison metaphor can and should be extended to embrace all the ideological processes through which we create and sustain meaning, not just the unconscious.

In this regard, the metaphor can be criticized for placing too much emphasis on the role of *mental* processes in creating, sustaining, and changing organizations and society. For many, it may seem more appropriate to talk about organizations as prisons rather than as psychic prisons, since the exploitation and domination of people are often grounded as much in control over the material basis of life as in control over ideas, thoughts, and feelings.

This view builds on a long-standing debate between humanists and materialists and will be placed in better perspective in the flux and transformation and domination chapters, where we give more attention to the idea that organizations and society may be shaped by forces that have a logic and momentum of their own. In the meantime, we must note that a change in consciousness or an appreciation of the role of the unconscious may not itself be enough to effect major change in the basic structure of organization and society.

■ **The metaphor underestimates the power of vested interests in sustaining the status quo.**

The metaphor's promise of liberation from undesirable psychological constraints often encourages utopian speculation and critique. While it does contribute certain insights on how to improve the conduct of day-to-day affairs, particularly in showing how we can challenge taken-for-granted mindsets or achieve a better understanding of the psychodynamics of change, many of its implications ignore the realities of power and the force of vested interests. Of course, the fact that reform may be dismissed as utopian adds power to the argument that our imprisoned state prevents us from imagining and realizing alternative modes of existence. If proposals for change must always be judged feasible and realistic, we are restricted to modifications of the status quo. However, the criticism of utopianism still remains.

- **There is a danger that the insights of the metaphor can be used to exploit the unconscious for organizational gain.**

A final limitation, and indeed danger, of the metaphor is that it raises the specter of an Orwellian world where we attempt to manage each other's minds. We noted in the culture chapter how an awareness of the importance of corporate culture has sent many managers and management theorists hurrying to find ways of managing culture. In highlighting the role of the unconscious in organization, there is a danger that many will now want to find ways of managing the unconscious as well.

This, of course, is impossible because the unconscious is by nature uncontrollable. While it is possible to act in a way that is sensitive to the existence and role of the unconscious in everyday life, knowledge of the unconscious does not produce blueprints for reform. The psychic prison metaphor promotes a style of critical thinking and awareness that can help us penetrate many of the complexities of organizational life. But it does not provide the easy answers and solutions to problems that many managers may wish to find.

8 Unfolding Logics of Change: Organization As Flux and Transformation

WHAT HAPPENS WHEN WE LOOK BEYOND THE SURFACE APPEARANCE OF ORGANIZATIONS and see them as the expressions of deeper processes of transformation and change?

- We gain insights into the fundamental nature of change.

- We see that deep systemic forces are constantly either locking organizations into the status quo or driving their transformation.

- We acquire new and powerful perspectives for intervention, using images of spirals, loops, and contradictions to help organizations shift from one pattern of operation to another.

The ideas explored in this chapter lead us into the new sciences of autopoiesis, chaos, complexity, and paradox with powerful implications for our understanding of organization and environment in the broadest sense.

AROUND 500 B.C. THE GREEK PHILOSOPHER HERACLITUS
NOTED THAT "YOU CANNOT STEP TWICE INTO THE SAME RIVER,
for other waters are continually flowing on." He was one of the first Western philosophers to address the idea that the universe is in a constant state
of flux, embodying characteristics of both permanence and change. As he
noted, "Everything flows and nothing abides; everything gives way and
nothing stays fixed. . . . Cool things become warm, the warm grows cool;
the moist dries, the parched becomes moist. . . . It is in changing that things
find repose." For Heraclitus, the secrets of the universe were to be found in
hidden tensions and connections that simultaneously create patterns of
unity and change.

In our own time, the late David Bohm has developed a theory that
invites us to understand the universe as a flowing and unbroken wholeness.
Like Heraclitus, he views process, flux, and change as fundamental, arguing that the state of the universe at any point in time reflects a more basic
reality. He calls this reality the "implicate" (or "enfolded") order and distinguishes it from the "explicate" (or "unfolded") order manifested in the
world around us. Bohm argues that the empirical world realizes and
expresses potentialities existing within the implicate order.

Imagine a whirlpool in a river. While possessing relatively constant
form, it has no existence other than in the movement of the river. The anal-
ogy illustrates how an explicate order (whirlpool) flows out of the implicate
order in accordance with a coherent process of transformation.

This theory has important consequences, for it suggests that in order
to understand the secrets of the universe we have to understand the generative processes that link implicate and explicate orders.

FOUR "LOGICS OF CHANGE"

In this chapter we explore four generative processes that we will call
"logics of change":

- The first draws on the theory of autopoiesis, an interesting new perspective that puts the relationship between systems and their environment in a new light.

- The second draws on some of the latest insights of chaos and complexity theory, with a view to explaining how ordered patterns of
  activity can emerge from spontaneous self-organization.

- The third draws on related cybernetic ideas suggesting that change is
  enfolded in the strains and tensions found in circular relations.

- The fourth suggests that change is the product of dialectical tensions
  between opposites.

Each perspective offers a metaphorical frame for explaining how the explicit reality of organizational life is formed and transformed by underlying processes that have an order or logic of their own.

As you read, remember the whirlpool. Think about what it might take to change its configuration. Because that's what the following ideas are ultimately about. They seek to explain the nature of organizational whirlpools. Why·do they exist? How do they sustain themselves? What can be done to influence their course?

AUTOPOIESIS: THE LOGIC OF SELF-REFERENCE

Traditional approaches to organization theory have been dominated by the idea that change originates in the environment. As we saw in the organism chapter, the organization is typically viewed as an open system in constant interaction with its environment, transforming inputs into outputs as a means of creating the conditions necessary for survival. Changes in the environment are viewed as presenting challenges to which the organization must respond. Although there is great debate as to whether adaptation or selection is the primary factor influencing survival, there is agreement that the major problems facing modern organizations stem from changes in the external environment.

This basic idea is challenged by the implications of a new approach to systems theory developed by Humberto Maturana and Francisco Varela. They argue that all living systems are organizationally closed, autonomous systems of interaction that make reference only to themselves. The idea that living systems are open to an environment is, in their view, the product of an attempt to make sense of such systems from the standpoint of an external observer. Their theory challenges the validity of distinctions drawn between a system and its environment and offers a new perspective for understanding the processes through which living systems change.

Maturana and Varela base their argument on the idea that living systems are characterized by three principal features: autonomy, circularity, and self-reference. These lend them the ability to self-create or self-renew. Maturana and Varela have coined the term *autopoiesis* to refer to this capacity for self-production through a closed system of relations. They contend that the aim of autopoietic systems is ultimately to produce themselves; their own organization and identity is their most important product.

To illustrate these ideas, consider how Maturana and Varela reinterpret the way the human brain and nervous system operate. As we saw in the brain chapter, one of the most familiar images of the brain is that of an information processing system, importing information from the environment and initiating appropriate responses. The brain is viewed as making representations of the environment, recording these in memory, and modifying the information stored through experience and learning. In contrast, Maturana and Varela argue that the brain is closed, autonomous, circular, and self-referential. They argue that the brain does not process information from an environment as an independent domain and does not represent the environment in memory. Rather, it establishes and assigns patterns of variation and points of reference as expressions of its own mode of organization. The brain organizes its environment as an extension of itself.

If one thinks about it, the idea that the brain can make true representations of its environment presumes some external point of reference from which it is possible to judge the degree of correspondence between the representation and the reality. This implicitly presumes that the brain must have a capacity to see and understand its world from a point outside itself. Clearly, this cannot be so. Hence, the idea that the brain represents reality is open to serious question. Maturana and Varela's work identifies this paradox and suggests that the brain creates images of reality as expressions or descriptions of its own organization and interacts with these images, modifying them in the light of actual experience.

To those of us who have become used to thinking about organisms and organizations as open systems, this kind of circular reasoning may seem very strange indeed. We have learned to see living systems as distinct entities because we insist on understanding them from *our* point of view as observers rather than attempting to understand their inner logic. As my colleague Peter Harries-Jones has put it, in doing this we tend to confuse and mix the domain of organization with that of explanation. If we put ourselves "inside" such systems we come to realize that we are within a closed system of interaction and that the environment is *part of* the system's organization because it is part of its domain of essential interaction.

The theory of autopoiesis accepts that systems can be recognized as having "environments" but insists that relations with any environment are *internally* determined. There may be countless chains of interaction within and between systems, A being linked to B, to C, D, E, and so forth, but there is no independent pattern of causation. Changes in A do not cause changes in B, C, D, or E because the whole chain of relations is part of the same self-determining pattern. The system's pattern has to be understood as a whole and as possessing a logic of its own. It cannot be understood as a network of separate parts.

ENACTMENT AS A FORM OF NARCISSISM: ORGANIZATIONS INTERACTING WITH PROJECTIONS OF THEMSELVES

As metaphor, the theory of autopoiesis has intriguing implications for our understanding of organization.

- First, a creative interpretation of the theory helps us see that organizations are always attempting to achieve a form of self-referential closure in relation to their environments, enacting their environments as extensions of their own identity.

- Second, the perspective helps us understand that many of the problems that organizations encounter in dealing with their environments are intimately connected with the kind of identity that they try to maintain.

- Third, it helps us see that explanations of the evolution, change, and development of organizations must give primary attention to the factors that shape the patterns embracing both organization and environment in the broadest sense.

In the culture chapter, we discussed Karl Weick's idea that organizations enact their environments as people assign patterns of meaning and significance to the world in which they operate. The ideas on autopoiesis are very consistent with this perspective, encouraging us to view organizational enactments as part of the self-referential process through which an organization attempts to tie down and reproduce itself.

Consider the cartoon in exhibit 8.1. We find here a typical process of organizational self-reference. A meeting has been convened to discuss certain policy issues:

- Where do we stand?
- What's happening in the environment?
- What business are we in?
- Is it the right business?
- How can we penetrate new markets?

Questions such as these, which parallel those required to generate the kind of double-loop learning discussed in the brain chapter, allow those asking them to make representations of themselves, their organization, and the environment in a way that helps orient action to create or maintain a desirable identity. The charts that decorate the walls of the meeting room are really mirrors. Like the reflecting globe in Escher's lithograph (also exhibit 8.1), they allow members of the organization to see themselves within the context of their ongoing activity. The figures and pictures that

Autopoietic systems are closed loops: self-referential systems that strive to shape themselves in their own image.

Hand with reflecting globe. Self-portrait by M. C. Escher (lithograph, 1935).

Well Jack, where do we stand ?

Exhibit 8.1. Systems that look at themselves. Escher self-portrait reprinted by permission of Haags Gemeentemuseum, The Hague, and courtesy of Vorpal Gallery, San Francisco and New York City, by permission of the heirs of M. C. Escher. © M. C. Escher heirs c/o Cordon Arts-Baarn-Holland. Boardroom cartoon reproduced by permission of the artist.

an organization produces on market trends, competitive position, sales forecasts, raw material availability, and so forth are really projections of the organization's own sense of identity, interests, and concerns. They reflect its understanding of itself. It is through this process of self-reference that organizational members can intervene in their own functioning and thus participate in creating and maintaining their identity.

When we view the enactment process as an attempt to achieve a form of closure in relation to the environment, the whole idea of enactment assumes new significance. We come to realize that enactment is not just an arbitrary mode of perception whereby we see or emphasize certain things while ignoring or downplaying others. It is a core process that projects, defines, and produces a particular way of existing.

IDENTITY AND CLOSURE: EGOCENTRICISM
VERSUS SYSTEMIC WISDOM

Nowadays, many organizations are preoccupied with understanding their environment as a "world out there" that has an existence of its own. The ideas discussed above show the dangers in this kind of thinking and suggest that if one really wants to understand one's environment one must begin by understanding oneself.

Many organizations encounter great problems in dealing with the wider world because they do not recognize how they are a part of their environment. They see themselves as discrete entities faced with the problem of surviving *against* the vagaries of the outside world, which is often constructed as a domain of threat and opportunity.

Dangers of egocentricism

This is most evident in the practices of what I call *egocentric organizations*, which have a rather fixed notion of who they are or what they can be and are determined to impose or sustain that identity at all costs. This leads them to overemphasize the importance of themselves while underplaying the significance of the wider system of relations in which they exist.

When we look at ourselves in a mirror we create a relation between "figure," the face that we see, and "ground," the context in which our face is located. When we focus on our face, our context is nearly eliminated from view. The egocentric enactments through which organizations attempt to structure and understand their environments often manifest a similar imbalance. In their quest to see and promote their own sense of identity and perceived self-interest against that of the wider context, they create an overassertive relation between figure and ground. Just as a face in a mirror is dependent on a host of conditions for its existence, such as the biological processes that create and sustain the face and the physical and cultural conditions required for the existence of the mirror, the defining features of organizations are dependent on a host of less obvious contextual relations that must be maintained if the organization is to continue to exist. The figure and its ground are part of the same system of relations and exist only in relation with each other. In enacting and dealing with their environment in an egocentric way, organizations often do not understand their own complexity and the numerous recursive loops on which they depend.

As a result of this egocentricism, many organizations end up trying to sustain unrealistic identities or to produce identities that ultimately destroy important elements of the contexts of which they are part.

A good example of sustaining unrealistic identities is found in the watch and typewriter manufacturers that failed to take account of developments in digital and microprocessing technology. Seeing themselves as "watchmakers" or "typewriter firms," they continued in the production of traditional products with traditional technologies, failing to understand that these identities were no longer relevant or realistic. As a result, many were obliterated by new forms of competition. We can correctly say in retrospect that all firms serving the traditional markets *should have* seen and included the new developments as part of their environment. But this misses the important point: that their understanding of the environment was *a product of their identity* as watchmakers or typewriter manufacturers. The closure that this entailed blocked their ability to gain or create new information that would allow them to challenge and question the status quo. To be successful, they needed very different conceptions of themselves and of what their future might entail.

Good examples of how egocentricism can destroy the context on which an organization depends are found in many modern industries. Producers of toxic chemicals create all kinds of environmental and social hazards as a side effect of their interest in making profits. They implicitly treat the physical and social environment as a kind of external dumping ground, setting the basis for long-run problems that challenge their future viability. The pollution and health problems created by toxins are likely to eliminate or severely constrain the operations of this industry in the long term. Similarly, in agriculture the use of fertilizers, pesticides, fungicides, and other chemicals together with mechanized methods of farming can bring short-term profits while destroying the soil and other aspects of the ecology on which farming ultimately depends. The commercial fishing business is also in the process of destroying itself because, historically, the key actors involved have seen themselves as being separate from the fish. They have enacted identities in pursuit of short-term goals with the result that their actions have, in many parts of the world, already depleted the resource on which their business relies.

Egocentric organizations draw boundaries around narrow definitions of themselves and attempt to advance the self-interest of this narrow domain. Part of the problem rests in the very idea of what it means to be "an organization." The concept implies an entity, "a thing," something with a discrete existence. The principles of autopoiesis highlight the self-referential loops that this creates. An organization sees itself as separate, views its environment with separateness in mind, acts to sustain its separateness, interprets reactions to those actions from a separatist viewpoint, and so on. Many of the social ills of our time are associated with this kind of egocentric enactment and the kind of free-standing individualism it implies.

Systemic wisdom: Evolving identity

Egocentric organizations tend to see survival as hinging on the preservation of their own fixed and narrowly defined identity rather than on the evolution of the more fluid and open identity of the system to which they belong. As discussed in the politics chapter, part of the problem rests in the fact that it is often difficult for them to relinquish identities and strategies that have brought them into being or provided the basis for past success. Yet this is what survival and evolution often require. As in nature, many lines of organizational development, although viable and successful for a while, can prove to be dead ends. In the long run, survival can only be survival *with*, never survival against, the environment or context in which one is operating.

In seeing how our suppliers, market, labor force, local, national, and worldwide community, and even competition are really parts of the same system of organization, it becomes possible to move toward an appreciation of systemic interdependence. Many organizations have succeeded in making major breakthroughs by breaking and reshaping the boundaries traditionally drawn between themselves and their customers and competition, creating a new sense of identity for themselves and the system as a whole.

The challenge presented by the theory of autopoiesis is to understand how organizations change and transform themselves along with their environment, and to develop approaches to organization that can foster open-ended evolution. At times, this may seem a daunting task. But human systems, like organizations, have a special character in that they are able to reflect on their identities and on the processes and practices that sustain them. In doing so, they can often initiate meaningful patterns of change.

By learning to see themselves and the way they enact their relations with the broader environment, they create new potentials for transformation.

The three other logics of change that we will review in this chapter contribute to the transformation process. They offer different yet complementary ways of understanding how patterns of change unfold and how we can use this understanding to influence future development.

SHIFTING "ATTRACTORS": THE LOGIC OF CHAOS AND COMPLEXITY

Our metaphorical development of the theory of autopoiesis has emphasized the close links between organization and environment. Although it is common to draw a clear distinction between the two, it seems systemically wiser to view organization and environment as elements of the same interconnected *pattern*. In evolution, it is pattern that evolves.

In recent years, major insights on how pattern evolves have emerged from two related lines of development: the theory of chaos and self-organization, and complexity theory. Using physical experiments and computer simulations as metaphors for understanding what happens in nature, they contribute important elements to a holistic theory of change. The essence of their view is as follows:

> Complex nonlinear systems like ecologies or organizations are characterized by multiple systems of interaction that are both ordered and chaotic. Because of this internal complexity, random disturbances can produce unpredictable events and relationships that reverberate throughout a system, creating novel patterns of change. The amazing thing, however, is that despite all the unpredictability, coherent order *always* emerges out of the randomness and surface chaos.

Consider how order emerges from chaos when the behavior of complex systems is simulated through computer models that speed up the course of evolution. Patterns form and re-form over and over again:

- Create a multitude of computerized "birds," "bats," or "fish" that can move in any way they wish by establishing three simple rules: don't bump into one another; keep up with your neighbors; don't stray too far away. The result: dynamic flock patterns where the detailed movements are completely unpredictable, yet reflect the synchronized behavior of real birds, bats, and fish.

- Create computer "viruses" in a closed environment that are able to self-replicate, mutate at random, and compete for limited space. The result: simulation of evolutionary patterns, whereby one species secures dominance, is almost pushed to extinction by new forces, is modified and makes a comeback, is accompanied by dozens of new species, and so on! A diverse ecology of artificial life emerges with all the familiar characteristics of predator and prey and the parasitic and symbiotic relations found in nature.

- Observe a colony of termites building their nest, moving earth randomly. Variations in the terrain emerge. These then become the focus of attention. The termites add to the emerging mounds. "Columns" begin to develop. These are connected to form arches and tunnels producing a wonderful piece of termite "architecture." Random movements eventually produce coherent structures.

- We see a similar pattern in the emergent intelligence of the human brain and in the behavior of the mobots discussed in the brain chapter. Unpredictable events and behaviors acquire coherent form.

SPONTANEOUS SELF-ORGANIZATION

Whether we are examining the flocking of birds, the changing relationships between predators and prey, the development of weather patterns, complex chemical reactions, termite colonies, the hive behavior of bees, or the way in which organizations and social systems are transformed over time, we can detect common processes of spontaneous self-organization. If a system has a sufficient degree of internal complexity, randomness and diversity and instability become *resources* for change. New order is a natural outcome.

The influence of attractors

In their investigations, chaos theorists have paid particular attention to the way system behaviors tend to fall under the influence of different "attractors." For example, the attractor pattern mapped in exhibit 8.2 illustrates how a system can be caught in a trajectory where events are unique yet patterned, and how the behavior of the system can "flip" from one pattern to another.

To understand the significance of an attractor, engage in the following experiment. Imagine that you are sitting in the early morning sun on an open veranda. Before you there is a scene of complete tranquility: a perfectly smooth lake reflecting the bright blue sky and the greens of the forest surrounding the lake. Loons are calling. Occasionally they dive and resurface. The scene draws you into a mood of complete peace and harmony.

Now, let your attention drift to the room behind you. You focus on the click, click, click of the electric clock, on the gurgling of a noisy refrig-

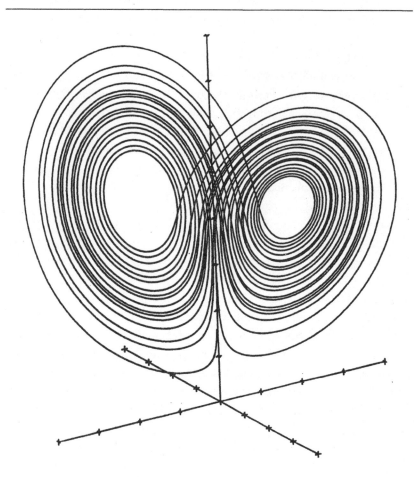

This image, based on the work of mathematician and meteorologist Edward Lorenz, has established itself as a powerful example of how complex systems combine order and disorder. The data plotted in this three-dimensional space show that although there is a clear pattern in the data, the behavior of the system is never repeated in exactly the same way. The "flip" or crossover from one "wing" of the pattern to the other results from random, nonlinear events that bring the system under the influence of a new set of attractions.

Exhibit 8.2. The Lorenz attractor, reproduced from J. Gleick, *Chaos: Making a New Science*, p. 28. © 1987, Penguin.

erator. A kitchen tap is also dripping. The sounds pull you out of the tranquil scene. Though your eyes may still be focused on the water, your mind is elsewhere.

In a very elementary sense you are caught between two attractors that define the context of two completely different situations. As you get pulled toward the one, the other becomes insignificant. When you are completely drawn into the lakeside scene, there are no discernible household noises. You only hear the loons. But if you are drawn to the clock, tap, and refrigerator, as many brainwashing techniques have revealed, the annoying noises *become* the dominant, indeed the all-embracing, reality.

Complex systems seem to have a natural tendency to get caught in tensions of this kind, falling under the influence of different attractors that ultimately define the contexts in which detailed system behaviors unfold. We see this in the examples presented earlier. Create a context defined by a few simple points of reference that are equivalent to the "minimum specs" discussed in the brain chapter, and random fluctuations will self-organize into a coherent form.

Chaos theorists have noted that complex systems can fall under the influence of different types of attractors. Some pull a system into states of equilibrium or near equilibrium, for example, as a result of negative feedback loops that counteract destabilizing fluctuations. Other attractors have a tendency to flip a system into completely new configurations, as in the case of the "Lorenz attractor" in exhibit 8.2, which illustrates how a system can be drawn under the influence of different sets of reference points that define competing contexts. The detailed behavior of the system depends on which context dominates.

Bifurcation points: Forks in the road of change

In explaining how systems can transform themselves, chaos theorists have become particularly interested in understanding what happens when a system is "pushed" far from its equilibrium toward an "edge of chaos" situation.

Here, it encounters "bifurcation points" that are rather like "forks in a road" leading to different futures. At such points the energy within the system can self-organize through unpredictable leaps into different system states. If the old dominant attractor can dissipate the energy and instability, potential changes get dissolved and the system reverts to a variation of its former state. If, on the other hand, a new set of influences gains the upper hand, it can "attract" the energies to a new configuration.

Bifurcation points and associated attractors always exist as latent *potentials* within any complex nonlinear system. They signal potentials for self-organization and the evolution of new form. However, the path of system evolution is completely unpredictable because, given the complexity and nonlinearity of the system, seemingly insignificant changes can unfold to create large effects.

The famous image is of the "butterfly effect," whereby a small change as insignificant as a butterfly flapping its wings in Peking can influence weather patterns in the Gulf of Mexico. Or, as science writer Kevin Kelly has put it, in complex nonlinear systems "2 + 2 = apples."

Under conditions of nonlinearity and randomness, incremental changes that may themselves seem insignificant can precipitate major discontinuous or qualitative changes because of the emergent properties triggered by marginal adjustments. The butterfly in China doesn't "cause" a new weather pattern. That's the old linear logic at work. The significance of the butterfly is that it triggers a small change that perhaps triggers another small change and another and another that by chance proves to be a significant random element, catalyzing changes that ultimately shift a system from the influence of one attractor pattern to another. Quantum and qualitative change occur *incrementally!* Thus 2 + 2 does not necessarily lead to 4 or even 5 or 6. It leads to the emergence of qualitatively new system states.

MANAGING IN THE MIDST OF COMPLEXITY

These insights have enormous implications for modern management, giving rise to at least five key ideas for guiding the management of change. In a nutshell, they suggest that it is important to

- rethink what we mean by organization, especially the nature of hierarchy and control,
- learn the art of managing and changing contexts,
- learn how to use small changes to create large effects,
- live with continuous transformation and emergent order as a natural state of affairs, and
- be open to new metaphors that can facilitate processes of self-organization.

The emergent nature of organization, hierarchy, and control

As we saw in our discussion of the emergent character of learning and intelligence in the brain chapter, complexity theory invites managers to rethink the nature of order and organization. Instead of seeing these qualities as states that can be externally imposed on a situation through hierarchical means or through the predetermined logic that we bring to the design of bridges or buildings, managers are invited to view them as *emergent* properties. New order emerges in *any* complex system that, because of internal and external fluctuations, is pushed into "edge of chaos" situations. Order is natural! It is emergent and free! But most interesting of all, its precise nature can *never* be planned or predetermined.

Note that in all of our discussions of complexity, whether in the preceding pages or in our discussion of the brain in chapter 4, no mention has been made of any grand design. There has been no mention of a master manager or grand architect. There *has* been discussion of how order can evolve under the influence of a number of simple rules (minimum specs). But no mention has been made of any absolute ordering or predesign.

This can have frightening consequences for managers who have become used to the props of planning, structure, hierarchy, and other traditional modes of control. But the message of chaos and complexity theory is that while some kind of ordering is always likely to be a feature of complex systems, structure and hierarchy can have no fixed form, hence cannot function as predetermined modes of control. Patterns have to emerge. They cannot be imposed.

Consider the activities of a self-organizing work team involved with the development of a new product, or an autonomous work group operating in a just-in-time, flexible factory. Hierarchical and other structural patterns are likely to develop as different team members, functions, or activities take a leading role, or as different priorities create a focus of attention. But the pattern evolves and finds its own form.

Under such conditions, hierarchy and associated patterns or organization and control are temporary conditions or *outcomes*. They are no more than "snapshot points" on a self-organizing journey. Moreover, the hierarchies that emerge are likely to be created and driven from any point within the system. Authoritarian "top-down" hierarchies found in mechanistic organizations give way to emergent hierarchies generated by the need to cluster and direct activities to address the contingencies at hand. Managers functioning in the midst of this kind of complexity are part of the flux. They need mindsets that allow them to facilitate the process and flow with the change rather than try to predesign and control in a more traditional way.

The art of managing and changing "context"

A second extremely important implication of a chaos-complexity perspective rests in the idea that *the fundamental role of managers is to shape and create "contexts" in which appropriate forms of self-organization can occur.* Managers have to become skilled in helping to shape the "minimum specs" that can define an appropriate context, while allowing the details to unfold

Let's use the image of a Lorenz attractor as a creative metaphor for thinking about organizational change. Here are some of the questions that are raised:

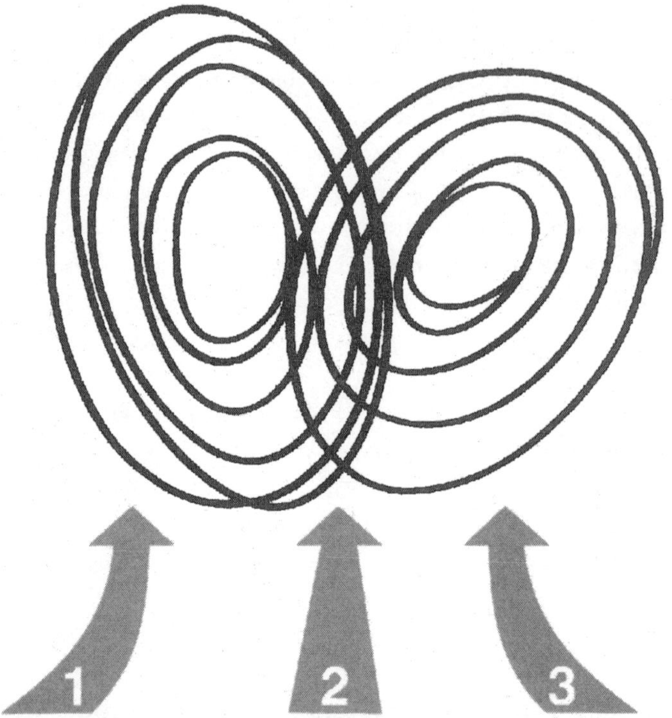

1 What are the forces locking an organization into its existing "attractor" pattern?

Structures?
Hierarchies?
Rules?
Controls?
Culture?
Defensive routines?
Power relations?
Psychic traps?

Is the "attractor" appropriate? Should it be changed?

2 If change is required, how is the transition from one attractor to another to be achieved?

How can small changes be used to create large effects?

3 What are the ground rules of the new attractor going to be?

How can we manage through the "edge of chaos" of stage 2 while remaining open to emergent self-organization?

Exhibit 8.3. Attractor patterns and organizational change

within this frame. In this way, they can help to shape emergent processes of self-organization, while avoiding the trap of imposing too much control.

The focus on attractor patterns creates a powerful perspective for the management of stability and the management of change, suggesting that *transformational change ultimately involves the creation of "new contexts" that can break the hold of dominant attractor patterns in favor of new ones.* The key principles underlying this approach are summarized in exhibit 8.3.

To illustrate the challenge of maintaining stability, consider the case of a hospital emergency operating room. The challenge here is to create a relatively stable space within which the surgical team can self-organize around the contingencies and challenges being faced. The context will be bombarded by all kinds of random influences: unanticipated or uncontrollable risks of infection, patients with unknown medical histories, an unpredictable case-load, unexpected changes in personnel. The challenge is to hold such a situation under the influence of a strong attractor pattern that minimizes disrupting influences so that the surgical team can do an effective job.

In other situations where the dominant attractor pattern is sustaining an undesirable state, the challenge will be to open the door to instability, or even to *create* the instability that will help a new pattern of behavior to emerge.

Continuing with our hospital-based example, consider the challenge of shifting major medical services out of the hospital into the community by using new modes of service delivery. This change may be hindered by the forces of the dominant attractor system within the hospital, such as those sustained by established mindsets, power-bases, vested interests, and existing codes of practice. Typically, these forces will undermine the change by pulling the new initiative back under the control of the established system, creating a long-term pattern of business as usual.

To break the power of the established attractor, our manager will have to find ways of creating a new context. One strategy may be to transform the mindsets of key physicians and administrators by dramatizing the fiscal realities, by demonstrating the viability of new innovations, or by highlighting the new forms of emerging competition that are underpinning the need for change. Another way may be to change the context by mobilizing a powerful coalition of key individuals that can launch and protect a prototype of a new system. Or, steps may be taken to transfer the responsibility for delivery of these services to a completely new organization, for example, through some kind of subcontracting arrangement.

Such proposals or actions would create great instability within the established system. This instability would have to be nudged and pushed toward the critical point at which key players are inclined to reconsider the viability of the hospital's established sense of identity so that the system can evolve into a new form, for example, where principles of community-based health care define key elements of the new context.

It is important to note that the manager acting on the insights of chaos and complexity theory cannot be in control of the change. He or she cannot define the precise form that the new attractor pattern will take. While it is possible to shape or nurture key elements of the emerging context by opening the old system to new information, new experiences, new modes of service delivery, new criteria for assessing quality, and so on, the resulting attractor will find its own form. The important point is that the manager helps to create the conditions under which the new context can emerge. To the extent that the system remains locked into the old context, no significant change is possible. This is the key problem that blocks so many organizations that are trying to transform themselves. Because of the power of the established context, they end up trying to do the new in old ways.

As chaos writer Jeffrey Goldstein has noted, much of the literature on organizational change has focused on the problem of "resistance," instead of focusing on how new attractors can "pull" the latent energies of a system to a point where they can organize into a new form. Resistance arises when the forces of an established attractor are more powerful than those of a new or emergent one. The challenge is to shift the balance.

This is what the art of creating new contexts helps us to do. New contexts can be created by generating *new understandings* of a situation, or by engaging in *new actions*.

New understandings can transform the autopoietic processes of self-reference through which a system produces and reproduces its basic sense of identity by exposing the system to new information about itself or its environment and by encouraging the kind of double-loop learning discussed in the brain chapter. The system can begin to challenge and change its operating norms, paradigms, and assumptions and free itself from the cognitive and other psychic traps that sustain its established attractor pattern.

As noted in our discussion of autopoiesis, the very idea that an organization thinks about itself as a discrete organization may be a key feature of its dominant attractor, leading it to try and survive as a discrete entity instead of allowing itself to evolve into a new form. For example, as a result of a new understanding of its situation, the hospital in our earlier example may be able to develop a new identity where it becomes part of an evolving network of services rather than hanging onto an unsustainable one.

New contexts can also be created by engaging in *new actions* that help to push the system into a new state more directly. Experiments, prototypes, changes in rewards, changes in key personnel, a fiscal crisis, staff layoffs, and numerous other events, actions, and experiences can themselves embody powerful messages that catalyze other changes in the context as the system adjusts itself to the new reality.

While new understandings can create a heightened sense of the need for change and a direction in which an organization may feel it needs to go, new actions help to get it there. The conventional way of thinking about organizational change follows this sequential order. But from a chaos perspective, it often needs to be reversed: new action can catalyze new understandings.

A hospital that creates a powerful prototype of new service delivery in action or subcontracts an important set of services to an organization that could develop into a potential competitor can create a dramatic new understanding of the status quo. The generation of new understandings and new actions, in whatever order they evolve, are the keys to contextual change.

Using small changes to create large effects

A third major implication of the chaos-complexity perspective, and one that brings a great deal of pragmatism to the task of managing and changing contexts, rests in the idea that in "edge-of-chaos" situations, small but critical changes at critical times can trigger major transforming effects. The image from the natural world is of the butterfly effect. But in complex human systems the principle assumes a new and even more powerful dimension because human beings have the ability to reflect on their contexts and to choose the points at which they intervene. It follows that any persons wishing to change the context in which they are operating should search for "doable" high-leverage initiatives that can trigger a transition from one attractor to another.

Chaos theory also gives clear indications of where managers should look for these initiatives. As will be recalled, the tensions between competing attractors generate bifurcation points leading to different paths of future development. Most often these manifest themselves as paradoxes or tensions between the status quo and alternative future states.

In our hospital situation, the drive toward a new system of community-based health care may generate all kinds of oppositions from the status quo, expressed as potential crises. For example, physicians or senior administrators may feel that community-based services will lead to poorer quality, less control, falling standards, and loss of power. Normally these fears and concerns will generate actions seeking to reinforce the current situation.

The chaos manager must recognize these forks in the road and create a context supporting the new line of development by finding interventions that transcend the paradoxes or make them irrelevant. For example, by creating a successful prototype or by getting key opinion leaders behind the initiative, he or she may be able to create the crucial time and space in which success can be demonstrated, publicized, and made irreversible. The task of creating new context often hinges on the management of this kind of paradox.

The basic ideas involved here allow us to talk about the skills of creating new contexts in precise terms. In particular, they suggest that if managers can learn to identify emerging paradoxes, or if necessary, create paradoxes that embody the tensions between the status quo and a desired future, they can identify important points of leverage that can be used to undermine the force of the status quo in favor of a new future. The task hinges on finding new understandings or new actions that can reframe the paradox in a way that unleashes system energies in favor of the new line of development.

Chaos theorists who have begun to look at the implications of this perspective for the management of change talk a great deal about the need to push systems into far-from-equilibrium states by generating instabilities and crises that will "flip" a system from one trajectory to another. The above ideas refine what is involved here and help to show how the chaos manager can begin to tread the fine line that often arises between nudging or flipping the trajectory of a complex system, on the one hand, and the creation of sheer anarchy on the other.

The challenge of managing complex systems often seems completely overwhelming. The complexity defies comprehensive analysis, and it is often difficult to know where to intervene. The above ideas encourage us to cut through this complexity and focus on a few key principles that offer the promise of achieving quantum change *incrementally!*

In much of the management literature, quantum and incremental change are seen as opposites. Quantum change is seen as being produced through large initiatives. Incremental change is viewed as the route to marginal improvements. While this is true under conditions of linearity, in complex nonlinear systems small incremental changes can produce large quantum effects. If people focus on finding high-leverage initiatives within their sphere of influence that have the capacity to shift the context, potentials for major change can be unleashed.

There are at least two ways in which this can occur:

- First, small changes may in themselves catalyze a major change because the change itself proves pivotal. In our health care example, a successful experiment prototyping a new health care delivery system may prove to be the crucial change that transforms the context of opinion among key power holders in the hospital.

- Second, small changes can also create a *critical mass effect*. Though small and insignificant in themselves, together they build an overwhelming force.

In the management of complex systems, both processes can be mobilized in a way that overcomes the conventional dichotomy drawn between incremental and quantum change.

Living with emergence as a natural state of affairs

In complex systems no one is ever in a position to control or design system operations in a comprehensive way. Form emerges. It cannot be imposed, and there are no end states. At best, would-be managers have to be content with an ability to nudge and push a system in a desired direction by shaping critical parameters that can influence the course of system evolution. In developing mindsets and skills appropriate for this task, they can benefit from understanding the principles of holographic self-organization, discussed in the brain chapter, especially in terms of the point that a focus on the role of limits and minimum specs can play in creating a space in which coherent self-organization can emerge. These concepts can be crucial in helping managers encourage the emergence of desired forms without dictating their detailed nature.

Managers can also benefit from a perspective that views every initiative as a systemic "probe" and learning opportunity. In discussing the art of creating new contexts, much has been made of the use of experiments and prototypes as a means of shifting attractor patterns. Successful experiments can go a long way in creating a foothold on a new reality. In particular, they offer important insights on the feedback loops and defensive routines that sustain a dominant attractor pattern and on what can be done to help a new one emerge.

The chaos manager must also develop a heightened awareness of the importance of "boundary management." New experiments often get neutralized by the status quo, so it is vital that the chaos manager become skilled in the art of managing boundaries: building them when it is necessary to shield an initiative from the forces of an old attractor and breaking them when the initiative is strong enough to survive on its own.

A manager seeking to promote the transformation to community-based health care in our hospital example may need to hide and protect radical experiments in their early stages or they will never get off the ground. But once successful, he or she may wish to drive their extensions in a very visible way. New images and metaphors of the manager's role are often needed to help in this task and to cope with the ambiguity, paradox, pressures, and uncertainties that the absence of fixed states and clear endpoints entails.

The challenge of nurturing processes of continuous self-organization demands that we find new metaphors for conceptualizing the task. The research on chaos and complexity is full of resonant images based on the behavior of termite colonies, beehives, and other processes that illustrate the nature of self-organizing systems. They provide a valuable resource for carrying organization and management theory into a new domain.

LOOPS NOT LINES: THE LOGIC OF MUTUAL CAUSALITY

The theories of autopoiesis, chaos, and complexity encourage us to understand how change unfolds through circular patterns of interaction and how organizations evolve or disappear along with changes occurring in the broader context. They invite managers to think more systemically about this context and the evolving pattern to which they belong. This requires that we think about change in terms of loops rather than lines and to replace the idea of mechanical causality, for example, that A causes B, with the idea of mutual causality, which suggests that A and B may be co-defined as a consequence of belonging to the same system of circular relations.

Numerous cyberneticians have attempted to develop methodologies for studying mutual causality and how systems engage in their own trans-formation. One of the most notable contributions is found in the work of Magorah Maruyama, who focuses on positive and negative feedback in shaping system dynamics. Maruyama observes that

- processes of negative feedback, where a change in a variable initiates counteracting forces leading to changes in the opposite direction, are important in accounting for the stability of systems, and

- processes characterized by positive feedback, where more leads to more and less to less, are important in accounting for escalating patterns of system change.

Together, these feedback mechanisms can explain why systems gain or preserve a given form and how this form can be elaborated and transformed over time.

The power of feedback loops was dramatically illustrated in the Club of Rome's project on the predicament of mankind, which pioneered the idea that we should understand world economics as a system of loops. Its report, *Limits to Growth,* focused on trends in world population, pollution, food production, and resource depletion, suggesting that these are driven by loops of positive feedback. Its analysis demonstrated how systems of positive feedback that do not have stabilizing loops can result in exponential change that cannot be sustained in the long run.

The characteristics of exponential change are beautifully illustrated in the story of an ancient Persian courtier who presented a chessboard to his king. In return he asked to receive one grain of rice for the first square on the board, two for the second, four for the third, and so on. The king readily agreed, ordering rice to be brought from his store. The fourth square required eight grains, the tenth 512, the fifteenth 16,384, and the twenty-first topped the million mark. By the fortieth square a million million grains had to be brought forth. The entire rice supply was exhausted long before the sixty-fourth square was reached!

Exponential change is change that *increases* at a constant rate, in this case doubling at each stage. And the moral is easy to see. The change seems fine for a while but soon runs completely out of control, just as a constantly increasing rate of pollution or overfishing that begins by killing a few fish will soon kill them all. Many aspects of economic and social life seem to be changing in this way.

Magorah Maruyama has developed this kind of loop analysis, showing how positive feedback accounts for the differentiation of complex systems. For example, a small crack in a rock may collect water, which freezes and makes the crack larger, permitting more water to collect and the crack to get bigger and bigger, allowing small organisms and earth to collect, a seed to grow, and the rock to be transformed by the growth of vegetation and perhaps even a tree. The runaway process creates differentiation, which may then be sustained in a given form by processes of negative feedback. Or, to take another of Maruyama's examples, a large homogeneous plain attracts a farmer, who settles on a given spot. Other farmers follow, and one of them opens a tool shop. The shop becomes a meeting place, and a food stand is established next to the shop. Gradually, a village grows as merchants, suppliers, farmhands, and others are attracted to it. The village facilitates the marketing of agricultural products, and more farms develop around the village. Increased agricultural activity encourages the development of industry, and the village gradually becomes a city. In the process, the homogeneous plain has been transformed by a series of positive feedback loops that amplify the effects of the initial differentiation.

The secret of the growth of the city, like the growth of the crack that collects water and vegetation, does not rest in any simple cause but in the deviation-amplifying *process*. As in the case of the butterfly effect, small changes can produce large effects. Initial kicks of high probability (e.g., that water will collect in a crack or that a farmer will settle on a plain) can escalate to produce deviations that have a very low probability (e.g., that a particular tree will grow in a particular crack or that a city will develop at a particular point on a homogeneous plain). Random mutations in nature and accidental events and connections in social life, given favorable circumstances, initiate open-ended processes of self-organization in which positive and negative feedback interact to produce changing patterns that may at some point assume relatively stable forms.

The relevance of mutual causality for understanding the events and processes that shape organizations and their contexts is that it can be used to understand the dynamics of many different kinds of organizational problems.

MUTUAL CAUSALITY AND ORGANIZATIONAL PROBLEMS

Exhibit 8.4 presents a contextual analysis of some of the relations contributing to price inflation. Most analyses of this problem tend to "think in lines," searching for simple causes that lie at the root of the problem. The level of employment, money supply, trade union power, wage rates, interest rates, and government spending have all at one time or another been identified as the root cause.

Linear thinking sets the basis for linear solutions, such as to increase unemployment, reduce the money supply, reduce trade union power, introduce wage restrictions, increase interest rates, or reduce government spending. The contextual analysis diagrammed in exhibit 8.4 offers an alternative way of thinking about the problem by revealing the *pattern of relations* that create and sustain inflation. Our attention now is directed toward an understanding of how the network of positive feedback loops that amplify price rises can be stabilized through negative feedback. We are encouraged to find ways of redefining the total system to strengthen the pattern of relations that we wish to maintain.

The following account of Great Britain's "mad cow" problem applies feedback loop analysis to how the issue escalated completely out of control into a major European crisis, threatening the collapse of the beef industry.

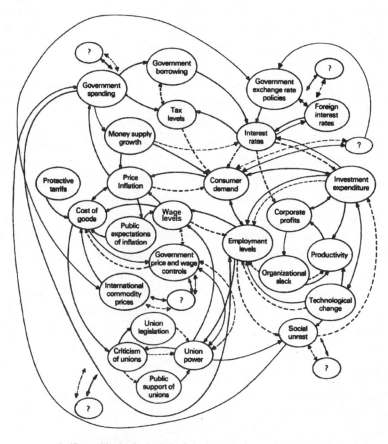

—— signifies positive feedback relations where more leads to more and less leads to less
◄----- signifies negative feedback relations where changes in one direction are associated with changes in the opposite direction

When we understand the problem of price inflation as a system of mutual causality defined by many interacting forces, we are encouraged to think in loops rather than lines. No single factor is the cause of the problem. Price inflation is enfolded in the nature of the relations that define the total system. Many of the links represented in this diagram are deviation amplifying (heavy lines); negative feedback relations (dotted lines) are more sparse. Positive feedback thus gains the upper hand. The system can be stabilized by strengthening existing negative feedback loops and creating others. Many government policies implicitly attempt to have this effect. For example, wage and price controls and unemployment policies introduce negative feedback loops that attempt to moderate the wage-price spiral. Government or media criticism of trade unions as unreasonable "villians" attempts to weaken the positive feedback loop between public support and union power.

In understanding this kind of mutual causality, we recognize that it is not possible to exert unilateral control over any set of variables. Interventions are likely to reverberate throughout the whole. It is thus necessary to adjust interventions to achieve the kind of *system* transformation that one desires, often by modifying key subsytems.

Exhibit 8.4. Price inflation as a system of mutual causality

"Mad cows"

The problem started in the early 1980s when diseased sheep brains were used in the production of cattle food. Several cows were observed "dancing" and stumbling in British fields and farmyards. The problem was identified as bovine spongiform encephalopathy (BSE) and labeled by the British press as "mad cow disease." Public fears about eating beef began to develop but were quickly countered by the British government and medical opinion: Beef, it was declared, was perfectly safe to eat. No real action or concern was necessary.

But still the problem festered. Media publicity continued.

In 1989, the British government began to take action by banning sale of diseased cattle. They hoped that this would make the problem go away. But the festering concerns continued until 1996, when the medical committee that had originally pronounced beef safe to eat reversed its position, announcing a connection between ten deaths of young British people from Creutzfeldt-Jakob disease, which seemed to be linked to BSE.

Panic hit the British media, with angry scenes in Parliament denouncing the "mind-boggling incompetence" of the British government in not taking swift action ten years before. The media carried forecasts of up to 500,000 human deaths and called for the slaughter of all eleven million British cattle at a cost of up to $40 billion. It was estimated that the eventual cost to Great Britain could be one percent of its gross domestic product.

The British government, backed by most scientific opinion, clung to its belief that beef was perfectly safe and that the ten deaths had resulted from contact with diseased animals, not from eating beef. The British public, fed by the media frenzy and dramatic scenes in Parliament, was unconvinced. Beef sales plummeted. McDonald's and other major food and retail chains joined the parade, declaring that they were no longer using British beef. The European Community, fearful about the collapse of the whole European beef market, tried to contain the problem to British shores. It declared a state of emergency, banning the import and sale of British cattle. Countries throughout the world quickly followed.

The British government still declared that British beef was safe. But there were no buyers in sight. The whole British beef market had collapsed: no confidence at home, let alone worldwide. Within days the government was obliged to completely reverse its position, agreeing to the slaughter of 4.7 million cattle, even though existing scientific evidence showed that virtually all British cattle were now completely healthy and disease free.

We see here the power of positive feedback loops and how they can run completely out of control. The case is undoubtedly an extreme one, but

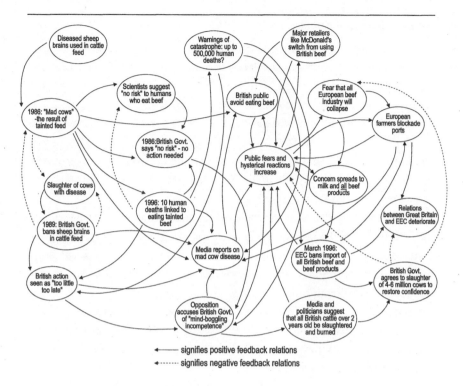

Exhibit 8.5. The "mad cow" phenomenon

the same process can be observed in countless situations: in how the Watergate burglary led to the fall of the Nixon administration in the United States; in the accumulating errors and oversights underlying the *Challenger* space shuttle disaster; and in the rapid collapse of the USSR, the Berlin Wall, and the political and economic structure of most of Eastern Europe. At a more modest scale, the phenomenon is experienced in millions of personal, family, and organizational situations where years of stalemate get flipped into patterns of anarchy and breakdown. Often, our explanations and analysis of such situations tend to focus on a search for villains or for a specific "cause." But more realistically, the phenomenon resides within the overall pattern of positive and negative feedback. Revisit the dynamics in exhibit 8.5. Negative feedback loops are very weak.

Identifying key patterns

When we analyze situations as loops rather than lines, we invariably arrive at a rich picture of the system under consideration. This can have its advantages in that the analysis highlights key connections and provides a way of identifying the configuration of positive and negative feedback loops defining a particular context or "attractor pattern." It also shows the points at which it may be desirable to intervene either to reinforce the existing attractor or to help the shift to a new one. But the richness and sheer complexity of the analysis can be overwhelming. So a balance often has to be struck to make the methodology pragmatic.

One of the tactics that can be used involves the search for key system patterns by trying to identify the particular configuration of positive and negative feedback loops that are shaping a situation. As Peter Senge suggests, it is often possible to detect distinct system *archetypes* that, once recognized, help to create general strategies of systems management. Applying this approach to the analysis of detailed organizational problems, Senge shows that many systems tend to be inherently unstable because of *delayed feedback and response* between elements, which leads people to underplay or exaggerate their behaviors.

The "mad cow" case offers a good example. No action, or "too little too late," can precipitate major swings in a system. The slaughter of a few thousand cattle in the 1980s could have saved the slaughter of four million later on. But in other situations, delayed action may be the best response because problems may prove to be nonproblems and disappear on their own.

Other systems may constantly *hit constraints* that prevent full development. For example, high production levels may hit manufacturing or resource constraints; the development of team skills or team spirit may plateau and then decline. In such situations, the systemically wise response will focus on removing the constraints that are holding key processes back.

In yet other systems, positive feedback loops may be *escalating* and driving a system into a destructive state. For example, team members may be so competitive that in trying to outperform each other they end up eroding each other's success. In such situations, the effective strategy may be to introduce system modifications through new loops that can create win-win outcomes.

Systems where individual elements can destroy the whole

In situations where individuals feed off a common resource without regard for the well-being of the whole system, we find a "Tragedy of the Commons" problem, where the resource ends up being completely destroyed.

This system archetype was originally identified by ecologist Garrett Hardin, who took the image of animals being allowed to graze common land and "grazing it to destruction" as a pattern that we find in the depletion of resources worldwide. There is short-term logic in farmers allowing their animals to eat as much of the common grass as possible. But the process pushes the system beyond the point of regeneration. The same process is destroying the world fishing industry and many aspects of the forestry and agricultural business. It is found in the dynamics of many social and corporate welfare systems and in the way individuals and organizations plunder long-term benefits for short-term gains. Solutions depend on the development of shared understandings of the problem, and an ability to reframe system dynamics so that short-term individual interest and long-term sustainability and development become more balanced and integrated.

LIMITATIONS AND STRENGTHS OF LOOP ANALYSIS

The complexity of most social systems is such that the analysis can rarely be complete because the problem or focus with which one starts often ends up being part of a larger problem requiring a broader focus. For example, in examining the details of exhibits 8.4 and 8.5 it is easy to see how new loops could be included to make the analysis even more comprehensive. In using loop analysis, short-cuts and compromises have to be struck. Otherwise, analysis leads to paralysis. In addition, since complex nonlinear systems are constantly unfolding, their form only becomes truly clear with hindsight.

But the methodology still has great power:

- It invites us to understand the key patterns that are shaping system dynamics, especially those that are locking the system into vicious circles because of clusters of positive feedback loops.

- It encourages us to approach organizational and social problems with a mindset that respects patterns of mutual causality and cultivates what Gregory Bateson has described as "systemic wisdom."

- Instead of thinking about problems mechanistically and trying to manipulate linear "causes" and "effects," it encourages us to develop mindsets and skills that focus on recognizing and changing patterns.

- It provides a methodology for acting on insights about the nature of autopoiesis and for modifying the self-referential processes that create system identity. It provides a methodology for analyzing a system's attractor patterns and for changing their trajectory.

- It provides further insights on how small changes can create large effects.

Loop analysis also raises some of the important questions that need to be asked in the management of complexity:

- What are the significant loops defining a system?

- Are there principal subsystems or nests of loops that hang together? What are the key connections? What are the key patterns?

- Can we use this understanding to go beyond surface appearance and superficial problems to identify the generative forces that are producing those problems?

- Given our understanding of system dynamics, where is the best place to intervene?

- Can we find manageable initiatives that will change the generative pattern, for example, by adding or removing positive or negative feedback loops?

- How can we learn to nudge key aspects of such systems to create new contexts, through our equivalent of the butterfly effect?

CONTRADICTION AND CRISIS: THE LOGIC OF DIALECTICAL CHANGE

THE STUDY OF OPPOSITES

Any phenomenon implies and generates its opposite. Day and night, hot and cold, good and evil, life and death, positive and negative are pairs of self-defining opposites. In each case, the existence of one side depends on the existence of the other. We cannot know what is cold without knowing what is hot. We cannot conceive of day without knowing night. Good defines evil, and life defines death. Opposites are intertwined in a state of tension that also defines a state of harmony and wholeness. Could this tension lie at the basis of all change? Could flux and transformation be a manifestation of contradictory tendencies through which phenomena change themselves?

This idea has a long history. Taoist philosophy, which originated in ancient China, has long emphasized how the way of nature (the word *Tao* means "way") is characterized by a continuous flux and wholeness shaped by the dynamic interplay of *yin* and *yang* (exhibit 8.6). These words, which originally denoted the dark and sunny sides of a hill, symbolize how the Tao is underpinned by a flow of complementary yet opposite energies through which all trends eventually reverse themselves. Whenever a situation develops extreme qualities, it invariably turns around and assumes opposite qualities, just as the brightest light of day begins to pass into the pitchest dark

The dynamic character of *yin* and *yang* is illustrated by the ancient Chinese symbol called *T'ai-chi T'u,* or "Diagram of the Supreme Ultimate."

This diagram is a symmetrical arrangement of the dark *yin* and the bright *yang,* but the symmetry is not static. It is a rotational symmetry suggesting, very forcefully, a continuous cyclic movement: The *yang* returns cyclically to its beginning, the *yin* attains its maximum and gives place to the *yang.* The two dots in the diagram symbolize the idea that each time one of the two forces reaches its extreme, it contains in itself already the seed of its opposite. From very early times, the two archetypal poles of nature were represented not only by bright and dark but also by male and female, firm and yielding, above and below. *Yang,* the strong, male, creative power, was associated with Heaven, whereas *yin,* the dark, receptive, female and maternal element, was represented by the Earth. Heaven is above and full of movement. The Earth—in the old geocentric view—is below and resting. Thus *yang* came to symbolize movement and *yin* rest. In the realm of thought, *yin* is the complex, female, intuitive main, *yang* the clear and rational male intellect. *Yin* is the quiet, contemplative stillness of the sage, *yang* the strong, creative action of the king.

Exhibit 8.6. Yin and yang: the primordial opposites guiding all change

of night. Taoist philosophy emphasizes that all of natural and human life is shaped by this cycle of coming and going, growth and decay, everything being in the process of becoming something else.

Many of these Taoist notions have had a strong influence on the work of Hegel and Marx, who developed the dialectical view that the world evolves as a result of internal tensions between opposites into powerful theories of social change. In the following sections we will use a neo-Marxian perspective to analyze social change and then shift to an organizational level to grasp some managerial applications of dialectical thinking.

With the political collapse of the USSR and Eastern Europe, Marxist ideology and philosophy seem distinctly passé. Yet, ironically, the basic method that propelled Marxian analysis has never been more relevant for understanding the core problems facing Western society.

Marx's three dialectical principles

Marxian method is a dialectical method that focuses on how the interplay of opposites fuels social change and how all societies have a tendency to transform and, in many respects, destroy themselves because of inner contradictions that cannot be contained. In the view of many social commentators, Western society, despite the political and ideological victories over Eastern communism, is now in such a position. It is being transformed by social and economic contradictions that will ultimately lay the grounds for a completely new kind of society to emerge. While it is clear that this society will have precious little in common with the communist utopia that Marx envisaged, it is very likely to be shaped by responses to the core contradictions that he identified as lying at the base of the capitalist system. Remembering that the substance of what follows is about *method*, not about the radical ideologies with which Marx is now most often associated, let's engage in some Marxian thinking about social change.

The thrust of Marx's social analysis can be understood as the expression of three dialectical principles that combine to provide a complex explanation of the processes that set the basis for both gradual and revolutionary kinds of change.

Principle 1 refers to the mutual struggle, or unity of opposites. It accounts for processes of self-generated change whereby phenomena change themselves as a result of tension with their opposites. This principle underpins the idea of contradiction and explains how one social arrangement inevitably gives way to another. For example, an act whereby one person attempts to rule or control another tends to set up a process of resistance or countercontrol that undermines the initial attempt at control.

The act of control *itself* sets up consequences that work against its effectiveness.

Principle 2 refers to the negation of the negation. It explains how change may become developmental in the sense that each negation rejects a previous form, yet also retains something from that form. An act of control may be negated by an act of countercontrol, which is in turn negated by a further act of control (the negation of the negation) and so on. Each successive pattern of control will retain an element of the previous negation.

Principle 3 refers to the transformation of quantity into quality. It accounts for processes of revolutionary change whereby one form of social organization gives way to another. In nature, there are many processes where changes in quantity eventually lead to a change in quality. Water will absorb increases in temperature until the boiling point, when it then changes into steam. A camel can be loaded with more and more weight until the final straw breaks its back. Similar processes can be observed in patterns of social organization. A process of control and countercontrol may continue until control is no longer possible, leading to a new phase of collaborative or destructive activity. Cumulative changes in society may provide the platform for a revolution that changes the underlying basis of that society.

When we combine these three dialectical principles, we arrive at a rich and complex picture of the nature of change. Marx's analysis of society stresses that social arrangements generate inner contradictions that defeat the purposes for which they were set up, leading to a continuing pattern of negation and counternegation. The negation of the negation allows for the progressive development of the system until a limit is reached where its inner contradictions can no longer be contained.

Marx and the contradictions in work organization

For Marx, "capital," by which he meant the surplus value that arises as a result of trading goods and services at a profit, embraces a fundamental contradiction because it puts people in a state of opposition. Buyers are pitted against sellers, just as employers (Marx's capitalists) depend for their profit on paying their employees less than what the product of their labor is worth in the marketplace. This view ignores the idea that employer and employee can come together in a value-creating relationship where both gain, but it grasps the dialectical tension that exists in situations where the relative gain accruing to one party (even in a value-adding relationship) defines an associated loss for the other. Dialectically, capital, wealth, and profit are based on antagonisms that have a momentum of their own.

Marx explains that the quest for profit or surplus value places the capitalist producer in constant antagonism with labor and competitors in the marketplace. These basic contradictions then unfold to create many problems. For example, the drive for surplus value leads the capitalist to reduce labor costs wherever possible. Labor, of course, resists, creating a continuing struggle in the workplace.

Similarly, profits are reduced through increased competition. This leads the capitalist producer to find ways of constantly beating the competition. Because price reductions of one's product, even though sometimes bringing short-term gain, ultimately reduce the level of profit, the capitalist system is launched into a constant search for new products and new markets. Historically, the push has been toward constant innovation and toward the search for new customers throughout the world. It is a never-ending process and is always intensified by the fact that when new ways of making a profit are found there is a natural tendency for them to be negated by the appearance of new forms of competition. Marx's economic analysis of the process makes much of the fact that, because of the inability of capitalists to isolate themselves from the long-term tendency toward declining rates of profit in all niches where a strong monopoly or exclusivity cannot be sustained, the system as a whole is constantly thrust toward a state of crisis.

Capitalism, in this view, is a social system riddled with, and driven by, contradictions. It is an endless treadmill because unless you can get into what Brian Arthurs has described as a world of "increasing returns," the driving logic is based on constant struggle. Competition becomes part of a runaway system that drives to ever-increasing levels of accomplishment in terms of productivity but with enormous contradictions and potentially negative consequences for the system at large.

We can see the Marxian dialectic playing itself out in the early struggles between capital and labor. To increase the efficiency of production, capitalists centralized the productive process under the factory system. Labor forces were *created* through this centralization. Gradually, they unionized and began to oppose the system that had created them.

The industrial system in the first part of the twentieth century was continuously shaped and reshaped by changing patterns of this dialectical opposition. For example, the mechanization of production *created* human relations problems, exacerbating the "them" and "us" division between capitalists and managers, on the one hand, and labor, on the other. This strengthened unionization, which strengthened management's resolve to break the power of unions.

The success of unionization, which succeeded in sustaining relatively high wages and undermined management control, led to all kinds of management innovation to eliminate labor or improve its efficiency, on the one hand, and to find ways of breaking labor control, on the other. The major solutions have been found in automation and the shift of production to Third World countries where wage rates are much lower than in the West and unions far less powerful. This, in turn, has created a high degree of structural unemployment in the West and a new crisis of long-term consumption. The irony of the spectacular achievements of Western corporations is that they have more or less mastered the problems of providing high-quality and relatively low-priced products, but in doing so, have eliminated, or are in the process of eliminating, their markets. The problem has been exacerbated by the fact that the structural crisis in employment has thrown an increasing burden on Western welfare states, which, faced with the declining tax revenue resulting from reduced employment levels, have moved into states of increasing crisis. This, in turn, has added to the basic problem because when you remove welfare payments you remove markets!

Every solution leads to a new problem. Modern managers experience this every day as they cope with the flux confronting them. But they rarely grasp the underlying social dynamic producing their problems. In a nutshell, they fail to see how the drive to increase efficiency through factory production (a solution) in effect *created* the power of unions (a new problem), which eventually led to increased automation and Third World production (a new solution) that undermines Western markets (a new problem). And so on.

We are in the midst of a dialectical unfolding, the future of which cannot be seen. Who knows whether the crisis currently being experienced by Western capitalism will prove to be a point of complete transformation of the system or just another stage in its evolution? What is clear, however, is that the mode of dialectical analysis explored here provides another powerful lens for understanding the unfolding logic of change of which we are all part. From a chaos theory perspective, Marxian analysis identifies key elements of the attractor system that has shaped much of the nineteenth and twentieth centuries. But Marx's vision of the new attractor—his ideal of a communist society—was completely wrong. It remains to be seen whether a new attractor will emerge to redefine the logic of the basic system or whether capitalism will continue to self-organize and refine itself into new variations on its existing pattern.

THE DIALECTICS OF MANAGEMENT

Dialectic analysis has at least two important implications for management:

1. It encourages us to put our heads above the flux and see the contradictions that are shaping detailed organizational life. The escalating levels of competition and the social problems and market potentials that are being lost as a result of corporate cutbacks and downsizings are systemic. They need to be understood in these terms and approached in a way that, using the language of chaos theory, addresses the basic attractor pattern producing the problems. They can be resolved only by modifying the basic rules of the game. Now that the ideological battle between Western capitalism and Eastern communism has been resolved, political and corporate leaders have an opportunity to go beyond ideological debate and address problems at a more substantial and systemic level.

   One way of approaching these issues rests in thinking about developments in modern capitalism as manifestations of "primary" and "secondary" contradictions.

   For example, widespread structural unemployment is an offshoot of the primary contradiction captured in the conflict between profit and costs. In turn, this generates secondary contradictions expressed in social oppositions, such as in the conflicts between employed and unemployed, between indigenous populations and new immigrants in their search for jobs, in the tensions between management and unions, and in all kinds of racial and social problems that arise along with difficult economic circumstances. These secondary, or "offshoot" contradictions cannot be completely resolved in themselves. They need to be tackled at a higher level, through an appreciation of the primary contradictions that are creating the context in which they are able to flourish.

   In a similar way, dialectic analysis encourages managers to recognize that corporate downsizings and associated global restructurings are not solutions to problems. They too are manifestations of deeper problems. Ultimately, they are best tackled through social and political initiatives that can address the rules of the game embedded in the primary contradictions shaping capitalism itself. Dialectical thinking provides a framework for approaching the policy issues involved.

2. It offers insights and methods for the micromanagement of capitalism at an organizational level. Managers cannot wait for the macroproblems described above to be resolved. They have to deal with the microflux even if it is the reflection of secondary contradictions. Dialectical analysis demonstrates that many detailed organizational problems hinge on the effective management of contradictions and

that innovation and development always rest in a process of "creative destruction."

Managing paradox

In our discussion of chaos theory, we described how systems that are moving away from the influence of a dominant attractor pattern toward a potential new configuration encounter bifurcation points or forks in the road. At these points, energies for change either dissipate and dissolve in a way that allows the old attractor to reassert itself or shift the system into a new form. An understanding of the dialectical nature of change offers important insights on the process, suggesting that the forks in the road usually arise around key paradoxes or contradictions that block the way to a new future. The successful management of change requires skill in dealing with these contradictory tensions.

Consider the following examples:

An organization is seeking to empower its staff by giving employees more control over the decisions influencing their work. This new development, which represents a shift toward a potential new attractor pattern, encounters opposition from the status quo. Existing decision-making systems and controls, and associated politics of hierarchy and careerism block or undermine the new developments. Staff members struggle to implement the new system. If they are successful in creating a context where they can exercise more autonomy and influence, there is a chance that new forms of empowered decision making will emerge and be accompanied by a transformation of the existing organization. If not, tradition will rule and the "empowerment exercise" will just be added to the organization's list of failed experiments and initiatives.

Potential new futures *always* create oppositions with the status quo. This dialectical principle gets played out in many forms:

Innovate ◄►Avoid mistakes

Think long term ◄► Deliver results now

Cut costs ◄► Increase morale

Reduce staff ◄► Improve teamwork

Be flexible ◄► Respect the rules

Collaborate ◄► Compete

Decentralize ◄► Retain control

Specialize ◄► Be opportunistic

Low costs ◄► High quality

These are just a few examples of how new initiatives or directions get mired in paradoxical tensions that undermine the desired change. Although there may be ways of resolving the paradoxes, the fact that the tensions are *experienced as contradictory* may in itself be sufficient to negate transformational change. For example, if people *feel* that the new demands for "more innovation," "improved morale," "more collaboration," "increased decentralization," and so on, are inconsistent with what seems reasonable or possible, inertia is the most likely outcome.

A dialectical view of change asserts that paradox is inevitable. It reflects the struggle of opposites and the fact that any system development always contains elements of a counterdevelopment, because each position tends to *generate* its opposite. In our empowerment example, the very act of seeking to empower staff is likely to *mobilize* awareness of existing modes of control, which, in turn, undermines the drive toward empowerment.

Managers interested in transformational change have to be skilled in managing these tensions. They need to be able to target those that are most important. As in the case of broad societal contradictions, there are often primary and secondary contradictions at a management level, and managers need to find ways of reframing them so that new patterns of development can unfold. Left to themselves, new initiatives often generate their negation, resulting in the stalemate described above, or in circumstances particularly favorable to the emergent dimension of the paradox, to a revolutionary swing to the polarity that it represents.

In our empowerment example, if the drive to empowerment was introduced in a context where the traditional control systems were particularly vulnerable to attack, the organization could end up with a situation of empowerment without any semblance of control. Such an extreme development may result in a situation as undesirable as the one the organization is trying to leave behind.

The first step in the successful management of paradox rests in *recognizing that both dimensions of the contradictions that accompany change usually have merit.* Casting your eye over the list of contradictions presented above, it is unlikely that as a manager you would want to build your organization around any one side of the dimensions presented. It is likely that you would want your organization to incorporate *both*. Just as staff may need to be empowered *and* controlled, you may want innovation with minimum mistakes; long-term development with an early return; high morale in a low-cost environment; improved teamwork with fewer staff; collaboration that is underpinned by a healthy competitive spirit along the right dimensions; faster, better quality production; and so on.

It is this requirement that distinguishes the management of paradox from the management of resistance to change. The idea of managing and removing resistance was pioneered by Kurt Lewin, who suggested that any potential change is resisted by forces working in the opposite direction. The idea is similar to the dialectical principle that everything generates its opposite. But within Lewin's framework, the forces tend to be external to the change, holding situations in states of dynamic equilibrium. His solution was to advocate that successful change rests in "unfreezing" an established equilibrium by enhancing the forces driving change, or by reducing or removing the resisting forces and then "refreezing" in a new equilibrium state.

The dialectical view differs in that it sees paradox as a product of *internal* tensions produced by the fact that elements of both sides of the paradox may embrace equally desirable states. The management task is to find ways of integrating the competing elements. Paradox cannot be successfully resolved by eliminating one side.

The second vital step in the successful management of paradox, then, rests in finding ways of creating contexts that can mobilize and retain desirable qualities on both sides while minimizing the negative dimensions. All the skills of managing in the midst of complexity, discussed earlier in this chapter, are relevant here. To the extent that the paradoxes created by change remain unaddressed, they become the stalemating context. The challenge is to transcend the stalemating context by *creating new contexts* that can reframe key contradictions in a positive way.

By applying the principles for managing complexity discussed earlier, managers can help to develop *new understandings* that will reshape the mindsets through which a particular paradox is approached. For example, by encouraging a view of empowerment that respects a few critical principles or rules (i.e., the minimum specs needed to deliver required control), it may be possible to integrate needs for both empowerment *and* control.

Alternatively, managers may seek to create a new context in which empowerment and control can flourish through *new actions* that prototype required behaviors. They may create a new empowered environment in relation to special projects, or prototypes of new team-based forms of production that break old patterns of control while recreating their essential contributions in a new form. The challenge is to find small changes that can unfold in a way that creates large effects that deliver on both sides of the paradox at the same time.

Paradox is one of the major forces stalling change at all levels of an organization. It tends to immobilize at both a psychological and action level. Yet it can be transformed into a major lever of change. For in dissolving or transforming paradox, we change the basic rules of the game.

Note how modern industry has transformed the traditional paradox between low cost and high quality. For decades, they were seen as opposites. But as a result of the Japanese idea that it is possible to reduce costs by improving quality, a whole new line of development has been unleashed. The reframing created a context where people recognized how they could reduce costs by eliminating waste and defects, by simplifying production through better product design, by taking the cost and time out of production, by eliminating excess resources in the production process, and so on. The new frame created a context in which the methods of just-in-time management and new relations between networks of firms involved in the production process could unfold and are still unfolding. Reframed paradoxes create new contexts in which radically new modes of operation can emerge.

Innovation as "creative destruction"

Dialectical thinking can also make a major contribution to how we understand and approach the process of innovation. The point is implicit in our discussion of paradox, but has been most fully developed by management writers who, following economist Joseph Schumpeter, invite us to see evolution and development as a process of creative destruction where new innovations lead to the destruction of established practice. New innovations tend to displace old innovations. In turn, they define the frontier for the next phase of innovation, creating a pattern where problems tend to generate new solutions, which set the basis for new problems, which lead to new solutions, to new problems, and so on. The process applies to the evolution of social life and the development of products, services, and business processes of all kinds.

This pattern has important implications. It means that innovations create the basis for their own downfall! Whenever an organization succeeds in creating a breakthrough in relation to one of its products and services, as Apple Computer did with the invention of the personal computer, this begins to define the frontier for new competition. Thinking dialectically, we can see that the breakthrough in effect *creates* the frontier for new competition. As Apple has found, numerous companies moved into the personal computer market with products and services that ultimately try to overcome the weaknesses of the original product, eroding the competitive edge that the innovation established.

Any organization wishing to sustain a competitive advantage must recognize how its successes are going to become weaknesses. It must be prepared to innovate in ways that will undermine current success so that new innovations can emerge.

The power of this strategy for promoting successful innovation has been widely recognized and practiced in many Japanese corporations that, as a consequence of Eastern comfort with dialectical thinking, have long used it as a method for continuous improvement of products and business processes. More recently, it has been advocated as a strategy for dealing with the turbulence and change of the modern corporate environment. For example, as Richard D'Aveni has suggested, many companies that succeed in sustaining competitive advantage in turbulent environments do so by systematically destroying the breakthroughs created by their own products and initiatives by coming up with better ones. Take, for example, the experience of Intel. The company's success in becoming a dominant force in the microchip business was propelled by its determination to produce innovations that could beat its own best innovations. In 1992 alone, the company produced nearly thirty new variations on its 486 chip as well as introducing the Pentium as a foundation for the next generation of chips. The company operates on a philosophy of launching multiple projects that in effect aim to make their developing products obsolete before they hit the market. It also tries to find ways of changing the rules of its industry by shifting business frontiers into domains that other competitors find it difficult to reach.

In the language of dialectical analysis, Intel's strategy celebrates the "negation of the negation": the second dialectical rule. It provides a powerful way of driving constant innovation and for directing creative energy and attention to the ideas and insights around areas of weakness that, if addressed, may help to avert downfall by propelling one's organization to higher and higher levels of innovation. It provides a way of challenging the psychic prisons explored in chapter 7, and other dimensions of the attractor patterns through which organizations get trapped by their own success.

But if taken to an extreme, the strategy leads to dangerous ground because it can unleash a spiral of destructive forces. To illustrate, return to the position adopted by Richard D'Aveni who suggests that the best competitive strategy under conditions of great turbulence, or what he calls "hypercompetition," is to develop strategies that systematically destroy or disrupt the advantages of others. The result is a world where survival seems to hinge on an ethic of kill or be killed.

Life is war!

In the anarchist movements of the nineteenth century, the slogan that "the most creative desire is the desire to destroy" become a rallying point for those wishing to overthrow capitalism. D'Aveni's position in effect uses the same principle to support innovation under conditions of advanced capitalism. In essence, it defines a "new anarchism," or as it is sometimes described in Europe, a "new brutalism." Destruction feeds on itself. Just as Hardin's "Tragedy of the Commons" created a cycle of destruction because the identity and needs of individuals took precedence over those of the collective, strategies of constant destruction can generate similar pathological patterns.

The process of negation, and the creative destruction that it implies, seems to be a natural quality of all systems. It is found in nature as well as in social life. But, for the most part, it needs no help. It is spontaneous. It is a part of the self-organizing process.

The danger of promoting creative destruction as a management policy is that the destructive potentials within a system get *over-emphasized*. It is a major paradox of social life. Evolution involves destruction. But destruction is a side effect or consequence, not a conscious aim. If we use an ethic of destruction to enhance evolutionary processes, the risk is that all manner of new instabilities and pathologies can arise.

STRENGTHS AND LIMITATIONS OF THE FLUX AND TRANSFORMATION METAPHOR

STRENGTHS

■ **The metaphor offers new understandings of the nature and source of change.**

We often take change for granted, viewing it as an independent force transforming the world around us and presenting us with all kinds of novel problems with which we have to deal. One of the major strengths of the ideas explored in this chapter is that they seek to fathom the nature and source of change so that we can understand its logic. This has immense significance for how we understand and manage organizations, for if there is an inner logic to the changes that shape our world, it may be possible to understand and manage change at a new and higher level. Instead of just responding to discrete events as novel happenings, we may be able to influence the processes that produce them.

The four sets of ideas explored in this chapter provide alternative yet complementary means of approaching this task.

1. *Autopoiesis* suggests that the way we see and manage change is ultimately a product of how we see and think about ourselves and consequently how we enact relationships with the environment. Much of the turbulence of the social world is a product of this enactment process.

Relationships between organizations and environment tend to be very truncated and egocentric. There is a poor appreciation of how organization and environment are part of the same broad pattern and how, in evolution, it is *pattern* that evolves. The theory of autopoiesis suggests that because of their capacities for self-reflection, organizations, like individuals, have an opportunity to enact new, more systemic identities that break the rigid boundaries between organization and environment, opening the way to more systemic patterns of evolution. In the long run, survival can only be survival *with*, never survival *against*, the environment or context in which one is operating. Organizations, like individuals, have to appreciate that they are always more than themselves. New mindsets redefining boundaries to embrace customers, competitors, and other significant elements of the environment are part of the required trend.

In the most fundamental sense, the distinction typically drawn between organization and environment is very problematic. Organizations do not exist in any way that is separate from their environment. We may feel that this idea is now well recognized through the idea that organizations are open rather than closed systems, but, paradoxically, this distinction just perpetuates the illusion of separateness. The concept of openness is flawed conceptually and also practically, for it works against organizations acquiring a deeper appreciation of the evolving or self-destructing pattern of relations to which they belong. The fundamental challenge is to think in terms of gestalt patterns—not just in terms of immediate organization-environment relations. The theories of chaos and complexity, mutual causality, and dialectical opposition provide complementary ways of understanding how pattern evolves.

2. *Chaos and complexity* teach us that organizations and their relationships with the environment are part of an attractor pattern. Key organizing rules—embedded in various aspects of structure, culture, information, mindsets, beliefs, and perceived identity—tend to hold organization-environment relations in a particular configuration. When pushed into edge-of-chaos situations the basic pattern can flip into new forms. The managerial challenge rests in nudging systems into desired paths by initiating small changes that can produce large effects.

3. *Mutual causality* encourages us to understand attractor patterns and the processes of change in terms of the positive and negative feedback

loops that define complete fields of relations. As we inspect the "mapping" that this perspective creates (exhibits 8.4 and 8.5) we quickly see the arbitrariness of any distinction between organization and environment. We see that the logic of the whole is embedded in the nature of the deviation amplifying or stabilizing loops and that the key to management results in shaping and reframing the nature of these loops.

4. *Dialectal analysis* offers yet another perspective of pattern and how it evolves. This time, the emphasis is placed on understanding the paradoxes and tensions that are created whenever elements of a system try to push in a particular direction. Each phase of development sets up conditions leading to its own transformation. The attractor patterns of chaos theory are now seen in terms of the core dialectical principles shaping a form of life—such as the dialectics of capital in capitalism and the emergent paradoxes and conflicts they generate. The perspective encourages us to recognize how the management of organization, society and personal life ultimately involves the management of contradiction. It invites us to find ways through which key tensions can be reframed to create new paths of development.

- **The metaphor offers new horizons of thought that can be used to enrich our understanding of management.**

  In this, perhaps more than in any other chapter, we have pushed the horizons of current management thought to embrace new disciplines. Each of the four perspectives has provided valuable insights. But our discussion only scratches the surface of possibility. In the theory of chaos and complexity alone, we find a completely new paradigm for management, and one particularly well equipped for dealing with the challenge of a turbulent world. The promise of this chapter is that we can mine each of the perspectives for many more new ideas for management practice

- **Leaders and managers gain a powerful new perspective on their role in facilitating emergent change.**

  Although all four ways of viewing change focus attention on different concepts and ideas, all share the view that change self-organizes and is an emergent phenomenon that cannot be predetermined or controlled.

  The insight that change self-organizes and cannot be controlled can be seen as both a strength and a limitation. The whole idea that change is an emergent phenomenon offers a powerful mindset for managing change. It encourages us to gain a reflective understanding of the logic driving the flux around us and to nudge and shape that logic whenever we can. Yet it also requires us to recognize that we can never be in control. The message is that, even though our actions shape and are shaped by change, we are just part of an evolving pattern.

The challenge is to cope with this paradox: by recognizing that even though we cannot exert unilateral power or control over any complex system, we can act through the power and control that we actually do have. Although we may be no more than "butterflies" in terms of our power on the overall system, we can have enormous effects, especially when we use our insights about systems dynamics and the nature of change to determine how and where to intervene. And, of course, the more butterflies the better!

LIMITATIONS

■ **Powerless power: Is this a message that managers really want to hear?**

The strength of the above ideas on emergent change may also be seen as a major weakness, for while they bring a message of hope that emphasizes the potential of "powerless power," it is not a message that many managers will want to hear or embrace. The whole history of organization and management theory is based on the idea that it is possible to organize, predict, and control. The insights of this chapter suggest that given the reality of complex systems this is not possible.

Ironically, all the perspectives on change explored in this chapter suggest that change is rule-bound. There is order in the chaos, whether we analyze that order by understanding attractor patterns, feedback loops, or unfolding contradictions. However, the order becomes apparent only with hindsight. As we look at the evolution of nature, of organizations, or of the artificial intelligence reflected in the computer simulations conducted by complexity theorists, we can discern distinct rules or patterns of behavior. But the key questions are: Are they generative or residual? Do they reflect the rules that have created the pattern that we see? Or are they just rules that we invent to capture and *describe* that pattern? Hindsight is always 20/20. Rules and patterns can always be found in nature and in history. The problem is, can we find rules that will predict the emergence of a pattern before it becomes reality?

This is a quest that drives much of science and indeed much of the ideology of Western civilization. There is an aspiration to predict and see the future, and thereby to be "in control."

But is this realistic?

Is it just part of our psychic prison? If so, the ultimate challenge of this chapter may be to recognize the emergent nature of change and let this aspiration go!

9 The Ugly Face: Organizations As Instruments of Domination

WHEN WE VIEW ORGANIZATIONS AS SYSTEMS THAT EXPLOIT THEIR EMPLOYEES, THE NATURAL ENVIRONMENT, AND THE GLOBAL ECONOMY FOR THEIR OWN ENDS, we are led to a powerful critique of almost every aspect of management throughout history.

- Whether viewing the construction of ancient pyramids or the activities of modern corporations, our attention is led to the processes of domination that underlie organized activity.

- Workaholism, occupational accidents and disease, and social and mental stress become seen as the price inflicted on one group of people to serve the interests of others.

- The role of global corporations in the exploitation of people and resources becomes seen as part of a deep process of exploitation running throughout the corporate world.

The metaphor creates a new level of social consciousness and an appreciation of why relations between exploiting and exploited groups can get so polarized. It invites managers to a deeper sense of the ethical dimensions of their work and its social impact.

OUR ORGANIZATIONS ARE KILLING US!

Ramparts magazine noted many years ago that the Western world is slowly eating itself to death. Our food is often adulterated with thousands of different synthetic flavors, colors, thickeners, acidifiers, bleaches, preservatives, package contaminants, antibiotics, and poisonous pesticides. Food and tobacco companies spend billions of dollars each year promoting health-damaging products, contributing to the high incidence of cancer and various forms of liver, kidney, heart, and lung disease. Although many argue that the scientific evidence is not conclusive enough to ban other than the most obvious hazards, many scientists believe that we are dealing with a human time bomb because the most damaging effects are likely to be long-term. Ingested toxins may well have an influence on mutations of the human gene pool, producing irreversible damage in generations to come.

Similar threats stem from environmental pollution. Every day, industrial organizations spew millions of tons of toxic waste into our waterways and the atmosphere or bury them in leaky containers underground. The economics of waste disposal is such that many organizations feel they have no choice but to continue in these damaging practices so long as they remain legal. As a result, it is now estimated that as many as two thousand toxins pollute the Great Lakes, and there are thousands of dangerous toxic-waste sites adding pollution to the groundwater. Over 160 such sites have been identified within three miles of the Niagara River, which feeds into Lake Ontario. The fish have cancer, and in areas of concentrated pollution such as the infamous Love Canal near the Niagara River, concern about pollution-related diseases has reached crisis proportions. As in the case of food and tobacco production, human health is adversely affected by corporate practices that place profits before human welfare.

Working in many organizations can be dangerous, too. Each year hundreds of thousands of workers throughout the world die of work-related accidents and illnesses. Over one hundred thousand deaths occur in North America alone. Hundreds of thousands of workers suffer from occupational diseases of varying severity, such as heart disease, eye strain, back pain, stress, or lung ailments. Only the worst hazards are closely monitored or controlled. Others occur within the law and are frequently treated as inevitable aspects of the lines of business in which they occur. Accidents and occupational disease, like pollution, are often viewed in a way that places more emphasis on costs and the "bottom line" than on the health of employees.

Throughout the Third World, large multinational corporations often ride roughshod over the interests of local people. As in the early years of the industrial revolution in Europe, people are legally and illegally dispossessed of their land and traditional ways of life. They are transformed into an urban poor who work for subsistence wages in sweatshops and factories. In the view of many analysts, the multinationals virtually rob their host countries of resources and labor power. At the same time, they engage in modes of strategic management that increase the dependence of these countries on their continued presence. Industrial accidents, occupational disease, pollution, and general degradation of the people and the land continue to occur at a level that vividly reproduces the conditions of raw exploitation and human despair experienced in the worst industrial centers of England in the late eighteenth and nineteenth centuries. Again, the logic of economics and the imperative of making large profits tend to be the dominant concerns.

In all these illustrations, we are talking about what former British Prime Minister Edward Heath once described as the "ugly face" of organizational life. Whether by design or by default, organizations often have a large negative impact on our world. Our purpose in this chapter is to gain insight on this aspect of organization by exploring how organizations can be understood as instruments of domination. Although we are usually encouraged to think about organizations as rational enterprises pursuing goals that aspire to satisfy the interests of all, there is much evidence to suggest that this view is more an ideology than a reality. Organizations are often used as instruments of domination that further the selfish interests of elites at the expense of others, and there is an element of domination in *all* organizations.

ORGANIZATION AS DOMINATION

A HISTORY BASED ON EXPLOITATION

Throughout history, organization has been associated with processes of social domination where individuals or groups find ways of imposing their will on others. Consider the incredible feat of organization, planning, and control required to build the Great Pyramid at Giza. It is estimated that its construction involved work by perhaps ten thousand persons over a period of twenty years. The pyramid is built from over 2.3 million blocks of stone, each weighing two and one-half tons. These had to be quarried, cut to size, and transported over many miles, usually by the Nile River when it was in flood. When we admire this and other pyramids today, it is the incredible ingenuity and skill of the early Egyptians that strikes us from both an aesthetic and an organizational standpoint. From another standpoint, however, the pyramid is a metaphor of exploitation, symbolizing how the lives and hard labor of thousands of people were used to serve and glorify a privileged elite.

In the view of some organization theorists, this combination of achievement and exploitation is a feature of organization throughout the ages. Whether we are talking about the building of the pyramids or the running of an army, a multinational corporation, or even a family business, we find asymmetrical power relations that result in the majority working in the interests of the few. Of course, important differences in practice can be observed, and over the ages much has changed. The conscription and slavery that provided much of the labor power required to build pyramids and empires have given way to use of paid employment where employees have the right to leave. Slave drivers have given way to managers, and employees now typically work in the interests of shareholders rather than of pharaohs, emperors, or absolute monarchs. However, in all cases, pursuit of the goals of the few through the work and labor of the many continues.

The domination aspect of organization has been made a special focus of study by radical organization theorists inspired by the insights of Max Weber, Robert Michels, and Karl Marx. As we saw in the machine chapter, Weber is famous among organization theorists for his work on the nature of bureaucracy. However, his main concern was to understand how different societies and epochs are characterized by different forms of social domination. He viewed bureaucracy as a special mode of social domination and was interested in the role of bureaucratic organizations in creating and sustaining structures of domination.

Weber's views of domination

For Weber, domination can occur in several ways. First and most obviously, domination arises when one or more persons coerce others through the direct use of threat or force. But domination also occurs in more subtle ways, as when a ruler imposes his or her will on others while being *perceived as having a right to do so*. This is the kind of domination that most interested Weber, and much of his effort was devoted to understanding the process through which forms of domination become legitimized as normal, socially acceptable power relations: patterns of formal authority in which rulers see themselves as having the *right* to rule, and those subject to this rule see it as their *duty* to obey.

- Charismatic domination occurs when a leader rules by virtue of his or her personal qualities that are perceived by followers to be extraordinary, such as prophetic or heroic. Followers are often described as falling under the leader's spell.

- Traditional domination occurs when followers accept the leader's rule as the custom or a given right, such as in inherited rulership.

- Rational-legal domination occurs when laws, rules, regulations, and procedures legitimize the leader's rule, such as in a bureaucracy. Followers give leaders the right to rule within the confines of the laws and regulations.

Weber believed that each mode of domination was accompanied by a particular kind of legitimacy and by a specific form of administrative organization. He was particularly concerned by the trend toward increasing bureaucratization and rationalization, which he saw as a very great threat to the freedom of the human spirit and the values of liberal democracy. He saw bureaucracy as a power instrument of the first order and believed that the bureaucratization of administration when completely carried through establishes a form of power relation that is "practically unshatterable." Hence his view of bureaucracy as an "iron cage." The strength of bureaucratic organization is, of course, now being undermined by developments in information technology that erode hierarchy and introduce new organizational power bases. But the process of rationalization and control to which Weber speaks is as strong as ever.

Michels's views of domination

Similar concerns to Weber's have been voiced by Robert Michels, whose famous "iron law of oligarchy" suggests that organizations typically end up under the control of narrow groups even when this runs against the desires of the leaders as well as the led. In his study of supposedly democratic organizations, such as trade unions and political parties, he found that the democracy was often no more than window dressing. Despite the best intentions, these organizations seemed to develop tendencies that gave their leaders a near monopoly of power. As leaders rise to power, they tend to become preoccupied with their own way of looking at things, and it seems that the most that can be hoped for is that they will attempt to keep the interests of their members in mind. But in Michels's view, even democratically elected leaders with the best intentions have a tendency to become part of an elite furthering their own interests and to hang onto their power at all costs.

The real value of these perspectives is that they show how even the most rational and democratic forms of organization can result in modes of domination where certain people acquire and sustain a commanding influence over others, often through subtle processes of socialization and belief. To take Weber's ideas as an illustration, we can become dominated by such basic and hidden forces as those underpinning the quest for rationality. Indeed, for Weber the process of rationalization is itself a mode of domination. As we become increasingly subject to administration through rules and engage in strict calculations relating means and ends and costs and benefits, we become increasingly dominated by the process itself. Impersonal principles and the quest for efficiency tend to become our new slave drivers.

Marx's views of domination

Weber's ideas resonate with those of Karl Marx, especially those discussed in the flux and transformation chapter. For Weber, the logic driving modern society is found in the process of domination through rationalization. For Marx, it is found in the domination generated by the quest for surplus value and the accumulation of capital. Many "radical" theorists have brought the ideas of Marx and Weber up to date, showing how organization in the modern world is based on processes of domination and exploitation of many kinds.

In the remainder of this chapter we will explore the ideas of these radical organization theorists, especially those of Karl Marx. We will be focusing on how the forces of domination embedded in the ways we organize often lead organizations to exploit their employees and the social and economic contexts in which they operate.

RADICAL ORGANIZATIONAL THEORY: HOW ORGANIZATIONS USE AND EXPLOIT THEIR EMPLOYEES

Arthur Miller's well-known play *Death of a Salesman* explores the tragic life and death of Willy Loman.

> Willy had been a salesman with the Wagner company for thirty-four years, traveling through New England year after year as Wagner's "New England man." However, at the age of sixty, Willy feels that he can no longer cope with the demands of life on the road. After a number of nervous breakdowns, he reluctantly decides to ask for a posting in New York City so that he can work at his home base. His family has grown up, and his financial needs are modest. He feels confident that Wagner will be able to find a niche for him, even though his sales performance is nowhere near what it once was.
>
> However, on raising the subject with Howard Wagner, Willy is rudely disappointed. Howard has little time for Willy's plight. Willy talks about his time with the firm, his close association with Howard's father, and the promises that had been made. But it has no effect on

Howard. Within a matter of minutes, Willy finds himself suggesting that his wages could be reduced from sixty-five dollars per week to fifty and finally to forty since he needs only to earn enough to get by.

Howard is uncomfortable with Willy's pleading but insists that there's no room for favors. After various attempts at escaping the situation by claiming that he has no more time and must move on to his next appointment, Howard finally ends the conversation by telling Willy that the company no longer needs him. Willy is shattered. He feels like "an empty orange peel." The company has eaten thirty-four years of his life as if it were a piece of fruit and is now throwing the rest of him away.

He ends up committing suicide.

Miller's play stands as a metaphor for the way organizations often consume and exploit their employees, taking and using what they need while throwing the rest away. Of course, there are exceptions. But many workers and managers at all levels of organization find their health and personal lives being sacrificed on the altars created by modern organizations. Willy's story, though extreme in its end result, is not extreme in substance. In the world today, individuals and even whole communities find themselves being thrown away like empty orange peels when the organizations they serve have no further use for them. Individuals find themselves permanently unemployed even though they feel that they have many good years of useful work ahead of them. Communities find that they are unable to survive once the organizations on which they have depended for their economic livelihood decide to move their capital elsewhere. Increasingly, many managers find themselves ending lives of workaholic involvement with their employer as the victims of cutbacks or "early retirement plans." Even though sometimes cushioned by "golden handshakes" and comfortable pensions, the blow to their egos and self-confidence can be shattering.

Somewhat ironically, those with the most privileged access to important information or with pivotal positions in their companies are often those who receive the hardest blow to their self-esteem. Many important executives, on being told that they are no longer needed, are also told that their termination is immediate. They will not be required to turn up at work ever again because, despite their glowing reputation, the organization fears that resentment may lead them to carry away documents that could be used to help competitors or to damage the organization in some way. In these cases, insult is added to injury.

In the opinion of many radical organization theorists, even though we have advanced a long way from the naked exploitation found in slavery and in the developing years of the industrial revolution, the same pattern continues today. They find particularly striking evidence of this in the way organizations structure job opportunities to produce and reproduce the class structure of modern societies; in the way organizations approach the problems of hazardous work situations, industrial accidents, and occupational disease; and in the way organizations perpetuate structures and practices that promote workaholism and associated forms of social and mental stress.

ORGANIZATION, CLASS, AND CONTROL

A strong case can be made for the idea that organization has always been class-based. The first types of formal organization probably arose in hierarchical societies where one social group imposed itself on another, often through conquest. Such societies became further stratified as certain individuals placed themselves in the service of the ruling class as priests, scribes, bookkeepers, traders, and merchants. Because these people were not involved in producing the goods necessary to sustain their livelihood, they formed an intermediate class of people between the ruling class and the peasants or slaves involved in the actual production of goods. We find the same system reproduced in modern organization in the distinctions between owners, managers, and workers.

Thousands of years intervene between the emergence of the first formal organizations and the corporations that we see around us today. We can pick up the story in the period of the industrial revolution in Great Britain around the 1760s and in the industrialization of the United States from the early 1800s.

The industrial revolution in Great Britain was set against the background of an agrarian society with a "domestic" or "cottage" system of production, supplemented by a small amount of mining and construction and a system of industrial workshops run by merchant-craftsmen organized in craft guilds. These workshops were typically stratified according to skill and status, in terms of masters, journeymen, and apprentices. The guilds controlled entry and working conditions and managed to secure a reasonable livelihood for their members, especially when compared with the poor farmers or landless poor who had lost their source of livelihood as a result of the enclosure of land during the sixteenth century.

The industrial revolution changed this picture as capitalist producers sought to overcome the uncertainties of output and quality associated with domestic production; to serve the new markets created by expanding world trade and a growing population; and, most important of all, to take advantage of mechanical systems of production. The development of factory production transformed the structure of the work force and intensified the growth of urban areas. Increasing numbers of people who had formerly been self-employed in workshops and cottage industry assumed new roles as part of an emerging wage-earning class. Labor increasingly became viewed as a commodity to be bought and sold. Because these changes eliminated earlier systems of production, for the new wage earners the process was irreversible, making them dependent on the wage system.

Similar developments occurred in the United States. At the beginning of the nineteenth century, capitalist production for profit using wage labor was insignificant outside the major cities. Most of the population lived in rural areas, and over 80 percent of the labor force was employed in agriculture, over 20 percent being slaves and indentured laborers. About 80 percent of the nonslave workforce were property holders and professionals—farmers, merchants, craftsmen, small manufacturers, doctors, lawyers, and others.

Slavery remained important in agriculture for much of the century. There were almost 4.5 million slaves in 1860, and even after emancipation many continued in feudal servitude under sharecropping and other systems of farming. In manufacturing, systems of capitalist production had an increasing impact, replacing cottage industry and small business with a system of wage labor. Immigrants, Native Americans, women and children, and displaced artisans and agricultural workers swelled a labor force that, as in Great Britain, found it increasingly difficult to find alternative sources of livelihood. The growth of capitalist organization has been accompanied by a decline in the number of self-employed persons and an increase in the number of wage and salary earners, though this trend has now started to reverse as a result of the flattening and decentralization of large bureaucracies and the rise of small business.

The growth of a capitalist system of production usually depends on the existence of a supply of wage labor, unless it is to rely on slaves or on some system of subcontracting. Slavery runs against important social norms and can be inefficient; and subcontracting, until the revolutions created in information technology, just-in-time management, and new forms of electronic control, was highly unpredictable from the capitalist's standpoint. Early capitalism in North America combined elements of slavery and subcontracting, but as the century progressed, a consistent trend toward the use of wage labor occurred—and with it the rise of the profession and activities of management as we know it today.

Wage labor creates a focus on efficiency and control

In many respects, it is possible to say that the system of wage labor created modern management, since for the first time outside slavery, profits depended on efficiency in the use of labor time. Under systems of domestic manufacture and subcontracting, the profit of the merchant-capitalist who bought and sold the goods produced did not necessarily depend on how the goods were produced. The merchant paid an appropriate price and lived off the profit margin. Great inconvenience arose when private producers failed to deliver the appropriate quantity or quality on time, but the problems involved were outside the merchant's direct sphere of interest.

With the appearance of the factory system, however, every second of wasted time or inefficient use of time represented a loss of profit, so the employment of wage labor led the capitalist to place primary emphasis on the efficiency of labor time and to seek increasing control over the process of production. The establishment of a wage system carried with it implications for the organization of the labor process and, as a corollary, institutionalized class divisions in the workplace, particularly between managers involved in the design and control of work and the workforce engaged in productive activity.

The development of a system of wage labor tends to be followed by increasingly strict and precise organization, close supervision, and increasingly standardized jobs. Skilled and semiskilled workers are increasingly replaced by cheaper unskilled workers, leading to what is sometimes described as "degradation" or "deskilling" of work and "homogenization" of the labor market. The extent of the deskilling has been graphically illustrated in a British study that showed how, in some organizations, over 80 percent of manual workers exercised less skill in their jobs than they used in driving to work.

Primary and secondary labor markets emerge

The labor market has also become increasingly segmented into two categories, sometimes described as primary and secondary sectors. The primary labor market is a market for career-type jobs that are especially crucial or that call for a high degree of skill and detailed knowledge, often of a corporation-specific nature. This market has grown along with the proliferation of bureaucratic and technocratic enterprises whose members are enticed to work not only for money but for nonmonetary rewards such as job satisfaction, the promise of career advancement, and security of employment. Members of the primary labor market are usually deemed worthy of significant investment. They are regarded and treated as "corporate assets" or "human capital." Such employees are expected to become committed and loyal. Corporations typically go to great lengths to foster and reward these traits and use extensive and rigorous selection mechanisms to eliminate high-risk candidates. However, as developments in information technology have created increasingly sophisticated subcontracting or outsourcing processes, increasing numbers of professionals once regarded as a core part of the primary labor market are finding themselves working on limited contracts where long-term commitments are neither desired nor possible.

The secondary labor market is a market for lower-skilled and lower-paid workers in offices, factories, and open-air jobs who are more dispensable and more easily replaced. It calls for little capital investment in the form of training and education, and workers can be hired and fired along with the vagaries of the business cycle. This type of labor provides a "buffer" that allows the organization to expand output in good times and to contract in bad, leaving the organization's operating core and elite primary labor force relatively unaffected. Increasingly, secondary labor is employed on a subcontracting basis.

A class system results

The existence of the two categories of labor gives an organization a great deal more control over its internal and external environment. The fact that primary workers are committed to the firm increases the predictability of its internal operations, whereas the existence of the secondary buffer facilitates its general ability to adapt. However, this means of control creates a differential system of status and privilege within the organization that parallels and sustains broader class divisions outside. It means that the vagaries of the business cycle have the harshest effects on the poorer sections of society, who belong to the secondary sector, and on special groups such as women, ethnic minorities, the handicapped, and poorly educated youths, who form a large part of this labor market.

If we examine the occupational structures of many Western societies we find that, on average, minorities and socially disadvantaged groups have a greater chance of having to perform dirty work for relatively low wages with little security of employment and few fringe benefits. Secondary-sector jobs are usually left for those who can't get any other. Employment patterns in this sector of the economy reflect social attitudes and patterns of prejudice and discrimination in society as a whole.

Some European countries have institutionalized this pattern by allowing migrant or "guest" workers from other countries to enter the workforce on temporary visas to perform the jobs that no one else wants. It is estimated that as many as ten million migrant workers are employed in Europe, making up as much as 11 percent of the workforce in Germany and 27 percent in Switzerland. Historically, the ranks of the British working class have always been swelled by immigrants, most recently by immigrants from the West Indies, India, Pakistan, and other countries in Asia, Europe, and the Commonwealth. In the United States, it is estimated that anywhere between 2 and 12 percent of the labor force consists of undocumented workers from Mexico, the Caribbean, and elsewhere, and African American workers have formed a substantial part of the working class ever since the days of slavery. Since the 1920s, they have become increasingly involved in manufacturing and service sector jobs and, despite affirmative action programs, still remain overrepresented in the secondary labor market.

Institutionalized discrimination? Or an unintended consequence of industrial development? The debate continues. It is clear that even though the domination and exploitation of disadvantaged groups may not be a stated aim of the modern corporation, it is definitely a side effect. Despite many major advances in employment equity legislation, the implicit or explicit exploitation of employees persists. Modern organizations continue to play an important part in creating and sustaining a relatively underprivileged working class that is now more appropriately described as an "underclass" because many of the working class are no longer working and have poor prospects of ever doing so. In creating and reinforcing the market system for labor, modern organizations continue to favor and reinforce a power structure that encourages people with certain attributes while disadvantaging others. The process reproduces patterns of favor and privilege that symbolize and reinforce underlying socioeconomic divisions. From this perspective, modern corporations play a crucial role in producing and sustaining the ills and inequities of modern society.

Although the focus has been placed on studying the evolution of organization under capitalism, it is important to recognize that a similar pattern is also evident in noncapitalist societies. As the Berlin Wall has tumbled in a political as well as a physical sense, it has become increasingly clear that state-run communist societies reveal similar features. China and the former USSR have always had a clear class structure, with Weber's vision of the iron cage of bureaucracy and Michels's "iron law of oligarchy" much in evidence. Organization, whatever ideological cloak it wears, seems to give form to systemic patterns of exploitation and social domination.

WORK HAZARDS, OCCUPATIONAL DISEASE, AND INDUSTRIAL ACCIDENTS

In one of the most vivid and moving chapters of *Das Kapital*, Karl Marx gives detailed attention to how many employers of his day were working their employees to death in horrific conditions. Quoting from the reports of factory inspectors and magistrates, his account bristles with incredible detail. In the lace industry in Nottingham, "children of nine or ten years were dragged from their squalid beds at two, three, or four o'clock in the morning and forced to work for subsistence wages until ten, eleven, or twelve at night, their frames dwindling, their faces whitening, and their humanity sinking into a stone-like torpor, utterly horrible to contemplate." Mr. Broughton Charlton, the county magistrate whose words are quoted above, castigated the system as one of "unmitigated slavery, socially, physically, morally, and spiritually . . . . We declaim against the Virginian and Carolinian cotton planters. Is their lash, and the barter of human flesh, more detestable than this slow sacrifice of humanity which takes place in order that veils and collars may be fabricated for the benefit of capitalists?"

In quoting reports on the pottery industry in Staffordshire, Marx produces similar facts, relating the story of William Wood, nine years old, who had been working for over a year from 6 A.M. until 9 P.M. six days a week. Quoting from health reports on how potters were dying at an alarming rate from pulmonary diseases caused by dust, fumes, vapors, and so on, he notes the observations of three physicians who had reported how each successive generation of potters was more dwarfed and less robust than the previous one. For example, Dr. J. T. Arledge reported in 1863 how the potters as a class of both men and women represent a "degenerated population . . . stunted in growth, ill-shaped, and frequently ill-formed in the chest . . . prematurely old, and . . . short lived . . . [dogged by] disorders of the liver and kidneys, and by rheumatism . . . [and] especially prone to pneumonia, phthisis, bronchitis, and asthma."

- Reports on match factories in the large cities documented how half the workers were children and young persons under eighteen, and how tetanus, a disease long associated with match making, was rife.

- Reports on the wallpaper industry tell how young girls and children were obliged to work from 6 A.M. until at least 10 P.M., with no stoppage for meals. Working seventy or eighty hours a week, they were often fed at their machines.

- Reports on the baking industry document how bakers often worked from 11 P.M. until 7 P.M. the following evening with just one or two short intervals of rest. They were among the most short-lived workers, rarely reaching the age of forty-two.

- Reports on the clothing industry document how girls and young women were being worked to death on sixteen-hour shifts and on shifts of up to thirty hours in peak seasons. They often worked without a break, being kept awake by occasional supplies of sherry, port, or coffee.

- On the railways, men often worked fourteen to twenty hours a day, forty or fifty hours of continuous work being common in peak travel periods.

- In the steel mills, boys nine to fifteen years old were reported working continuous twelve-hour shifts in high temperatures, often at night, and not seeing daylight for months on end.

It was Marx's opinion that capital lived "vampire-like . . . sucking living labor" and that, in general, capital took no account of the health or length of life of the worker unless society forced it to do so.

Many people conducting research on health and safety at work today believe that, although the working conditions in the majority of organizations are much better than those described above, many basic problems remain. Many employers take account of work hazards only when legislation requires them to do so. Workers in the Third World still often suffer under conditions exactly like those described above, working in subcontracted sweatshops for global corporations, and child labor is rife. Even in developed Western countries, accidents and occupational disease continue to take an alarming toll on human life:

- In the United States, the Occupational Safety and Health Administration (OSHA) reports that every year work-related accidents and illnesses cost an estimated 56,000 American lives. On an average day, 17 people are killed in safety accidents, 16,000 are injured, and 137 die from occupational disease. Each year, 700,000 days are lost to injuries and illnesses related to musculoskeletal disorders because of overuse of particular parts of the body. It is estimated that safety accidents alone cost the American economy over $100 billion a year.

Data on occupational illness and disease are more difficult to tie down than those on accidents because the links are often harder to document in an authoritative way. However, U.S. government estimates suggest that as many as 100,000 U.S. citizens a year die as a result of work-related illnesses. It is estimated that anywhere between 23 and 38 percent of cancer deaths may be work related. To put the figures in perspective, the number of people killed by occupational diseases and accidents each year exceeds the number of American lives lost in the duration of the Vietnam War.

We're a long way from the industrial revolution in terms of general working conditions, but these figures speak for themselves. Despite the major advances in occupational health and safety legislation, the issue of costs versus safety looms large on the unofficial agenda in many corporate decisions. Often, it is the issue of cost that wins. As one safety officer in an automobile factory described it, although the explicit policy is "safety first," the reality is "safety when convenient." Many industrial accidents occur because of problems unintentionally built into the structure of the plant and buildings because of poor maintenance or because it is easier or more efficient to work without using safety equipment. Because it is either expensive or inconvenient to remedy such problems, nothing tends to get done until someone gets hurt or until the organization is forced to introduce changes by government regulation.

Similar problems arise in relation to the hazards underlying occupational disease. It is estimated that industry at present creates and uses over 63,000 chemicals, perhaps 25,000 of which would be classified as toxic. Many of these are new, and their long-term effects are unknown. The effects of their interaction are impossible to predict in a comprehensive manner because of the number of possible permutations. In the view of some safety experts, the approach commonly adopted is a kind of trial and error using people in the workplace as human guinea pigs until concrete risks are identified.

It is often the most gruesome problems that are brought to our attention, such as the dangers presented to coal miners by black lung, the hazards of brown lung for those exposed to cotton dust, the dangers of working with asbestos, or the risks of radiation from nuclear power plants and uranium mining. However, toxic substances of one type or another affect the majority of occupational groups. In a survey of production workers conducted by the Survey Research Center at the University of Michigan, 78 percent reported some exposure to work hazards. Occupational groups such as carpenters, construction workers, laboratory technicians, agricultural workers, dry cleaners, firefighters, hospital staff, and even hairstylists increasingly work with chemical substances whose long-term effects are unknown. Even in the modern office building, poor ventilation or exposure to radiation from video display terminals can add to the risk of occupationally induced illness of one kind or another.

While such risks can be seen as an inevitable side effect of industrial development, those directly involved with the promotion of health and safety at work suggest that employers are often reluctant to admit to hazards even when there is plenty of evidence or early warning signs.

The classic case is found in the history of the asbestos industry, which, even now, accounts for approximately 50,000 deaths annually in the United

States alone. The risks have been long known. As early as 1918, insurance companies in both the United States and Canada stopped selling life policies to asbestos workers. Yet the industry continued to allow employees to operate without respirators, sometimes in dust so thick that it was impossible to see beyond a few yards. The industry also systematically overlooked the tragic consequences.

Documents in product liability suits against the asbestos industry in the United States suggest an organized cover-up of the ill effects. A 1980 report on corporate crime by a subcommittee of the U.S. House of Representatives noted that a number of firms in the asbestos industry made out-of-court settlements to asbestos workers who had registered claims, many in the 1930s, well before the firms admitted to having recognized the hazard presented by asbestos.

The history of the modern asbestos industry is every bit as bad as that of the lace and pottery industries in the mid-nineteenth century. Asbestos-related deaths among shipyard and insulation workers continue at high rates; it is estimated that 20 to 25 percent die from lung cancer, 10 to 18 percent from asbestosis, and 10 percent from gastrointestinal cancer. Additional asbestos-related deaths in industries as diverse as steel, automotive-parts manufacture, construction, and building maintenance continue at high levels. Although this case history is one of the more extreme and serious ones, it is by no means untypical. Just as the tobacco industry long denied links between smoking and lung cancer in the interests of profitability, toxic industries seem to resist acknowledging key problems and are reluctant to take action until forced to do so.

The problems continue in the Third World, where international corporations engage in the same dangerous practices, free from the health regulations now imposed in the West. The evidence on hazardous factories operated for Western corporations suggests that health and safety practice is often fifty years behind standard practice in their home countries. Besides the hazards in the factories, dangerous chemicals are often dumped in places where other humans, especially children at play, are subject to direct exposure.

Economics rules! Just as the early manufacturers of the nineteenth century often worked their employees to death because of losses associated with idle machines, modern industrialists often seem compelled to keep their plants in operation despite statistics suggesting that all is not well. Although workers may prove careless, and bad management and negligence often occur, many of the problems are systemic. If accidents are built into the structure of a plant or if the use of toxic chemicals is essential for continued productivity or for gaining a competitive edge, the welfare of the worker frequently takes second place.

The limitations of legislation

Despite an early start in Great Britain with the Factory Acts of 1833, legislation has often appeared too late to deal with critical problems and is often difficult to enforce, especially in relation to the threat presented by exposure to toxins: many employees bringing compensation claims have found it hard to show employer liability. Of the half million people in the United States severely disabled as a result of occupational disease, fewer than 5 percent have received formal compensation.

Since the passage of the 1970 Occupational Safety and Health Act in the United States and similar legislation elsewhere, the situation has improved. OSHA intervention in the United States has been accompanied by a 50 percent reduction in the workplace fatality rate. Action in relation to specific problems such as brown lung disease in the cotton industry, lead poisoning in battery and smelting operations, accidents on building sites, and grain dust explosions, to name a few, has led to major improvements.

But problems still abound. The fact that it is often cheaper to pay accident compensation than to eliminate accidents or diseases by making work safe, and the fact that penalties on firms that continue to operate high-risk plants are not stiff enough to close them down perpetuate the underlying problem.

Also, issues of liability and the threat of class action suits from employees with a common grievance lead organizations to adopt a defensive posture. Many corporations, like the tobacco industry, marshal their resources to demonstrate that no risk exists. When accidents do occur, organizational prudence suggests that it is much better to let the injured worker sue for compensation than for the organization to acknowledge any responsibility.

Legislation often requires the appointment of safety officers in high-risk organizations. But because they are paid by the corporation concerned, they often get caught in role conflicts between economics and safety. Many end up performing a role designed to make their employers look good in the eyes of government inspectors. As a result, the relations between safety officers and inspectors often become an elaborate organizational game.

As a safety officer in a manufacturing plant tells it:

> The tactics employed depend on the government inspector. There's one who usually likes to issue a few minor directives. He's nearing retirement, does not want a fuss, and wants to avoid the paperwork that stems from issuing serious directives. . . . In this case, the

tactic is to create obvious minor infractions so that the inspector does not have to search for problems. . . . [Thus] items such as exit signs with burnt-out bulbs or guard rails that are not high enough are left unrepaired near inspection time. . . . In the case of another, younger inspector, renowned to be thorough and wishing to make a name for himself as having promotion potential, everything must be up to scratch. Thus, in this case, a particular machine or process which is known to be in marginal condition is examined before the inspection so that modifications can be planned and budgeted. Then, when the inspection occurs, the inspector indirectly is encouraged to shut down the machine and thus satisfy his own requirements. The approach is successful in minimizing inconvenience and projecting a good image in that we get few instructions for improvement.

Organizations work hard to look good in official records by reducing the number or severity of potential hazards actually *identified* through various kinds of window dressing. They may do this by influencing the way accidents or hazards are classified or by reducing the number of days lost to injury by encouraging injured employees to turn up for work in return for assignments to easy jobs. The attempt to control accidents through legislation often encourages this type of response, leaving underlying attitudes and hazards unchanged.

Of course, while there are many employers who do not take health and safety seriously, there are also many who do. Similarly, there are many workers who take advantage of the rules, regulations, and compensation schemes. The Marxian idea that the majority of employers are unscrupulous "vampires" who willfully suck the blood of labor is no doubt an exaggeration, as is the widespread idea that the majority of workers are fakers and scroungers. While there are many cases at the extremes, the truth stands somewhere in between: in a place consistent with the general idea that in many situations the bottom line tends to come first and safety second. The radical critics of modern organization make a strong case in asserting that many organizations continue to advance their interests by exploiting and dominating the health and welfare of employees.

Stress and workaholism

Our discussion up to now has placed principal emphasis on work-related hazards of a physical kind. As such, many of the victims belong to the secondary labor market, a fact that again emphasizes the differential impact of organizations on different sections of the working population. However, those in the primary labor market also become victims of certain hazards, especially those producing various kinds of stress. Although white-collar workers are, on average, less likely than blue-collar workers to be killed or seriously injured by accidents while working on the job or to be directly exposed to toxic hazards, they are often far more likely to suffer from work-related coronary disease, ulcers, and mental breakdown.

Stress as an occupational hazard

Coronary disease, often labeled the "management killer," is being increasingly recognized as a problem affecting many people in stressful work situations. Not only white-collar workers but also blue-collar workers and women faced with the problem of managing a family as well as holding down a part- or full-time job often suffer from this disease. The problem is endemic to stressful situations of all kinds and seems to be the product of a complex network of factors. One's working conditions, role, career aspirations, and quality of relations at work interact with one's personality to influence personal stress levels and physical and mental well-being. The "Type A" personality, driven by the compulsion to control his or her work environment, ambitious, achievement oriented, competitive, impatient, and perfectionistic, is always a good candidate for coronary problems. Even those who work with such a person run risks as well, for the Type A personality often creates considerable tension for others in the workplace. The tension, frustration, and anger that often accompany a sense of powerlessness, such as that experienced by people in dead-end blue-collar and clerical jobs, also increases the risk of physical and mental breakdown.

It is estimated that somewhere between 75 and 90 percent of visits to physicians in the United States are stress related, with an estimated cost to industry of between $200 billion and $300 billion per annum. Insurance industry surveys of American workers have found that over 40 percent of employees find their jobs very or extremely stressful. For women, stress is identified as the number-one problem, highlighted as a major concern by an average of 60 percent over all occupational groups. The figures are as high as 74 percent for women in their forties in professional and managerial roles and 67 percent for single mothers. Overwork, impossible schedules, high uncertainty, fear of job loss, economic problems, work-family conflicts, and other contextual factors are important factors across many occupational groups.

High stress also correlates with increasing physical violence in the workplace. Data collected by the U.S. Department of Justice reveal that the number of work-related assaults is now in the region of one million per annum. Homicide ranks as the second leading cause of workplace death overall and ranks number one for women. Each month, five or six employers are killed in employer-directed homicides.

Although much can be done to modify the levels of stress and tension experienced at work—for example, through appropriate design of jobs and the attempt to develop balanced relations between work and outside life—it seems that a certain amount of stress is endemic. Indeed, organizations thrive on and at times actively create stress as a means of promoting organizational effectiveness. Although in the view of many experts a certain amount of stress may be beneficial, undue stress has a costly long-term impact on organizations because of illness and lost working time and its negative impact on overall quality of life. The feeling in many quarters is that the problem is almost out of control. The hypercompetition in the global economic environment with the constant drive toward continuous improvement and creative destruction is reflected in hyperstress in the workplace.

Few people feel completely secure in their roles. They have seen Arthur Miller's "orange peel phenomenon" all too often in relation to friends, family, or community. The flattening of organizations and associated resource reductions have removed a lot of the slack that used to provide a cushion through which people could moderate organizational pressures.

The stressful impact of information technology

Information technology has created an expectation of instantaneous action, even on difficult problems. It has also led to increased surveillance. Through the use of sophisticated software and on-line information systems, salespeople, telephone operators, production teams, and service staff can be subject to constant control. Their productivity can be measured and updated every minute of the day. In some offices and manufacturing situations, the latest on-line productivity statistics of individuals or groups may be displayed continuously as a constant reminder of how well or badly one is doing against expectations. Needless to say, work stress in such situations is at an all-time high.

Workaholism as an occupational disease

Even when people enjoy their jobs, work pressures in the modern corporation can carry the "enjoyment" too far. To get ahead or just keep their current positions, many executives and aspiring newcomers often feel that they must demonstrate complete identification with what their organization stands for and comply with organizational norms that demand rushed or missed meals and long hours of work six or seven days a week.

The product, of course, is the workaholic. Work becomes an addiction and a crutch, resulting in unbalanced personal development and creating many problems for family life. The workaholic tends to be always under pressure, to have little spare time for his or her spouse and children, and to be frequently absent from home. Very often, progress on the career ladder requires frequent change in jobs, often involving moves from one anonymous city to another. The negative impact on home life and the incidence of marital and family breakdown is of course enormous. In the case of dual-career families, the strains and tensions are often amplified many times. While the individuals involved ultimately make the choices that shape these events, they are in many cases driven by their desire to comply with the norms and values that have become standard practice in the corporate world.

ORGANIZATIONAL POLITICS AND THE RADICALIZED ORGANIZATION

The idea that organizations use and exploit their employees commands a great deal of support and accounts for important attitudes, beliefs, and practices in many organizations. It helps us understand why labor and management have often found themselves in such bitter conflict and why, with the downsizings in executive ranks, many managers now find themselves sharing the same uncertainty and skepticism with regard to their role in the modern corporation. From the point of view of a member of the secondary labor market who suffers periodic unemployment with the ups and downs of the business cycle, or who is engaged in a low-status job that values and uses few of his or her abilities, or who has suffered from a work-related accident or toxic hazard without compensation, it may make much more sense to understand organizations as battlegrounds than as united teams or friendly coalitions. Workers ask themselves the following questions:

- How can we feel we belong to a team if we are uncertain whether we will still be employed next week?
- How can we believe that we are part of a community of shared interests when differences in status and privilege are obvious and rife?

It seems quite reasonable in these circumstances for workers to see themselves as part of an exploited and disadvantaged group of people and to band together with their fellows to see what gains and benefits can be extracted from their employers. This is what has made unions thrive, making organizations become divided worlds reflecting and entrenching class divisions found in the wider society.

In extreme cases, these divisions have often become as sharp as those between warring factions, creating "radicalized organizations" such as those often found in mining and heavy manufacturing industries. Here, the difference between white- and blue-collar workers has always been very clear, being symbolized and reinforced every day in terms of the rights and privileges of the different groups.

On average, white-collar workers have enjoyed cleaner and safer work conditions, more regular work hours, more fringe benefits, longer vacations, and higher wages than their blue-collar colleagues. They have enjoyed corporate cultures that reflect their privilege and which, by implication, affirm the inferior status of their colleagues.

Consider the British vehicle assembly firm where separate dining rooms were provided for shop-floor workers and white-collar staff. The rooms were next to each other but were worlds apart. In the staff dining room one could enjoy lunch and a glass of wine served by uniformed waitresses at an attractive table. In the plant dining room one had to line up for self-service food to be eaten at long bare tables with plastic knives and forks. Metal cutlery could be used—provided one paid a deposit!

Needless to say, there was no feeling on the part of the workforce that they belonged to the same team as management, let alone that of the shareholders. They knew they were on opposite sides and behaved accordingly. A battleground atmosphere was the norm.

Interestingly, with the fiscal cutbacks and job reductions of the 1990s, many white-collar workers have begun to adopt the same position. Even white-collar bureaucracies that used to be regarded as secure and privileged middle-class institutions have become radicalized through strikes, lockouts, and battles over job security. In the aftermath, relations often remain strained and hostile, with people acting with minimum trust on the premise that they are always in danger of being exploited in some way.

In the 1970s and 1980s when open conflicts between management and labor were at their height, representatives of senior management tended to adopt a unitary or pluralist ideology, emphasizing the need for team efforts or a "stakeholder" approach to problem resolution, as a means of reframing the "us and them" attitudes. But since the 1980s, the battleground has shifted, and new tactics and strategies have emerged.

The shift to automated manufacturing and the decision on the part of many major companies to relocate operations in lower-wage, nonunionized Third World countries have undermined the power of Western trade unions. Faced with a lower demand for labor and the increasing structural unemployment created by plant relocations, support for militant action among union membership has declined. Fear and uncertainty have replaced the sense of power, confidence, and strength that characterized earlier times. This has opened the way for management to more or less dictate the terms of labor-management negotiations and to obtain a reversal in basic conditions of employment that in the heyday of unionism would have been completely unthinkable.

A "new brutalism"?

The trend toward management domination has been so dramatic and extreme that in continental Europe it has become known as the "new brutalism." The ruthless drive for efficiency and bottom-line profits at the expense of human concerns and considerations is seen as more or less shifting capitalism back into the nineteenth and early twentieth centuries. Management ideology is seen as serving the needs of capital accumulation above all else. News of the latest layoffs is frequently accompanied by news of record profits, highlighting the conflict of interest between labor and capital.

Interestingly, the critique is no longer confined to left-wing radicals. It has become mainstream. Amid the corporate downsizings of the mid-1990s, *Newsweek* magazine ran a cover-page article on "Corporate Killers." It featured the photographs of leading chief executives accompanied by details of their salaries, often many millions of dollars per annum, and the number of employees who had been downsized during the previous few years: 74,000 at GM, 60,000 at IBM, 50,000 at Sears, and 40,000 at AT&T, to name just a few. The fact that such a conservative magazine would use such an extreme image to capture the reality of corporate life symbolizes the increasing concern and cynicism that people hold about the role and interests of the modern corporation.

In Germany, where the system of codetermination has established joint labor-management committees at the most senior corporate levels, the trend has been resisted. There has been a deliberate attempt to integrate the interests of labor and capital. Work sharing has often replaced layoffs, and there has been a deliberate attempt to maintain wage levels and social benefits. But with the development of globalized low-wage production systems, it is very difficult to preserve national policies. The global economy doesn't respect national boundaries insofar as the economics of production are concerned. While rules about local content may require global corporations to produce locally if they are to sell in these markets, the tendency in many globalized industries is to shift to low-cost manufacturing centers wherever they may be. Now the battle between labor and management is being fought on a global stage and is intimately connected with the role of multinationals in the world economy. It is to this dimension of the radical critique of organizations that we now turn.

RADICAL ORGANIZATIONAL THEORY:
MULTINATIONALS AND THE WORLD ECONOMY

The operation of the world economy is dominated by the activities of giant companies, usually called "multinationals" or "global" or "transnational" corporations. They now account for over 70 percent of world trade. There are more than two thousand corporations with sales of over $2 billion per annum. Many of these corporations have sales over $50 billion. The largest corporations, including Mitsubishi, Mitsu, Itochu, Sumitomo, GM, Marubeni, Ford, Exxon, Royal Dutch Shell, Toyota, and Wal-Mart, have annual sales figures that exceed the gross national products of many nations. No wonder they have been described as sovereign states that have a major impact on international politics and the world economy.

Multinational corporations with headquarters in Japan and the United States dominate the list of the largest companies. Up until the early 1970s hegemony of the United States was undisputed, but Japan has now become the dominant force. The largest multinationals include electronics, automobile, oil, insurance, retail, and a variety of other firms and typically operate in countries throughout the world. Most have diversified interests and are controlled by shareholders; some are fully or partly government owned.

In the late nineteenth and early twentieth centuries we witnessed the growth and proliferation of multinationals along with developments in the capitalist world economy. Large, specialized corporations were among the first to appear, amassing a great concentration of economic resources and near-monopoly power with operations in many countries. Around the middle of the twentieth century, a new development emerged along with antitrust legislation designed to curb the influence of such organizations, namely, the emergence of diversified conglomerates. Diversified conglomerate multinationals developed as firms attempted to control supplies of crucial raw materials, to develop a portfolio of different types of investment, to hedge the risks associated with location by operating in many places at once, to engage in defensive foreign investment that protected them from the vagaries of the business cycle or the policies of any single host government, and to open up new markets for products that were reaching a stage of maturity in older markets.

This strong pattern of centralized *control* has been sustained throughout the century, but as Peter Drucker has noted, it has been accompanied by an increasingly broad-based pattern of ownership through the influences of pension funds and other channels of institutionalized investment. The trend has produced a form of "postcapitalist society" where the logic of accumulating capital still drives the system, but with rewards accruing to a new, detached group of owners.

MULTINATIONALS AS WORLD POWERS

The proliferation of multinationals has had major repercussions on power structures throughout the world. Many modern organizations are larger and more powerful than nation-states, but unlike nation-states, they are often not accountable to anyone but themselves. The activities of many multinationals are highly centralized, their foreign subsidiaries being tightly controlled through policies, rules, and regulations set by headquarters. The subsidiaries have to report on a regular basis, and their staff are often allowed very little influence on key decisions affecting the subsidiary. Chief executives in foreign countries often become branch managers, developing local initiatives but within the policies set at the center. Because it is head-quarters that actually controls the executive's future in the corporation, central concerns will almost always override local ones. The resources of multinationals are also usually managed in a way that creates dependency rather than local autonomy.

Global dominance

Whenever we examine multinationals we are quickly brought face-to-face with their monolithic power and the fact that the twentieth century has witnessed a worldwide transformation. The power is not just economic. It is cultural and political as well. Note the global marketing alliance struck between McDonald's and Disney. In coming together, the two companies have created a global force that will have a massive socializing impact on youths throughout the world.

Of all organizations, multinationals come closest to realizing Max Weber's worst fears with regard to how bureaucratic organizations can become totalitarian regimes serving the interests of elites, where those in control are able to exercise power that is "practically unshatterable." Even though ownership is now widely diversified, and in an idealistic sense reflects what Peter Drucker calls "pension fund socialism," governance is still highly centralized. The "owners" are not really in a position to know what is happening, especially on a detailed level, because multinationals usually control a network of subsidiary companies. Power is firmly concentrated in the hands of senior management.

Historically, multinationals have tried to achieve global dominance through worldwide sourcing of raw materials at the lowest possible price with a view to producing and selling goods and services in the most profitable markets. The old model was one where the multinational would operate from its home base and penetrate foreign markets at a distance. Now the tendency is to create a strong simultaneous presence in a number of key areas of the world.

Kenichi Ohmae suggests that the late twentieth century has seen a shift toward what he calls "triad power"—a simultaneous penetration and presence in Japan, the European Community, and North America. Instead of selling "clone" products and services throughout the world, international companies now find ways of getting inside these three power bases with differentiated goods that tap regional markets to an optimum degree. This calls for new strategies and the use of joint ventures and international consortia through which different companies lever each other's strength. These strategies create strange bedfellows. Consider the alliance between companies like GM and Toyota. Competitors such as these can lever each other's distribution, production, and other strengths in mutually beneficial ways. If a U.S.-based manufacturer can link with European and Japanese companies with strengths in distribution, considerable gains can accrue to all.

Multinationals have long engaged in this kind of collaboration through the medium of international cartels, even though these are illegal in many countries. They have also reduced competition by entering into home-market protection agreements that establish exclusive territories that competitors will avoid or where competitors will content themselves with existing market shares, leaving the dominant firm with no competition except from small domestic firms outside the cartel. "Hunting ground" agreements have often defined the degree of competition that is to be allowed in foreign markets, with preference usually being given to patterns of traditional market dominance. Agreements in relation to the exchange and transfer of technology and patent rights have reduced competition in this sphere as well.

With the new patterns of international alliances, these practices have developed to a new level of sophistication and add to the already immense power of multinationals in an important way, not least because they help to prevent mutually destructive battles between the giants by controlling the ground and terms on which they will fight.

Political impact

The efforts of multinationals to control their environment also extend into the realm of politics itself. Big corporations often use their immense lobbying power to shape the political agenda and to create political outcomes favorable to themselves. In this, perhaps more than any other single activity, the political significance of multinationals as world powers comes to the fore as they are often in a position to exert major influence on host governments, especially when a nation is critically dependent on their presence or on some aspect of their operations.

While the issues on which a multinational wishes to exert its influence are usually economic, the corporation often becomes directly and sometimes illegally involved in the political process. For example, when the economic aims and objectives of a multinational are in conflict with the line of development favored by a host government, it is very easy for the multinational to become embroiled in activities designed to shape the economic and social policies of the government. As a result, it may be drawn into the political arena and become explicitly political and ideological in its activities, although usually acting behind the scenes.

The classic and infamous case is ITT's involvement in the affairs of Chile where it plotted in 1970 to stop the election of Marxist President Salvador Allende. Conspiring with the CIA, ITT sought to create economic chaos within Chile and thereby encourage a military coup, with the company offering to contribute "up to seven figures" to the White House to stop Allende coming to power.

Multinationals are, for the most part, a political force without political accountability. The Chilean episode, although extreme in its characteristics, highlights the contradictions that arise when strong authoritarian powers like multinationals are allowed to exist in democratic states, for they are in a position to oblige governments to be more responsive to corporate interests than to those of the people who elected them.

We can see now why advocates of the radical frame of reference point to the existence of multinationals as yet further evidence of the general antagonism of interests between people and corporations. The sheer power of multinationals, and the associated cartels, alliances, and interlocking patterns of ownership and control that bind them together, combine to create a world economy dominated by organizations where the power of the corporate official often dwarfs that of the elected politician and that of the public-at-large.

MULTINATIONALS: A RECORD OF EXPLOITATION?

Advocates of multinationals often see them as positive forces in economic development, creating jobs and bringing capital, technology, and expertise to communities or countries that might have difficulty developing these resources on their own account. Their critics, though, tend to see them as authoritarian juggernauts that are ultimately out to exploit their hosts for all they can get. The argument identifies the horns of a major dilemma in that the policies that serve the interests of a multinational firm may not be in the best interests of the community or nation in which the firm is located.

Hence, given the immense power of the multinational firm, its hosts often find themselves having to rely on a benevolent social responsibility on the part of the multinational.

The record of multinationals in this regard, however, leaves a great deal to be desired. The highly centralized systems of decision making frequently mean that centralized corporate interests relating to the profitability, growth, or strategic development of the multinational as a whole take first place in decision making with localized community or national interests taking second. When strategic considerations lead the executive staff of a multinational to divest its holdings in a particular industry, to close down a particular plant, or to restructure its operations internationally, the consequences can be devastating for the communities and countries involved.

Consider how the shift in search of cheaper, nonunionized labor has led many firms to leave relatively high-priced cities in Canada and the northern United States for locations in the southern states, Mexico, Brazil, or Asia. The effect has been to create large areas of regional and urban decline. The effects are particularly marked in small communities where the decision of the multinational to close down operations of a major plant can remove the economic lifeblood of the community. Regional exodus also creates massive structural unemployment, increasing welfare rolls and intensifying the fiscal problems faced by governments. The bitter irony is often that many of these decisions are made not because a particular plant or set of operations is unprofitable, but because the corporation believes that it is possible to earn greater profit elsewhere.

Similar developments are found in the decaying industrial and mining centers of Europe, where the closure of coal mines and steel mills leads to the economic and social decline of whole regions. These communities often feel they have been used and sucked dry and are now being thrown away because they are no longer needed. The feelings of resentment and exploitation are particularly severe when the plants or mines being closed are profitable but not profitable enough from a corporate standpoint.

Conflicts with host nations

That corporate and community interests are not always synonymous is a truism common to all organizations, not just multinationals. But the scale of operations among the latter is so enormous that it makes the consequences of their decisions especially great. We have illustrated the point by focusing on how changes in corporate strategy, even if only to *increase* rates of profit, can set the basis for widespread socioeconomic change. In a similar way, the decisions of multinationals to move their liquid capital from one country to another to take advantage of interest rate differentials can have a major effect on the international balance of payments of the countries concerned. Or a decision to pursue a particular line of corporate development can have a major effect on national and regional economic planning, distorting the pattern of relations that the host region or nation wishes to encourage.

For these and many other reasons, communities and nations often find themselves wishing to attract multinationals while also fearing the consequences because they know that the underlying sets of interests may be in fundamental conflict. Some nations, such as Canada, where foreign ownership in many sectors of industry is at levels well over 50 percent, have formally recognized that such conflicts exist and have tried, without success, to codify the conditions under which multinationals will be allowed to operate within their domains. However, there is a dilemma in that the more a host government attempts to control the practices of multinationals, the less attractive their investment in that country becomes. So multinational and nation-state often end up in a relation of dominance and dependency or as rival power blocs, each attempting to shape the conditions under which the other is to operate. Up to now, it seems that the multinationals are winning the battle. Increasingly, nations are having to recognize that they cannot really manage or control what goes on within their own boundaries.

The impact of multinationals on Western countries may be damaging, but their impact on the Third World has undoubtedly been much worse. Critics see them as modern plunderers, exploiting natural and other resources for their own ends. Of course, the multinationals do not see themselves in this way. They see their activities as helping develop the underdeveloped world amid the difficulties created by unfavorable publicity about the wrongdoings of a socially irresponsible minority, by propaganda against big business leveled by critics on the left, and sometimes by hostile and ungrateful foreign governments who fail to honor contracts. Although multinationals recognize that their activities must be subjected to appropriate rules of conduct, they argue that their influence is positive and that multinationals and host nations can operate in a way that benefits both. The debate is a hot one, and arguments can be made for either side.

Criticisms of multinationals in the Third World

1. *Multinationals' effect on the economies of host nations is basically exploitative.* Multinationals in Third World countries traditionally have been heavily involved in the extraction of raw materials and foodstuffs. More recently they have become involved in manufactur-

ing. In both cases, control of operations, technology, and revenues rests with the multinationals and their parent nations, the end result being that the Third World countries are *more* dependent on them than when the process first started.

The introduction of multinational enterprise tends to eliminate local agriculture and traditional craft and industry, creating a dispossessed labor force and a market for unskilled labor. Skilled artisans and farmers go to work on plantations and in factories for subsistence wages exactly as they did in Europe and North America centuries before. And just like the factory owners in the industrial revolution who exploited this workforce, corporations continue to do so in the Third World today.

2. *Multinationals exploit local populations, using them as wage slaves, often as a substitute for unionized Western labor.* In multinational-owned Third World factories, men, women, and children sometimes work ten, twelve, or more hours for less than one dollar a day. No wonder that industry drifts from Western cities to Third World factories at an incredible rate. The AFL-CIO has estimated that the United States alone loses around one million jobs every five years to these sources of cheap and exploited labor.

3. *While multinationals claim to be taking capital and technology to underdeveloped countries, the result is usually a net outflow of capital and continued control over the technology they introduce.* It has been estimated that multinationals sometimes raise as much as 80 percent of their capital from local sources. Their own direct investment is often relatively small, boosting the return generated by overall profits on their own capital to quite staggering heights. In certain industries, the estimated rate of return on capital invested by the multinationals sometimes runs as high as 400 percent per annum. Given that it is usual to repatriate a major proportion of profits to headquarters, and hence the parent nation, it is easy to see how a net outflow of capital from the host nation can arise. It becomes extremely difficult for Third World countries to derive any long-term benefit from the presence of multinationals as host governments usually do not build any real equity in their industry.

The severity of this problem has been exacerbated by the kinds of foreign aid extended by agencies such as the World Bank, the International Monetary Fund, and the United States Agency for International Development. Frequently, this aid is tied in ways that promote links with multinational enterprises, and in the long run it contributes to the net outflow of capital. This problem is vividly illustrated by the fact that the outstanding interest on the international debt of Third World countries is now greater than the capital originally borrowed, and their annual interest payments often exceed the amount of incoming aid. It is estimated that Third World debtor countries make net transfers of over $20 billion per annum. In other words, international aid has resulted in their paying to the West much more than they have received.

Similar criticisms apply to the export of technology. Although much is often made of how multinationals bring valuable expertise to the Third World, they bring only what they want and ensure that they retain control. Much of the technology exported to the Third World is Western technology that is often not appropriate to local conditions and is no longer at the cutting edge. Technology reaching maturity in the West often finds a ready market in the Third World, especially when supported by foreign aid. Western technology also makes the Third World user dependent on the Western supplier for spare parts, modernization, and often the expertise necessary to maintain and develop the technology. Critics argue that multinationals are doing no more than a form of intelligent marketing that ultimately serves their own interests. For example, most research and development continues to be done in the parent country, so no real opportunity is created for a Third World country to build technological expertise of its own. What the export of technology really exports is a new form of dependency.

4. *Multinationals often disguise excess profits and avoid paying appropriate taxes in their host nations through creative "transfer pricing."* It has been estimated that a staggering one-third of world trade is intracompany trade. In terms of value, each multinational corporation is often its own most important customer, with one subsidiary buying from another. Such trading gives the corporation great scope for manipulating profit figures for a subsidiary in a given country. By buying materials from one fellow subsidiary at high prices and selling its products to another at low prices, a subsidiary can make an operating loss or a high profit according to the impression it wishes to give to the outside world. The profits of subsidiaries in high-tax countries may be kept artificially low and those in low-tax countries inflated. Or profits can be switched from one industry to another to take advantage of special incentives offered by host governments. Such

transactions often play a big part in the politics of organization, especially in relation to negotiations with trade unions, and in producing rationales for plant closure. The simple statement that a plant is "unprofitable" is often backed by creative accounting that deceives all but the most discerning members of trade unions, investors, and members of the general public.

5. *Multinationals often drive unduly hard bargains with their host nations and communities, playing one group or country against another to achieve exceptional concessions.* These bargains may take many forms: rights to retain a controlling interest for a set period of time; excessive rates of return; local tax concessions or access to subsidies and other forms of host government support; freedom from government regulation; or regulations of reduced stringency. The multinational often achieves a position where it can do pretty much as it wishes. Some of the most obvious examples of abuses are found in the field of occupational health and safety and in the general conduct of multinationals in relation to the safety of the communities and markets they serve. Free of government regulations, they often end up operating hazardous factories or dumping hazardous products onto an unsuspecting public. It has been suggested that safety standards in some multinational plants in the Third World are decades behind those in the West. The ever-present danger posed by such plants was vividly illustrated by the 1984 tragedy at the Union Carbide plant in Bhopal, India, which took over twenty-five hundred lives and maimed thousands more.

For all these reasons, critics of multinational operations tend to stress that multinationals can create economic, political, and social havoc, distorting rather than benefiting the development of their host country. Of course, the blame is not seen as lying entirely with the multinationals, as they are usually invited into the countries where they operate and often do so with the active cooperation and encouragement of ruling governments, dictatorships, or powerful elites. The critics also place a heavy measure of blame on the ruling classes within those countries for participating in the domination and exploitation of their nation's human and material resources. Sometimes, multinationals engage in explicit or implicit agreements with ruling authorities regarding the conditions under which they will operate. Elsewhere the arrangements tend to be more subtle and the result of careful and continuous political lobbying.

The radical critique emphasizes that the modern state and multinational corporations act as partners in systematic domination. The defenders of modern practice, however, tend to see such activities in a more favorable light. State and multinationals are viewed as partners in progress, modernization, and development, and in the view of advocates of this partnership, the majority of multinationals usually behave in an exemplary way. These advocates would argue that it is necessary to focus on the exemplary behavior as a model of what overall practice could look like and to develop codes of conduct and accountability to create a constructive framework for world development, such as those developed by the United Nations in relation to the dumping of hazardous products and by the International Labor Organization in relation to good corporate citizenship.

STRENGTHS AND LIMITATIONS
OF THE DOMINATION METAPHOR

The negative impact that organizations often have on their employees or their environment or that multinationals have on patterns of inequality and world economic development is not necessarily an intended one. It is usually a consequence of rational actions through which a group of individuals seeks to advance a particular set of aims, such as increased profitability or corporate growth.

What, then, do we mean by rationality? If rationality has unintended negative impacts that lead even the most celebrated and excellent organizations to create problems for others, why is such action rational?

STRENGTHS

■ **The metaphor shows that rationality is a mode of domination.**

The overwhelming strength of the domination metaphor is that it draws our attention to this double-edged nature of rationality, illustrating that it always reflects a partial point of view. Actions that are rational for increasing profitability may have a damaging effect on employees' health. Actions designed to spread an organization's portfolio of risks (e.g., by divesting interests in a particular industry) may spell economic and urban decay for whole communities of people who have built their lives around that industry. What is rational from one organizational standpoint may be catastrophic from another.

Viewing organization as a mode of domination that advances certain interests at the expense of others forces this important aspect of organizational reality into the center of our attention. It leads us to appreciate the wisdom of Max Weber's insight that the pursuit of rationality can itself be a mode of domination and to remember that, as discussed in the conclusions to the politics chapter, in talking about rationality we should always be asking the question "Rational for whom?"

- **The ideological and ethical aspects of organization become central concerns.**

The metaphor provides a useful counterweight to much of traditional organization theory, which has for the most part ignored values or ideological premises. Most discussions of organization attempt to be ideologically neutral, often by presenting theories of organization as theories that can be used to serve many different ends and by identifying questions of business ethics as topics for special and isolated study. Through such means, it is possible to talk or write about how one can design a bureaucratic or matrix organization, or create or manage an organizational culture, or play organizational politics without paying too much attention to the way the ideas will be used. The facts that they may be used to improve the production of food or of bombs, and that in improving the rationality and efficiency of an organization one may be providing the basis for action that is profoundly irrational for many other groups of people are not addressed.

- **We see that domination may be intrinsic to organization.**

The domination metaphor also forces us to recognize that domination may be intrinsic to the way we organize and not just an unintended side effect. It shows us that there is often a seamy side to otherwise excellent organizations and suggests that this should be a mainstream concern of managers and organization theorists.

- **The metaphor provides a way of turning the table on existing power structures.**

Used in an even more proactive mode, the domination metaphor also shows a way of creating an organization theory for the exploited. In exposing the seamy side of organizational life, whether in terms of structured inequality, institutionalized racism, occupational accidents and disease, or exploitation in the Third World, and in attempting to develop theories to account for these phenomena, the organization theorist has a means of using organization theory as an instrument for social change. Those interested in pursuing this agenda turn to radical organization theory to counter the influence of more conventional theory, which they see as serving and reinforcing vested interests embodied in the status quo.

- **We gain an increased understanding of why the history of organization has been so conflict prone and polarized.**

As we have discussed, many organizations become radicalized in ways that stress "them and us" attitudes. In understanding how organizations foster dual labor markets, symbolized and extended in differential systems of privilege, or how these operate as opportunity structures that open the doors to success for some employees while closing them to others, we catch a glimpse of the kinds of segregation and division that millions of people experience on a daily basis. As we begin to appreciate the reality of factory workers who see no future in their organization other than an extension of their dingy present or the sense of exploitation experienced by those who are forced to work under oppressive conditions because they have no other means of survival, we can begin to understand that industrial unrest is not necessarily the work of troublemakers or of unions that have outlived their usefulness.

Many organizations are literally divided societies that perpetuate class warfare in the workplace. They are societies that naturally generate radical leaders hell-bent on changing the circumstances of their followers even if this means a long and arduous battle that may ultimately be lost. Hence, employees may frequently engage in what their employers see as a senseless or futile struggle for wage increases they feel they deserve, or they may even put a company out of business rather than return to work on unfair terms. The popular notion that organizations serve the interests of all often blinds us to the fact that the radical ideology is not just ideology but an accurate description of the reality of masses of people.

- **The perspective challenges managers to develop a deeper appreciation of corporate responsibility.**

The domination metaphor encourages us to recognize and deal with perceived and actual exploitation in the workplace rather than dismiss it as a radical distortion of the way things are. Clearly, if those managing organizations were to attempt to deal with the radical frame of reference by accepting rather than denying its legitimacy, as tends to be the situation at present, this would help initiate a new era of employee relations and conceptions of corporate responsibility. A new and aggressive form of social consciousness would oblige corporate decision makers to take personal responsibility for the inhuman consequences of so many conventional practices.

LIMITATIONS

The strengths of the domination metaphor provide the basis for a truly radical critique of organization and organization theory. However, in the view of many it goes too far and has a number of serious limitations.

- **The metaphor can add to the polarization between social groups if domination is interpreted as an aim rather than an unintended result.**

This limitation arises when the perspective is linked to a crude conspiracy theory of organization and society. Although there is much evidence to suggest that patterns of domination are class based, that there is a tendency for the interests of ruling elites to converge in centralized ownership and control, and that government policies often work in ways that sustain and serve the interests of dominant social groups, this does not necessarily support the idea that there is a conspiracy in the way one group or social class is pitted against another.

Let us return to a question raised implicitly throughout this chapter: *Does organizational domination occur by default or by design?* A conspiracy theory tends to imply the latter, suggesting that the process of domination in society is rooted in some callous structure of motivation or in a conscious policy of exploitation. However, this is not necessarily the case. If we consider the ideas discussed in the flux and transformation chapter, it is easy to see that domination may be encoded in the logics of change through which social life is unfolding: organizational actions that promote structured inequalities, industrial accidents, occupational disease, environmental pollution, or exploitation in the Third World may all result from the way systemic forces dictate that business be done.

- **The metaphor can lead us to blame individual decision makers, rather than help us see that it is the "logic" of the whole system that needs to be addressed.**

For many, any explanation of social domination that emphasizes its systemic character is far too deterministic, serving to remove all responsibility from the powerful decision makers who are actively engaged in producing the organizational world, and who, in principle, have the power to change things. However, it does serve to raise a very real dilemma, for many top-level decision makers often feel caught "between a rock and a hard place," recognizing the social consequences of their actions and yet knowing that a sensitive social conscience or undue concern for people may prove economically paralyzing and prevent their organizations from operating in a decisive and efficient way.

To the extent that domination is seen as part of a social conspiracy or the responsibility of a few individuals, the latent consequence is to assign blame, arouse defenses, and entrench the fundamental problems. At best, it mobilizes social and political opposition to the problem, aiming for revolutionary change, but usually achieving no more than marginal change. Although such mobilization may be appropriate, a more systemic understanding would help to create a greater sense of collective responsibility and to find ways of reframing the basic problems to create new kinds of remedial actions. Such reframing may show that domination is embedded in processes of mutual causality or in dialectical logics of change that can be reshaped by giving attention to special system pathologies, new codes of social responsibility, new concepts of social accounting, and the like. We may be able to remove key problems by changing the rules of the game that produce them.

■ **The focus on systemic patterns of domination can lead us to overlook opportunities for creating nondominating forms of organization.**

This potential limitation of the metaphor stems from the danger that in asserting an equivalence between domination and organization we may blind ourselves to the idea that nondominating forms of organization may be possible. It is sometimes argued that the real thrust of the domination metaphor should be to critique the values that underlie different modes of organization and to highlight the differences between exploitative and non-exploitative forms, rather than to engage in critique in a broader sense.

■ **The metaphor is sometimes seen as too extreme.**

Finally, it is often said that the metaphor merely articulates an extreme form of left-wing ideology, serving to fan the flames of the radical perspective and adding to the difficulties of managers in an already turbulent world. The criticism has merit in that the perspective is ideological, but it is certainly no more ideological than any other. The chapters in this book show that all theories of organization are inherently ideological in that they tend to give us rather one-sided views. Although the domination metaphor may lead us to focus on the negative side of organization in an extreme way, it is really no more extreme than any other viewpoint, including the highly orthodox.

III Implications for Practice

Using metaphor to negotiate the demands of a paradoxical world

10 Reading and Shaping Organizational Life

ORGANIZATIONS AND ORGANIZATIONAL PROBLEMS CAN BE SEEN AND UNDERSTOOD IN MANY DIFFERENT WAYS. Limit your seeing and your thinking and you limit your range of action. Limit your range of action and you limit your effectiveness. This chapter shows how we can use multiple metaphors to "read" an organization and increase our options for effective interventions.

The ability to "read" and understand what is happening in an organization is a key managerial competence, especially now, when managing change is one of business's greatest concerns. When we broaden our understanding, we broaden the potential range of actions through which we can approach key problems and issues.

This chapter provides a concrete illustration of how to use the metaphors presented in earlier chapters in reading and interpreting the experience of a small organization called Multicom. In the next section, you will find a short case study describing life at Multicom during a key period of its development followed by two readings of the case from different points of view. One adopts the perspective of a manager-consultant seeking to deal with the problems presented in the case. The other presents a reading from the perspectives of a social critic and policy analyst. Together they illustrate how we can mobilize the insights of different metaphors to identify and understand key dimensions of a situation to serve the purposes at hand.

THE MULTICOM CASE

Multicom is a small firm employing 150 people in the public relations field. It was started by Jim Walsh, a marketing specialist, and Wendy Bridges, a public relations expert. They had worked together for several years at a medium-sized communications firm and decided to branch out on their own to realize their own ideas as to what a good PR firm could and should be. They felt that their combined expertise and extensive contacts provided an excellent base on which to do this.

Before submitting their resignations at their old firm, they persuaded two colleagues, Marie Beaumont and Frank Rossi, to join them as minority shareholders. Walsh and Bridges each held 40 percent of the equity in the new venture; Beaumont and Rossi were each given 10 percent. Rossi was an editor and writer with an excellent reputation, and Beaumont was a well-regarded film and video expert.

At first, business was difficult, and they were glad of the corporate clients that they had taken with them from their old firm. Competition was keen, and their old firm seemed subtly to be doing everything it could to block their progress. However, they worked hard, and their reputation steadily grew along with the size of their staff and their earnings. By the end of their second year, the four partners were each earning almost double their previous salaries and building a significant capital investment as well. They felt that they were well on the way to achieving the kind of top-notch company on which they had set their sights.

These early years were exciting ones.

When they established Multicom, the four partners adopted a client-centered mode of organization. Each partner had certain clients for whom he or she felt a special responsibility, and in effect each became a project manager for these clients. Each developed a reasonable competence in all aspects of the agency's work so that one could substitute for another when necessary. New staff were encouraged to develop the same all-around skills and capacities in addition to their specializations. While this was often time-consuming and expensive, it created great flexibility. The search for new business and continuing contacts with clients took a significant proportion of staff away from the office most of the time, so the existence of a number of good "all arounders" was a real asset. Besides that, it often made work more interesting and enjoyable and added to the general team spirit of the office.

The staff at Multicom worked hard, often starting early in the morning and working late at night. They also played hard, throwing regular parties to celebrate the completion of major projects or the acquisition of new clients. These parties helped keep morale high and project Multicom's image as an excellent and exciting place to work. The firm's clients often attended these parties and were usually impressed by the vitality and quality of interpersonal relations.

During the company's third year, however, things began to change. The long hours and pace of life at Multicom were getting to Walsh and Bridges. Both had heavy family commitments and wanted more leisure time. They increasingly talked about the need to "get more organized" so that they could exercise a closer control over staff and office activities, which, in their view, at times verged on the chaotic. Beaumont and Rossi, however, both of whom were single and at thirty and thirty-one, respectively, almost ten years younger than the senior partners, relished the lifestyle and were keen to maintain the firm's present character. They would have been happy to shoulder a greater share of the work and responsibility in return for a greater equity in the company, but Walsh and Bridges were reluctant to hand them this sort of control.

As time went on, it became clear that there were important philosophical differences about the way the office should be run. Whereas Walsh and Bridges regarded the ad hoc style of organization that had developed during the first two years as temporary—"necessary until we've sorted out our ideas as to how we want to put this organization together"—Beaumont and Rossi saw it as a desirable way of doing business in the longer term. Whereas Walsh and Bridges complained about the frequent absence of staff

from the office and the lack of clear systems of responsibility and office protocol, Beaumont and Rossi relished what they often described as their "creative chaos." To them, the firm was producing excellent results, clients were
happy and knocking at the door, and this was all that mattered.

By the fourth year, tensions were close to the breaking point. The four
principals frequently found themselves in long meetings about office organization, and the differences were as deep as ever. Walsh and Bridges argued
for "more system," and Beaumont and Rossi argued for the status quo. The
differences were straining personal relations and were having an unfavorable impact on life in the office generally. Many staff felt that Multicom was
in danger of losing its special character and was no longer quite the same
"fun place" at which to work.

All four principals sensed this change, and they talked about it frequently. However, there was simply no consensus as to what should be
done. As a result of general frustration, they began to break an unwritten
but golden rule set in the early days of Multicom: that all four would always
be involved in major policy decisions. Walsh and Bridges began to meet
together and resolved that the only way forward was for them to exercise
their authority and to insist that a reorganization of the office be initiated.
They agreed to propose this at a meeting with Beaumont and Rossi the following day.

Walsh and Bridges were surprised. The idea produced little resistance
from their two colleagues. It was almost as if it was expected. Beaumont
and Rossi insisted that the decision should not be taken without a lot of
thought because it represented a major departure. They reiterated their view
that no change in office organization was necessary other than a streamlining of a few financial procedures. They were by no means happy with the
proposal, but it was clear that they weren't going to fight it.

The following week Walsh and Bridges called a meeting of all staff to
outline their plans. In operational terms, these involved a clearer definition
of job responsibilities, a more formalized procedure governing the exchange
of staff between projects, and a closer control over the conditions under
which staff were to be away from the office during business hours. A number of other office procedures were also introduced.

The meeting was unique in Multicom's history in tone and nature.
For weeks there was talk about a rift among the four principals and about
how winds of change were blowing through the firm. Some members of the
staff welcomed the greater degree of structure; others resented the new
developments. Staff continued to work hard at their jobs with the profes-
sionalism they knew Multicom demanded, but everyone knew that things

were not quite the same. Multicom was no longer working—or playing—the Multicom way.

Walsh and Bridges, however, were well pleased. They felt a lot more secure with the way things stood and could see the time ahead when they would be able to take a lot of pressure off themselves and let the office run itself within the framework they had begun to develop. Beaumont and Rossi continued to work hard as usual, and their project teams were least affected by the new developments. Within a year, however, they had left Multicom and set up a new company of their own, taking a number of key staff and clients with them.

Thanks to a large number of faithful clients, Multicom continued to produce sound financial results, but it gradually lost its reputation as a leading-edge agency. It could be relied on to produce good solid work but was, in the eyes of a number of disaffected clients, "uninspiring."

Beaumont and Rossi's new firm, Media 2000, picked up many of these clients and, adopting the organizational style pioneered at Multicom, re-created a "fun business" employing eighty people. The firm quickly established itself as a talented and innovative agency. Beaumont and Rossi take satisfaction in the firm's reputation and financial success and look back on their days with Multicom as "a great learning experience." In retrospect, they view their differences with Walsh and Bridges as part of a "lucky break" that spurred them to find an even more lucrative and satisfying work situation.

INTERPRETING MULTICOM

Many different metaphors can be used to understand the pattern of events at Multicom. Yet the tendency for many people is to seize on one particular point of view—for example, that "Multicom offers a clear case of organizational politics"—and elevate this to THE VIEW of the situation. Instead, it is critical to recognize that, as illustrated in exhibit 10.1, many different interpretations and meanings may all have a measure of validity in understanding what is happening. A reflective reading of Multicom requires that we remain open to as many possibilities as we can and then find ways of integrating the insights to further our objectives.

I find it helpful to think about this kind of reflective reading in terms of two interdependent processes:

- a *diagnostic reading,* whereby we strive to gain as comprehensive an understanding as possible, accompanied by
- a *critical evaluation* that integrates key insights.

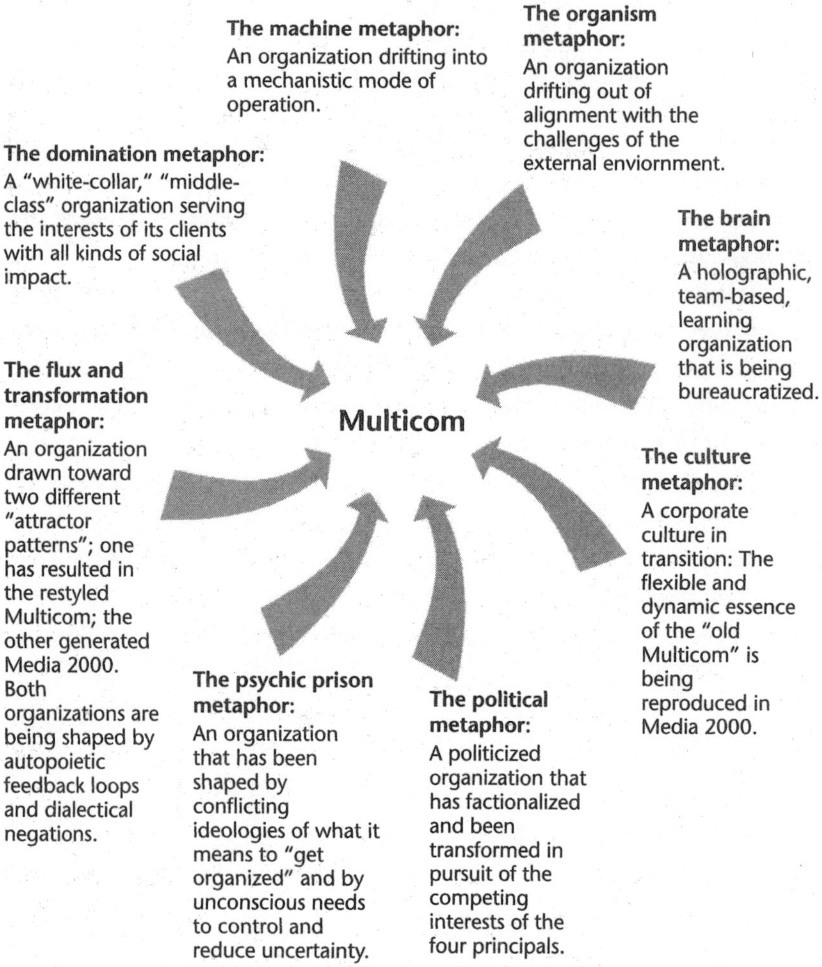

The machine metaphor: An organization drifting into a mechanistic mode of operation.

The organism metaphor: An organization drifting out of alignment with the challenges of the external enviornment.

The domination metaphor: A "white-collar," "middle-class" organization serving the interests of its clients with all kinds of social impact.

The brain metaphor: A holographic, team-based, learning organization that is being bureaucratized.

The flux and transformation metaphor: An organization drawn toward two different "attractor patterns"; one has resulted in the restyled Multicom; the other generated Media 2000. Both organizations are being shaped by autopoietic feedback loops and dialectical negations.

Multicom

The culture metaphor: A corporate culture in transition: The flexible and dynamic essence of the "old Multicom" is being reproduced in Media 2000.

The psychic prison metaphor: An organization that has been shaped by conflicting ideologies of what it means to "get organized" and by unconscious needs to control and reduce uncertainty.

The political metaphor: A politicized organization that has factionalized and been transformed in pursuit of the competing interests of the four principals.

Exhibit 10.1. "Reading" Multicom

The diagnostic reading allows us to remain in an open-minded mode. The evaluation brings us into a more focused perspective. [The trouble, for many people, is that they often want to jump into the evaluation mode too quickly instead of allowing themselves to be influenced by the insights of different views.]

A good diagnostic reading seeks to generate a comprehensive range of insights that allows us to discern the unfolding tendencies and character of a situation:

- What is happening at Multicom, and in the emergence of Media 2000?

- What understandings or lessons can we take away from the experience?

- How can we use the knowledge we have gained?

The answers to such questions, of course, ultimately depend on the point of view and interests that we bring to the task of understanding the organization in the first place.

If we are examining Multicom from a detached academic standpoint, we may enjoy exploring the paradox of competing viewpoints as an end in itself. But if we are in a position that requires that we take action in relation to Multicom, we will want to drive beyond this relativism and use the metaphors in a way that will offer a basis for action:

Key!! A basis for action.

- A new manager or management consultant charged with advising the organizations on their recent history and what Multicom or Media 2000 should do next will want to integrate insights to serve this purpose.

- However, a social critic or policy analyst will want a reading to serve quite different purposes in terms of policy agenda or critique.

This is where the *critical evaluation* stage of the reading process comes into play. It involves creating a kind of *storyline* that can advance our objectives. Whereas the diagnostic phase generates a range of insights that can open avenues for creative interpretation, the storyline brings them together in a meaningful way.

Developing a detailed reading and "storyline"

To illustrate, let us adopt the perspective and role of a new manager or management consultant charged with making recommendations to Multicom. As we "read" through various metaphors, we find ourselves being pulled into the different metaphors' ways of seeing. We begin to identify key insights, such as those illustrated in exhibit 10.1. Some of the insights strike us as particularly resonant or meaningful and worthy of further investigation, so we choose to investigate in more depth.

A DIAGNOSTIC READING
The organismic metaphor

If we choose to follow the insights of the organismic metaphor, we find ourselves asking questions about the relationships between Multicom and Media 2000 and the broader environment:

- What is the nature of the business environment?

- What are the critical tasks influencing each organization's ability to survive?

- Have Multicom and Media 2000 found an appropriate niche?

- Are they adopting appropriate strategic organizational and managerial styles?

Pursuing this line of inquiry, we may choose to perform a "contingency analysis" using the framework offered in chapter 3 (exhibit 3.4) and map the relationships between organizational and environmental characteristics (exhibit 10.2). As a result, we would conclude that Multicom's trend toward increased bureaucratization, which slows down communication and action capabilities, is dangerous because it creates an incongruent relationship with the challenges of the media sector's rapidly growing business and technological environment. Using the same framework (exhibit 10.2) we note that Media 2000, with its flexible, holographic style, is much better adapted to the media-services environment than Multicom.

Viewing both organizations as part of a wider ecology of competitive and collaborative relations involving similar and dissimilar organizations and rapid developments in multimedia technology, we find ourselves reflecting on various paths for future strategic development. Can each firm survive as a distinct entity? Are new alliances necessary to cope with new technologies and the patterns of organization shaping the multimedia sector as a whole? In this way, the detailed insights of the organismic metaphor help us build a comprehensive reading of where the two organizations stand.

The brain metaphor

Using the brain metaphor, we can see that the early years of Multicom implicitly built upon holographic characteristics, especially those of "requisite variety" and "redundant functions." The client teams were microcosms of the whole organization. The firm's leaders allowed employees to use a full range of skills at every level of the organization that effectively serviced the clients and that, at the same time, encouraged flexibility, learning, and development. We note how the same principles underpin the organizational style of Media 2000.

The culture metaphor

Viewing the situation through the lens of the culture metaphor, we note how the holographic style of operation in Multicom's early years was underpinned by a highly cohesive corporate culture built around the shared values of the four leaders of the organization. The corporate philosophy

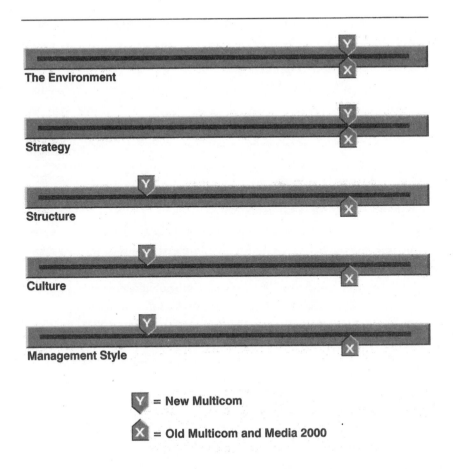

Exhibit 10.2. Rough profiles of Multicom and Media 2000 (based on the contingency model presented in exhibit 3.4, p. 54)

stressed the importance of working and playing hard in a way that affirmed the corporate identity. The culture was undermined by the bureaucratization at Multicom but was perpetuated by its offshoot, Media 2000.

The political metaphor

Switching to the political metaphor, we note that the troubles of Multicom and the new success of Media 2000 were spawned by the divergent management styles and personal interests of the four leaders. History repeated itself. Just as Multicom was born politically when Walsh, Bridges, Beaumont, and Rossi broke away from their old firm, taking key clients with them, Multicom split into two separate elements. We note how this potential was seeded by the unequal ownership structure and power base that ultimately allowed an autocratic decision to be made by Walsh and Bridges.

The psychic prison metaphor

As we probe the psychic prison metaphor, we find ourselves asking new questions: Were unconscious factors driving Walsh and Bridges's desire for control? Could the problem of overwork and conflicting family obligations have been resolved in another way? Were Walsh and Bridges trapped by the idea that good organization ultimately means more bureaucracy?

DEVELOPING A STORYLINE
A manager–consultant's perspective

The challenge of using multiple readings, of course, is to convert them into a storyline that can help us deal with the complexity. Thus, as the new manager or management consultant faced with advising Multicom or Media 2000, we may find ourselves developing an integrated perspective along the lines illustrated in exhibit 10.3. Using the organismic metaphor as a dominant frame of reference, we see the main challenge facing both organizations as that of evolving with a changing environment. We see Media 2000 as well-adapted. We see Multicom as facing major problems.

Our advice to Media 2000 is to build on the organization's holographic style, using the strong corporate culture as a way of creating systems of shared meaning and understandings that continue to bind the organization together while maintaining a flexible, free-flowing style. We urge Beaumont and Rossi to look at the broader ecology of relations—with customers, competitors, and other organizations that offer complementary services—and to strike the alliances and connections that they will need to flow with change.

Our advice to Multicom is to understand what has happened and how the organization has become incongruent with the environment. We have to tread carefully here because there may be deep psychic and political forces behind the bureaucratization. Our task would be to explore these forces with Walsh and Bridges, learn more about the psychological and political factors that have driven the change, and advise accordingly. If the increased bureaucratization is indeed a psychological force, as opposed to a pragmatic time-management ("Let's get Multicom under control") strategy, we will probably have a difficult task launching any kind of restructuring. Entrepreneurial figures who create successful new enterprises are notoriously reluctant to let the reins of control go, even when it is in the best interests of the future enterprise. As we interact with Walsh and Bridges, it is likely

Multicom is an organization that has become bureaucratized and incongruent with its wider environment. It must recapture the flexibility and vitality of its old culture and style to achieve future effectiveness.

Several factors have contributed
to the problem.

Walsh and Bridges have entrenched a bureaucratic style. It suits their desire to have a large measure of certainty and control.	The old holographic qualities have been eroded and replaced by more formal work processes.	The corporate culture has lost its dynamism. The political struggle between the four principals and the departure of Beaumont and Rossi have left their mark.

Given the politicized history, any transformation of Multicom must first win the confidence of Walsh and Bridges. Hence: Use the above analysis to present the history of Multicom in a new light and to argue for a new mode of alignment with the enviornment.

Media 2000 seems adapted to its environment in every respect. Look to the future here: How can Media 2000 evolve with the broader enviornment?

Exhibit 10.3. An "adapt-to-the-environment" storyline

---

that a deeper reading will unfold, suggesting an appropriate course of action.

As should be clear from the above account, a storyline implies a course of action.

If Multicom is indeed out of alignment with its environment, the task of the new manager or consultant will be to help it strike a more effective configuration. The detailed insights about the psychological, political, cultural, and other factors that have created the malalignment provide clues as to how the bureaucratization should be approached and how the situation can be rectified. They are incorporated into the storyline within the overall framework presented by the organismic metaphor, offering detailed insights as to how the manager or consultant can shape his or her change strategy.

We will have more to say on the relationship between a storyline and the mode of action that it recommends later in this chapter. So, for the moment, let's stay with the process of developing an appropriate storyline. As summarized in exhibit 10.4, a storyline ultimately involves a prioritization of insights generated through one's diagnostic reading, usually by giving priority to a particular metaphor and supporting it with insights from other metaphors. In the above Multicom/Media 2000 analysis, our emerging storyline has given priority to insights generated by the organismic metaphor. The insights of other metaphors were brought in as subsidiary themes that are mobilized to inform and shape action around the primary task of helping Multicom and Media 2000 thrive in a rapidly developing media business.

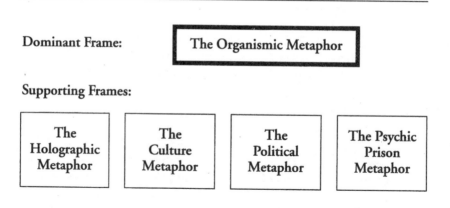

Exhibit 10.4. Storylines prioritize the insights of different metaphors

What if the manager-consultant intervened <u>before</u> Beaumont's and Rossi's defection?

The development of a storyline is always highly relative, depending on the precise circumstances being faced at the time of intervention. To illustrate, let's turn the clock back on the situation and assume a point of intervention in the middle of the chain of events leading to the schism within Multicom. Our manager-consultant would have found him- or herself dealing with a very different set of circumstances and evolving a very different storyline.

As illustrated in exhibit 10.5, it is likely that our manager-consultant would be seeing politics all over the place. The issue of whether Multicom

Multicom is being politicized in an extreme way. The challenge is to understand and defuse the political dimensions.

The insights of other metaphors can help this process.

| The holographic metaphor can help Walsh and Bridges understand that there are real alternatives to bureaucratization. Minimize the impact of bureaucratic thinking! | The culture metaphor can be used to show how the organization is being held together through core values and shared meanings. It can continue to flourish in this way. | The psychic prison metaphor can be used to explore the unconscious dimensions. | The organismic metaphor and contingency analysis can be used to frame a debate on the kind of organization that is required to meet external challenges. |

Dominant Frame:

The Political Metaphor

Supporting Frames:

| The Holographic Metaphor | The Culture Metaphor | The Psychic Prison Metaphor | The Organismic Metaphor |

Exhibit 10.5. A political storyline

was adapted to the environment would at first probably be nowhere in view. The primary aim of our new manager-consultant would be to understand the political dynamic:

- What are the key forces driving the four principals apart?
- Are they rooted in truly different sets of interests and styles?
- Do they hold different assumptions and beliefs about what it means to "get organized"?
- Is there a deep psychological dimension behind the actions of Walsh and Bridges?
- Can the organization be held together?

- Is there a different way of helping Walsh and Bridges manage the conflicts between work and family?

- Is there a gender dimension here?

- Can we use the insights of the holographic and culture metaphors to demonstrate how Multicom is already well organized?

- Can we use the contingency model generated by the organismic metaphor (exhibits 3.4 and 10.2) to make the case against bureaucratization?

- Will the insight that the firm has discovered a highly effective way of organizing for flexibility with a strong client orientation help the principals preserve their success?

And so on.

As illustrated in exhibit 10.5, when we intervene at this point, the political metaphor provides the principal frame for analyzing the situation. The other frames are used in a subsidiary role. The organismic metaphor, which provided the dominant frame for understanding the situation after Multicom and Media 2000 had split (see exhibits 10.2 and 10.3), now has less status. Although from a professional standpoint our manager-consultant may want to see the organismic metaphor as offering a dominant frame for understanding, since the ability to survive along with a changing environment is the long-term challenge facing Multicom, the political realities may require that it be used only as a supporting frame to bring a measure of detachment into a hot political situation. For example, the contingency analysis presented in exhibit 10.2 could be used to help reframe the politics by allowing the four principals of Multicom to see the proposed bureaucratization and its consequences from another viewpoint.

Now that we have a storyline dominated by political considerations, change strategies will be approached with the political factors firmly in mind, just as a storyline dominated by cultural considerations will require change strategies based upon cultural factors, and so on. Different storylines tend to favor different actions.

An effective diagnostic reading and storyline hinges on an ability to play with multiple insights and to integrate them into a coherent pattern. The metaphors, theories, and frames through which we implicitly scan the situations that we are trying to understand act as a kind of "radar" or "homing device" that draws our attention toward key features of a situation. These factors become elevated in importance, with others remaining invisible or in a background role. The way of seeing becomes a way of not seeing. The skilled reader of organizational life has a well-equipped radar system embracing many potential points of view and learns to marshal relevant insights in a way that provides a basis for effective action.

In describing the process, a clear distinction has been drawn between the *reading* and *evaluation* phases and the suggestion made that there is a temporal sequence here, with the evaluation implied in the storyline following the diagnostic reading. This is an oversimplification because in reality the elements are intertwined. As we read a situation through different metaphors we inevitably begin to form an evaluation as we become attracted to one line of interpretation over another. But the distinction drawn between the two stages is a very useful one because it warns us of the dangers of jumping prematurely into an evaluative mode. The challenge is to remain open to a range of possibilities so that an effective reading and storyline providing real insights and real leverage on situations and problems can emerge.

The process has been illustrated from the perspective of a manager-consultant, showing how readings and storylines have an unfolding character. They're not fixed. They're not absolute. They change over time. They vary with the objectives and perspectives of the reader. Although the process and skills are consistent, the content and product vary.

MULTICOM FROM ANOTHER VIEW: SEEING DIFFERENT DIMENSIONS OF THE SAME SITUATION

To illustrate and reinforce these important points, let's change perspective once again. Instead of adopting the role of a manager-consultant, let's view the developments at Multicom through the eyes of a social critic or policy analyst interested in the field of media relations.

The Multicom story now has a very different significance. There is probably little interest in the internal politics or the new Multicom's malalignment with its task environment. The horizon is set much wider. Both firms are likely to be viewed from a broader institutional perspective with a focus on understanding the role that Multicom and Media 2000 play in serving the interests and public relations needs of their clients. The domination and flux and transformation metaphors are likely to provide key frames (exhibit 10.6):

- What clients do the two firms serve?
- What services do they offer?
- What are the explicit and *unstated* functions of these services?
- How do they serve to legitimize their clients' activities?
- Is there a seamy side?

- Are there cover-ups?
- Is there government lobbying?
- What role do the activities of Multicom and Media 2000 play in creating a pattern of positive and negative feedback loops that create space in which their clients' activities can thrive?
- Are they, in effect, paid to dampen, mask, or gloss the negative social impacts of their clients?

The social critic is likely to zero in on signs of domination wherever they can be found. The insights and methodologies of the political and flux and transformation metaphors may be used to analyze key relationships and marshal the evidence relating to Multicom's and Media 2000's social role and impacts.

Multicom and Media 2000 belong to the ideological superstructure of modern capitalism. They are handmaidens of power. Their main role is to perform services that legitimize and enhance the interests of their clients. Their true nature can be revealed by studying their ultimate impacts on people, society, and the environment.

A detailed "political analysis" reveals the patterns of interest being served and can reveal the coalitions and webs of power that Multicom and Media 2000 help to sustain.

An analysis of the feedback loops and contradictions linking the activities performed by Multicom and Media 2000 to the broader context reveals their role in sustaining key social patterns and power relations.

Dominant Frame:

> ## The Domination Metaphor

Supporting Frames:

The Political Metaphor	The Flux and Transformation Metaphor

Exhibit 10.6. A social critic's storyline

Dominant Frame: ┌─────────────────────────────────────┐
                     │ The Flux and Transformation Metaphor │
                     └─────────────────────────────────────┘

Supporting Frames:

┌──────────────────┐   ┌──────────────────┐
│ The Political   │   │ The Domination │
│   Metaphor   │   │   Metaphor   │
└──────────────────┘   └──────────────────┘

Exhibit 10.7. A policy analyst's storyline

If our social critic was more of a policy analyst, however, it is likely that he or she would choose to use the flux and transformation metaphor as a primary frame (exhibit 10.7). The study of dialectical oppositions or loops of mutual causality (exhibits 8.4 and 8.5) may provide ideal frames for analyzing the institutional patterns and processes to which Multicom and Media 2000 contribute and for understanding where, from a policy point of view, it is most effective to intervene.

The point is that the way of seeing and reading that our social critic or policy analyst brings to the situation will be very different from that of our manager-consultant. Their different perspectives and interests favor different theoretical frames. They see completely different dimensions of the same situation. Indeed, the perspectives of the critic and policy analyst will lead them to break the boundaries of the case study presented earlier in the chapter and seek a completely different pattern of information. From these perspectives, most of what has been provided in the Multicom case description would probably be deemed irrelevant to the needs at hand.

In juxtaposing these different perspectives, we underscore the inherent partiality of any reading process. Whoever we are, it is impossible to obtain a complete point of view. Our perspectives always have horizons and limits dictated by the factors that we implicitly or explicitly value and deem important. We are back to Albert Einstein's point that our observations are always shaped by the *theory* through which we see.

One of our challenges as managers, consultants, critics, or policy analysts, and as individuals in everyday life is to cope with this problem. If we dwell on the impossibility of achieving an all-embracing understanding or comprehensive insight, we will surely be depressed and overwhelmed. But if we turn the problem around and focus on what *can* be achieved by refining our interpretive skills, a much more positive message emerges.

It must be emphasized that the aim of this case study is to provide just one simple illustration of the methodology in action. Readers who are interested in further applications and more advice on using the reading method will find detailed descriptions in this book's companion volume, *Imaginization: New Mindsets for Seeing, Organizing, and Managing.*

"READING" AND EMERGENT INTELLIGENCE

In the brain chapter we discuss how the human brain is characterized by a form of "emergent intelligence" whereby coherent order and pattern result from a multitude of possibilities.

It is useful to think about the process of reading organizational life in similar terms, for as we have seen, an effective reading requires that we remain open to different possibilities that can form and reform in a way that allows us to act appropriately.

The process is organic. There is a dynamic quality that unites the reader and the situation being read in an unfolding process through which the reader can begin to grasp, shape, and understand the pattern of events or circumstances being encountered.

By being open to the frames and concepts generated by different metaphors

- we can be sensitive to the different dimensions of a situation,

- we can be aware of when politics, culture, domination, or the insights of other frames call our attention and, in effect, say "take account of this point of view,"

- we can open ourselves to a variety of insights on which creative interpretation and synthesis thrive,

- we can learn to use different frames and subframes to explore, elevate, or diminish the significance of what we are seeing,

- we can be sensitive to the all-important relationship between figure and ground and realize that when we elevate the importance of a particular metaphor or group of metaphors we tend to push others into a background role,

- we can use our "reading" skills to open new horizons as well as deepen understanding of the territory we already know, and

- we can learn to keep open, reflective, and evolving as we search for meaningful insights that open new action opportunities or give new leverage on difficult problems.

The reading is not an end in itself. It does not rest in the mechanical application of a few favored metaphors or analytical schemes. Its purpose is to connect with the truly significant dimensions of a situation. Effective readings are *generative*. They produce insights and actions that were not there before. They open new action opportunities. They make a difference.

The criteria for judging an effective reading are not objective. They are pragmatic. Returning to the specifics of the Multicom case, for a manager this pragmatism may rest in understanding how the political dynamic of the "old Multicom" can be reframed through a contingency analysis that defuses the politics. For a social critic or policy analyst, the pragmatism may rest in discovering positive and negative feedback loops that can change the social impacts of key Multicom clients.

Another important point that must be emphasized is that the process of reading a situation is always *two-way*. In trying to discern the meaning of a situation, we create an interplay between the situation itself and the frames through which we are trying to tie it down.

To illustrate, consider the process of reading a book. The book presents us with words and sentences. But the reader also brings his or her personal perspective to the reading, and this plays a vital role in determining the meaning that the text conveys.

The same is true in organization and everyday life. Situations may call for our attention. But the interpretive frame of the reader also *shapes* what is read into that situation. As has been suggested, if we are dominated by an interest in structure, culture, or politics, this is what we will probably see. The dominant frame will push other potential insights from view.

In this sense the reader is also an author. He or she is not in a passive role. This is what makes the challenge of reading organizational life so powerful. The manager or social critic truly does have an opportunity to shape how situations unfold.

11 Using Metaphor to Manage in a Turbulent World

AS WE MOVE INTO THE TWENTY-FIRST CENTURY, we find ourselves living through a period of unprecedented change with major implications for the whole field of organization and management. Theories that were once viewed as providing sound foundations are becoming obsolete. New theories are emerging at a rapid pace. Each month, it seems, brings a crop of new perspectives through which managers are urged to understand and act on their problems.

Needless to say, the situation is often overwhelming. Managers at all levels are invited to embrace new paradigms, develop new competencies, integrate left- and right-brain thinking, become skilled political actors, and learn to be team players. In any single year, leading business journals invite managers to consider dozens of ways of structuring and managing their enterprises to create

- learning organizations,
- inverted pyramids,
- shamrocks,
- spider plants,
- third-wave organizations,
- virtual enterprises,
- cluster organizations, and
- lean organizations,

to name just a few.

Modern chaos theorists would describe this as an "edge-of-chaos" situation. We are shifting from a world dominated by bureaucratic-mechanistic principles into an electronic universe where new organizational logics are required. The intense theoretical and practical innovation is part of the transition and, given the fluid, self-organizing nature of a world dominated by electronic media, is likely to remain so.

This shift poses enormous challenges for any person wishing to stay abreast of new developments and cope with the flux in a positive way. Managers have to get beneath the surface and understand what is happening at a deeper level. Instead of being buffeted by the latest theories and trends, they need to be able to develop and take their own position.

This book shows how this can be done.

In a famous discussion on the nature of scientific understanding, quantum physicist Werner Heisenberg once observed that understanding ultimately rests in the ability to recognize how many different phenomena are really part of a coherent whole. Genuine understanding cuts through surface complexity to reveal an underlying pattern.

This is exactly what an understanding of the role of metaphor helps us to do. When we recognize that all organizational theories are just *metaphors,* we tackle organizational problems from new perspectives. Theories become building blocks, not fixed answers. We can learn to develop our own theories and create relevant implementation strategies—and to avoid blindly buying into the latest management fad. We can learn to see and tap metaphors' strengths and be aware of their inevitable limitations. We can set the grounds for a much more reflective approach to management practice, where people rather than theories are in charge.

The various chapters in this book have covered a great deal of ground, and in a conclusion such as this, it is not possible to cover all the ideas that have been presented. Nor is it desirable to do so. As suggested in Chapter 1, part of the message of this book rests directly in the *experience* of reading different chapters and of coping with competing points of view. So the focus in the remainder of this chapter is on four messages that capture some of the major implications for management. They can be summarized as follows:

- **Mobilize new ways of seeing. Be aware of the constant link between theory and practice.**

    In times of change it is vital to be in touch with the assumptions and theories that are guiding our practice and to be able to shape and reshape them for different ends. *Images of Organization* shows us how to do this, and it encourages us to bring a fluid perspective to the problems and challenges being faced. Traditional management perspectives often lock us into fixed frameworks. They offer a way of seeing that says, "This is THE WAY to see." As a result, we often get trapped by the metaphors on which they are based.

A part of the problem rests in the fact that in a world dominated by practical considerations there is often a reluctance to get involved with issues of a theoretical nature. People tend to think that theory gets in the way of practice. Yet, as Kurt Lewin has pointed out, "there is nothing so practical as a good theory." Also, as previous chapters illustrate, practice is *never* theory free. In any sustained endeavor, we are guided by implicit root images that generate theories of what we are doing. It is vital that we know what they are and the strengths and limitations they express. This has implications at all levels of management and policy making.

■ **Develop capacities that will help you evolve with new challenges.**

Managers at all levels must gain comfort in dealing with the insights and implications of diverse perspectives. In the organism and brain chapters, we mentioned the "law of requisite variety," which states that the adaptive capacity of any system depends on its ability to embrace the complexity of the environment being faced. This assumes new significance here. In being open to the insights of different metaphors and in learning to use metaphor to *create* new insights, we enrich our capacities for generating innovative ways of dealing with new challenges and of forging new evolutionary patterns.

■ **Remember that you are an "author" as well as a "reader" of organizational life.**

This book has emphasized the importance of being able to read and understand the complexity of organizational life. But it is also important to remember that the reading of a situation always implies a degree of authorship as well. In reading our organizations, it is important to place ourselves in an active mode. We are not passive observers interpreting and responding to the events and situations that we see. We play an important role in shaping those interpretations and, consequently, in the way events unfold.

■ **Imaginize!!! Don't just organize.**

Finally, we need to recognize that despite its roots in mechanistic thinking, organization is really a creative process of *imaginization.*

We organize as we imaginize, and it is always possible to imaginize in new ways. In appreciating this, we open the way to numerous possibilities and to a key competence for managing in turbulent times.

The imaginization process has been illustrated throughout this book, especially in those chapters that have sought to extend the boundaries of current practice by using creative metaphors to capture and develop new ways of organizing. Consider our discussion of the brain, where images of holograms, mobots, "corporate DNA," and fractal-like reproduction were used to create design principles for developing intelligent organizations.

The approach developed here begins to illustrate the possibilities. But, like the book as a whole, it only offers a sliver of the full potential. As I have shown in *Images of Organization*'s companion volume, *Imaginization: New Mindsets for Seeing, Organizing, and Managing*, we can use the style modeled here for rethinking almost every aspect of management. Organizational structure, strategy, management style, teamwork, organizational change, and even products and services can be vitalized and reformed through creative images that allow us to act in new ways. I have included an excerpt from *Imaginization* in an appendix to *Images* so you can see how this is done.

The concept of organization is a product of the mechanical age. Now that we are living in an electronic age, new organizing principles are necessary. The many ways we can use metaphor to theorize, organize, and manage our enterprises help us make the transition and meet the challenges of this new reality.

Appendix

There is no limit to the number of imaginative ways that we can think about organization. The ideas about metaphor that I've introduced in *Images of Organization* can be extended and developed to fit any situation.

The following excerpt from my book *Imaginization: New Mindsets for Seeing, Organizing, and Managing,* the companion volume to *Images,* shows how we can take inspiration from the activities of termite colonies to organize and manage in new ways. It is one of *Imaginization's* many examples of how we can put our understanding of metaphor into everyday practice. Enjoy!

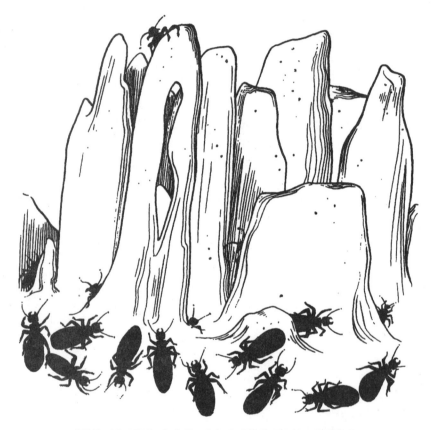

TERMITES ARE MASTER BUILDERS!

Termite nests are products of random, self-organizing activity where structures emerge and unfold in a piecemeal, unplanned way. They provide inspiration for developing coherent approaches to strategic management and change, without the straitjackets and problems imposed by trying to follow predetermined plans.

In times of change, plans and planning often prove ineffective because they create rigidities. In highly politicized contexts, they often serve as magnets for political opposition, catalyzing and crystalizing the views of those who do not want to travel in the planned direction. This creates an enormous dilemma for would-be leaders or managers, because they have to find ways of planning without plans or, at least, of creating some kind of visionary framework that can evolve and adapt as circumstances require.

This chapter explores some ideas that I've found particularly powerful in helping managers reimage their leadership role in such circumstances. They're based on the image of a "strategic termite." It's a humble metaphor and, for many people, a distinctly unflattering one. Who, after all, wants to be seen as a termite? But the image has enormous power for would-be leaders who wish to generate major change in difficult situations, safely, yet effectively. It provides a way of tapping many of the insights emerging from the new disciplines of cybernetics and chaos theory in an evocative, practical manner.

TERMITES AND EMERGENT SELF-ORGANIZATION

Termites! Small, blind creatures related to the cockroach.

Creepy, crawly things that eat wood and make houses crumble.

Whenever I mention the possibility of becoming a "strategic termite," most managers seize on negative interpretations.

"You want us to eat away at the bureaucracy?"

"You're inviting us to become subversive?"

The metaphor, at first sight, does have these negative associations. But they're not the ones that I want to emphasize here. Subversive behavior in an organization tends to attract the exterminator. The person who seeks to create change by directly undermining existing policies and structures often runs into trouble. Create a hole in bureaucratic functioning one week, and chances are that next week the basic structure will be twice as strong as before.

So let's redirect attention to some of the more positive aspects of termite behavior, especially those exemplified in the processes through which termites build their nests and engage in mutually supporting activities.

Imagine a termite colony somewhere in the Tropics. There are thousands of termites milling around.

The ground on which they start to build their nest is quite flat. The termites begin their work by moving earth in a random fashion. Gradually, distinct piles of earth begin to emerge. These then become the focus of sustained building activity, resulting in columns located *in more or less random positions*. These are built to a certain height, then construction stops. When columns emerge that are sufficiently close together, building resumes until they are joined at the top to form a rounded arch. In this way, the termite nest evolves as an increasingly complex structure, with the arch as the basic unit. The approach eventually results in a kind of free-form architecture, comprised of interlocking caverns and tunnels that are ventilated, humidity controlled, and beautifully formed. African termite nests may rise 12 feet high and measure 100 feet across. They can house millions of termites. In terms of scale, they're equivalent to human beings creating a building more than a mile high.

Needless to say, the accomplishment has attracted the attention of many scientists. How do these blind creatures manage to produce such architectural masterpieces? No one knows for sure. A queen termite occupies a royal cell in the center of the mound. It's suspected that she plays a crucial role in processes of communication within the colony. But, if there's a plan or blueprint, where does it come from?

How do the termites direct and control their activity?

How do they coordinate their work?

How do they acquire the ability to repair parts of nests when they are destroyed, returning them to states that are as good as new?

There are lots of unresolved issues here. Instinct, habit, and various forms of communication play an important role. For example, the termites' deposits of saliva are believed to form important parts of their communication system. But one thing is clear. Termites don't build their nests like humans build houses and office towers. They don't follow predetermined plans.

One exciting theory emerging from the study of termite behavior is that work in the termite colony reflects a self-organizing process where order emerges "out of chaos." While the nest always has a familiar pattern, it is infinitely variable in terms of detailed form. It is impossible to predict the detailed structure in advance, because it emerges as a result of the scattered pattern of droppings. This is what makes the construction process so different than that of human beings. The "masterpiece" evolves from random, chaotic activities guided by what seems to be an *overall* sense of purpose and direction, but in an open-ended manner.

We have in this view of termite behavior a splendid image for rethinking many aspects of the leadership process in human organizations. For example, it suggests that effective leadership or change management may not have to be based on a *detailed* strategic plan. It may not be something that has to be *imposed*. It may be something that can emerge and take form in a self-organizing, evolutionary way.

In my research on the management of change, I encounter many successful "strategic termites." They are managers who have clear aspirations about what they would like to achieve. But, instead of trying to force-fit their vision, or direct and control a situation to achieve the results they would like to see, they manage in a much more open-ended way, encouraging and allowing desirable initiatives to emerge form the evolving situations being faced. "Strategic termites" are incremental and opportunistic in their approach to change. They build on ideas, actions, and events that they initiate or that spontaneously come their way. They are *strategic* in the sense that, while their activity is open to the influence of random opportunity, decisions and actions are always informed and guided by a strong sense of what they are ultimately trying to achieve. They have "plans," but they don't implement plans and are not constrained by plans. They are people who know where they would like to go. But they do not always know the route by which they're going to get there!

In this positive, expansive, and free-ranging interpretation of termitelike behavior, I believe there's an important message for people who wish to undertake leadership roles in turbulent times. Here are some stories illustrating different aspects of the metaphor in practice. . . .

Bibliography

THE FOLLOWING REFERENCE list includes only those sources that were cited in this executive edition of *Images of Organization*. For a complete list of the many sources that contributed to *Images of Organization*, please consult the second edition (1997), or visit the World Wide Web at www.imaginiz.com. The references contain a 50-page guide to over nine hundred detailed works exploring various metaphors discussed in the previous chapters.

Andersen, E. *On Organizations as Brains.* 1992. Available at http:/~/~wwwl.usal.com/-self/orgbrain.htm.

Argyris, C. *Overcoming Organizational Defenses.* Boston: Allyn & Bacon, 1990.

Argyris, C. "Good Communication That Blocks Learning." *Harvard Business Review* (1994): 77–85.

Argyris, C., and D. A. Schön. *Organizational Learning: A Theory of Action Perspective.* Reading, Mass.: Addison-Wesley, 1978.

Arthurs, B. "Increasing Returns and the Two Worlds of Business." *Harvard Business Review* (1996): 100–109.

Bateson, G. *Steps to an Ecology of Mind.* New York: Ballantine, 1972.

Becker, E. *The Denial of Death.* New York: Free Press, 1973.

Berman, D. M. *Death on the Job.* New York: Monthly Review Press, 1978.

Bohm, D. *Wholeness and the Implicate Order.* London: Routledge & Kegan Paul, 1980.

Boulding, K. E. *Evolutionary Economics.* Beverly Hills, Calif: Sage, 1981.

Bridger, H. "The Kinds of Organizational Development Required for Working at the Level of the Whole Organization Considered as an Open System." In *Organizational Development in Europe*, Vol. 1. ed. K. Trebesch. Berne: Paul Haupt Verlag, 1980.

Brooks, R. A. "New Approaches to Robotics." *Science*, 1991.

Burns, T., and G. M. Stalker. *The Management of Innovation.* London: Tavistock, 1961.

Burrell, G. "Sex and Organizational Analysis." *Organization Studies* 5 (1984): 97–118.

Burrell, G. "The Organization of Pleasure." In *Critical Management Studies*, ed. M. Alvesson and H. Willmott, 66–89. London: Sage, 1992.

Burrell, G., and G. Morgan. *Sociological Paradigms and Organizational Analysis*. London: Heinemann Educational Books, 1979.

Business Week Reporters. "Ford After Henry II: Will He Really Leave?" *Business Week*, 30 April 1979, 62–72.

Chatov, R. "Cooperation Between Government and Business." In *Handbook of Organizational Design*, ed. C. Nystrom and W. H. Starbuck, 487–502. New York: Oxford University Press, 1981.

Dahl, R. A. "The Concept of Power." *Behavioral Science* 2 (1957): 201–215.

D'Aveni, R. A. *Hyper-Competition: Managing the Dynamics of Strategic Maneuvering*. New York: Free Press, 1994.

Delahanty, F., and G. Gemmill. "The Black Hole in Group Development." Presented at the Academy of Management Meetings, New York, 1982.

Denhardt, R. B. *In the Shadow of Organization*. Lawrence, Kans: Regents Press, 1981.

Dennett, D. C. *Consciousness Explained*. Boston: Little, Brown, 1991.

Devons, E. "Statistics as a Basis for Policy." In *Essays in Economics*, 122–137. London: Allen & Unwin, 1961.

Drucker, P. F. *The Practice of Management*. New York: Harper & Row, 1954.

———. *Managing in Turbulent Times*. New York: Harper & Row, 1980.

———. *Post-Capitalist Society*. New York: Harper Business, 1993.

Fayol, H. *General and Industrial Management*. London: Pitman, 1949.

Foucault, M. *Discipline and Punish*. New York: Vintage, 1979a.

———. *The History of Sexuality*. London: Allen Lane, 1979b.

Freud, S. *The Complete Psychological Works of Sigmund Freud*. London: Hogarth, 1953.

Garfinkel, H. *Studies in Ethnomethodology*. Englewood Cliffs, N.J.: Prentice Hall, 1967.

Gemmill, G., and J. Oakley. "Leadership: An alienating social myth?" *Human Relations* 45 (1992): 113–129.

Gleick, J. *Chaos: Making a New Science*. New York: Penguin, 1987.

Goldstein, J. *The Unshackled Organization*. Portland, Ore.: Productivity Press, 1994.

Gulick, L., and L. Urwick, eds. *Papers in the Science of Administration*. New York: Institute of Public Administration, Columbia University, 1937.

Hampden-Turner, C. *Maps of the Mind*. New York: Macmillan, 1981.

———. *Charting the Corporate Mind*. New York: Free Press, 1990.

Handy, C. *Gods of Management*. London: Pan Books, 1978.

Hardin, G. "The Tragedy of the Commons," *Science* 13 (1968): 1243–1248.

Harries-Jones, P. *Ecological Understanding and Gregory Bateson*. Toronto: University of Toronto Press, 1995.

Heisenberg, W. *A Physicist's Conception of Nature.* London: Hutchinson, 1958a.

————. *Physics and Philosophy.* New York: Harper, 1958b.

————. *Physics and Beyond.* New York: Harper and Row, 1971.

Helgesen, S. *Female Advantage: Women's Ways of Leadership.* New York: Doubleday, 1990.

Janis, I. L. *Victims of Groupthink.* Boston: Houghton Mifflin, 1972.

Jaques, E. "Social Systems as a Defence Against Persecutory and Depressive Anxiety." In *New Directions in Psycho-Analysis,* ed. M. Klein, 478–498. London: Tavistock, 1955.

Jung, C. G. *Collected Works.* London: Routledge & Kegan Paul, 1953.

Kakar, S. *Frederick Taylor: A Study in Personality and Innovation.* Cambridge: MIT Press, 1970.

Kamata, S. *Japan in the Passing Lane.* New York: Pantheon, 1982.

Kast, F. E., and J. E. Rosenzweig. *Contingency Views of Organization and Management.* Chicago: Science Research Associates, 1973.

Kelly, K. *Out of Control: The New Biology of Machines, Social Systems, and the Economic World.* Reading, Mass.: Addison-Wesley, 1994.

Klein, M. *Contributions to Psycho-Analysis: 1921–1945.* London: Hogarth, 1965.

————. *Envy, Gratitude, and Other Works.* London: Hogarth, 1980.

Lawrence, P. R., and J. W. Lorsch. *Organization and Environment.* Cambridge: Harvard Graduate School of Business Administration, 1967.

Lewin, K. *Field Theory in Social Sciences.* New York: Harper and Row, 1951.

Maccoby, M. *The Gamesman.* New York: Simon & Schuster, 1976.

Maruyama, M. "The Second Cybernetics: Deviation Amplifying Mutual Causal Processes." *American Scientist* 51 (1963): 164–179.

Marx, K. *Das Kapital.* Harmondsworth, England: Penguin, 1976.

Maslow, A. H. "A Theory of Human Motivation." *Psychological Review* 50 (1943): 370–396.

Maturana, H., and F. Varela. *Autopoiesis and Cognition: The Realization of the Living.* London: Reidl, 1980.

Mayo, E. *The Human Problems of an Industrial Civilization.* New York: Macmillan, 1933.

McLuhan, E., and F. Zingrone, eds. *Essential McLuhan.* Toronto: Anansi Press, 1995.

McLuhan, M. *Understanding Media.* New York: New American Library, 1964.

Menzies, I. "A Case Study in the Functioning of Social Systems as a Defense Against Anxiety." *Human Relations* 13 (1960): 95–121.

Michels, R. *Political Parties.* New York: Free Press, 1949.

Miller, A. *Death of a Salesman.* New York: Viking, 1949.

Miller, D. *The Icarus Paradox.* New York: Harper Business, 1990.

Mintzberg, H. *The Structuring of Organizations.* Englewood Cliffs, N.J.: Prentice Hall, 1979.

Morgan, G. *Imaginization: The Art of Creative Management*. Newbury Park, Calif.: Sage, 1993.

———. *Imaginization: New Mindsets for Seeing, Organizing, and Managing*. San Francisco: Berrett-Koehler, 1997.

Newsweek, "The Hitmen." 26 February 1996, 44–48.

Ohmae, K. *Triad Power*. New York: Free Press, 1985.

Ouchi, W. A. *Theory Z: How American Business Can Meet the Japanese Challenge*. Reading, Mass.: Addison-Wesley, 1981.

Pascale, R., and A. Athos. *The Art of Japanese Management*. New York: Warner Books, 1981.

Peters, T. J., and R. H. Waterman. *In Search of Excellence*. New York: Harper & Row, 1982.

Plato. *The Republic*. Oxford: Clarendon, 1941.

Presthus, R. *The Organizational Society*. New York: St. Martin's, 1978.

Pribram, K. *Languages of the Brain*. Englewood Cliffs, N.J.: Prentice Hall, 1971.

Pribram, K. "Problems Concerning the Structure of Consciousness." In *Consciousness and the Brain*, ed. G. Globus et al. New York: Plenum, 1976.

Reich, W. *Character Analysis*. New York: Farrar, Straus, Giroux, 1972.

Revans, R. W. *The Origins and Growth of Action Learning*. Kent, England: Chartwell-Bratt, 1982.

Roddick, A. *Body and Soul*. New York: Crown, 1991.

Roethlisberger, F. J., and W. J. Dickson. *Management and the Worker*. Cambridge: Harvard University Press, 1939.

Sampson, A. *The Sovereign State of ITT*. New York: Stein & Day, 1978.

Sayle, M. "The Yellow Peril and the Red Haired Devils." *Harper's*, November 1982, 23–35.

Schön, D. A. *Invention and the Evolution of Ideas*. London: Tavistock, 1963.

———. A. "Generative Metaphor: A Perspective on Problem Setting in Social Policy." In *Metaphor and Thought*, ed. A. Orotny, 254–283. Cambridge: Cambridge University Press, 1979.

Schumpeter, J. *The Theory of Economic Development*. Cambridge: Harvard University Press, 1934.

———. *Capitalism, Socialism, and Democracy*. New York: Harper, 1942.

Senge, P. *The Fifth Discipline*. New York: Doubleday, 1990.

Smircich, L., and G. Morgan. "Leadership: The Management of Meaning." *Journal of Applied Behavioral Studies* 18 (1982): 257–273.

Stopford, J. M., J. H. Dunning, and K. O. Itaberich. *The World Directory of Multinational Enterprises*. New York: Facts on File, 1980.

Taylor, F. W. *Principles of Scientific Management*. New York: Harper & Row, 1911.

Taylor, G. R. *The Natural History of the Mind*. New York: Dutton, 1979.

Trist, E. L. "Referent Organizations and the Development of Inter-Organizational Domains." *Human Relations* 36 (1983): 269–284.

Trist, E. L., and K. W. Bamforth. "Some Social and Psychological Consequences of the Longwall Method of Coal Getting." *Human Relations* 4 (1951): 3–38.

von Bertalanffy, L. *General Systems Theory: Foundations, Development, Applications.* New York: Braziller, 1968.

Weber, M. *The Theory of Social and Economic Organization.* London: Oxford University Press, 1947.

Weick, K. E. *The Social Psychology of Organizing.* Reading, Mass.: Addison-Wesley, 1979.

Whyte, W. F. *Human Relations in the Restaurant Industry.* New York: McGraw-Hill, 1948.

———. *Money and Motivation.* New York: Harper & Row, 1955.

Winnicott, D. W. "Transitional Objects and Transitional Phenomena." In *Collected Papers.* London: Tavistock, 1958.

Zaleznik, A. "Power and Politics in Organizational Life." *Harvard Business Review* 48 (1970): 47–60.

Index

About the Author

GARETH MORGAN has spent the last twenty years developing practical insights on how we can develop the competencies needed for managing in a turbulent world. He is author of seven books, including *Imaginization: New Mindsets for Seeing, Organizing, and Managing*, the companion book to *Images of Organization*.

After studying as an economist at the London School of Economics and Political Science, Gareth began his professional work as an accountant in England. His skill in integrating the insights of leading-edge theory and practice has since led to two equally successful careers: as a social scientist developing new ways of thinking about organization and management and as an international consultant and change agent implementing them in practice.

Gareth's speeches and workshops on imaginization and on the new management have helped thousands of executives develop new leadership and organizational styles. His services have been used by companies such as Continental AG, Digital, Esso, GE, Hewlett Packard, Merck, Northern Telecom, Royal Bank of Canada, Shell, and Volkswagen. He has also worked with numerous health care and educational organizations. He is a Distinguished Research Professor at York University in Toronto and has been elected a Life Fellow of the International Academy of Management.

Born in Wales, Gareth now lives in Toronto with his wife, Karen, and their two children, Evan and Heather.

Please visit the World Wide Web at www.imaginiz.com to receive further information on Gareth's work. Further information on his speeches, workshops, and senior management briefings can be obtained through his Toronto office by calling (416) 239-4794, or by e-mail via: morgan@imaginiz.com.

Berrett–Koehler
Publishers

A community dedicated to creating
a world that works for all

Visit Our Website: www.bkconnection.com

Read book excerpts, see author videos and Internet movies, read our authors'
blogs, join discussion groups, download book apps, find out about the BK Affiliate
Network, browse subject-area libraries of books, get special discounts, and more!

Subscribe to Our Free E-Newsletter, the *BK Communiqué*

Be the first to hear about new publications, special discount offers, exclusive
articles, news about bestsellers, and more! Get on the list for our free e-newsletter
by going to **www.bkconnection.com**.

Get Quantity Discounts

Berrett-Koehler books are available at quantity discounts for orders of ten or more
copies. Please call us toll-free at (800) 929-2929 or email us at bkp.orders@
aidcvt.com.

Join the BK Community

BKcommunity.com is a virtual meeting place where people from around the world
can engage with kindred spirits to create a world that works for all. BKcommunity
.com members may create their own profiles, blog, start and participate in forums
and discussion groups, post photos and videos, answer surveys, announce and
register for upcoming events, and chat with others online in real time. Please join
the conversation!

MIX
Paper from
responsible sources
FSC® C012752